Diners, Dudes, and Diets

Diners, Dudes, and Diets

*How Gender and Power Collide
in Food Media and Culture*

Emily J. H. Contois

The University of North Carolina Press CHAPEL HILL

*This book was published with the assistance of the
Anniversary Fund of the University of North Carolina Press.*

Set in Merope Basic by Westchester Publishing Services
Manufactured in the United States of America

The University of North Carolina Press has been a member of the
Green Press Initiative since 2003.

Library of Congress Cataloging-in-Publication Data
Names: Contois, Emily J. H., author.
Title: Diners, dudes, and diets : how gender and power collide in food media
    and culture / Emily J. H. Contois.
Other titles: Studies in United States culture.
Description: Chapel Hill : University of North Carolina Press, 2020. |
    Series: Studies in United States culture | Includes bibliographical
    references and index.
Identifiers: LCCN 2020013479 | ISBN 9781469660738 (cloth : alk. paper) |
    ISBN 9781469660745 (paperback : alk. paper) | ISBN 9781469660752 (ebook)
Subjects: LCSH: Advertising—Food—United States—History—21st century. |
    Men in advertising—United States—History—21st century. | Food Habits—
    United States—History—21st century. | Men—United States—Social life
    and customs—21st century.
Classification: LCC HF6161.F616 C66 2020 | DDC 659.19/6413—dc23
LC record available at https://lccn.loc.gov/2020013479

Cover illustration: Burger logo © iStock.com/DorukTR.

Portions of this book were previously published in a different form and I am
grateful for the permission to reprint them here. The preface includes material
from two sources: "I Was Trolled—Here's Why I'm Turning It into a Teaching
Opportunity," *Nursing Clio*, July 17, 2018, https://nursingclio.org/2018/07/17/i
-was-trolled-heres-why-im-turning-it-into-a-teaching-opportunity; and "Food
Culture at the Margins: Two New Books on Eating Disorders," *Gastronomica:
The Journal of Critical Food Studies* 17, no. 3 (2017): 104–5.

Chapter 1 includes material from "Blogging Food, Performing Gender," in
Cambridge Companion to Food and Literature, ed. J. Michelle Coghlan (Cambridge:
Cambridge University Press, 2020): 243–61. Chapter 2 includes material from
"Welcome to Flavortown: Guy Fieri's Populist American Food Culture," *American
Studies* (The Food Issue) 57, no. 3 (2019): 143–60. Chapter 4 includes material
from two sources: "Real Men & Real Food: The Cultural Politics of Male Weight
Loss," *Nursing Clio*, August 15, 2017, https://nursingclio.org/2017/08/15/real
-men-real-food-the-cultural-politics-of-male-weight-loss; and "'Lose Like a
Man': Gender and the Constraints of Self-Making in Weight Watchers Online,"
Gastronomica: The Journal of Critical Food Studies 17, no. 1 (2017): 33–43.

For Christopher, always.
Did you know . . . ?!!

Contents

Illustrations

Preface

These Are the Stakes

I have always been interested in how food expresses anxieties and fears alongside hopes and dreams. Like many food writers and scholars, I think about the ways food brings people together, but there is more to the story, and sometimes that story is difficult. Every year growing up, my exceedingly thin grandmother labored in the kitchen alongside my mother to cook our Thanksgiving meal. When she joined us at the table, she never partook in the bounty spread before us. Instead she ate a Lean Cuisine meal, piping-hot from the microwave, anemic wisps of steam escaping from a shallow, black plastic dish. Looking back, I see how that tradition began to reveal how food is a complex source of joy and conflict, freedom and control, pleasure and shame. Those contradictions not only led me to a decade-long battle with my own eating disorder but also to study dieting in American culture as an undergraduate.

Although I loved research and writing, my younger self worried that such bookish activities were not enough to make a difference in the world. Confident that fresh fruits and vegetables could fix everything, or at least put a dent in "diet-related diseases," I next went to the University of California, Berkeley, to study public health nutrition. I put my newly minted professional skills to work during my years in worksite wellness programming at a major health-care company. But I eventually began to worry that we shouldn't be telling people what to eat. Leafy greens couldn't actually fix problems caused by poverty and structural inequalities. I also yearned to think and write from the interdisciplinary, liberal arts perspective in which I had first been trained. I started buying used cultural studies textbooks and reading them on the weekends. I researched trophy kitchens and wrote about them in the evenings.

I juggled working remotely and nearly full time in worksite wellness as I studied in the Gastronomy Program at Boston University, the program founded by Julia Child and Jacques Pépin. In 1991 Julia was quoted in the *New York Times* as saying, "There's a lot more to the field than cooks piddling in the kitchen. It's high time that it's recognized as a serious discipline." She was right. I continued that serious study at Brown University in the

Department of American Studies. Mentored by scholars known for their public engagement, I developed into an unconventional academic, writing for many audiences every step of the way. These opportunities for public writing, speaking, and engagement made clear the stakes for my scholarship about media, food, gender, and justice. When the stakes are high, the responses can be loud.

In the summer of 2018, I published a short academic article inspired by the themes of this book. I examined the YouTube interview show *Hot Ones*, on which the host and a celebrity guest each eat ten chicken wings dressed with hot sauces of increasing intensity as they talk. I analyzed how these interviews combine a number of food-related phenomena that American culture typically genders as masculine: spicy flavors, bar food like chicken wings, competitive eating, and eating messily in public. Because of these cultural stereotypes, I argued, female guests had to perform their celebrity differently than male guests. I didn't expect saying so would make much of a splash, but then Breitbart wrote an article about it. So did *The College Fix*, *The Blaze*, *The Daily Wire*, *National Review*, and a small army of blogs. Their readers typed out their best attempts at derisive reviews of my work. They also sent me hundreds of trolling tweets, Facebook posts, Instagram comments, and emails, along with one deranged letter sent to my home address where I had lived for less than six weeks. It was shocking and painful but also bizarrely thrilling to see the central tenets of my research on American gender anxiety play out on my screen. (For every troll, I had friends who supported me through this ordeal with phone calls, social media messages, emails, letters, and care packages. There are too many to name, but I hope you each know how thankful I was and am for your kindness.)

That experience proved the central point of this book: food reveals a great deal about gender and power in the United States. Gendered online abuse proves no exception. It's not a coincidence that one of the most cited academic papers on the topic of online misogyny, written by Emma A. Jane, is titled "Back to the Kitchen, Cunt: Speaking the Unspeakable About Online Misogyny." It's not a coincidence that a couple of *Breitbart* comments instructed me to "fix me a sammich" or "get me a beer." It's not a coincidence that research on food or media (and heaven forbid, food *and* media) is construed, as my commenters called it, "pseudo-academic drivel" and "self-validating madness masquerading as science." This dismissal has everything to do with gender.

Prominent food scholar Warren Belasco has argued that such gender-based reactions to food studies are rooted in a classical dualism between the glorious (masculine) mind and the gross (feminine) body. He also argues that food studies' reputation has been held back by a relic of the Victorian era, separating the world into separate spheres—masculine and feminine, public and private, production and consumption. As this book will show, much work remains to unpack and break down such binaries.

The fact remains that many readers inside and outside the academy still wonder why something like "dude food" or the "dad bod" should be worthy of serious analysis and debate. As a scholar of popular consumer culture, I am familiar with this challenge. The simple answer is that when we look at the stuff of everyday life as it transpires all around us, placing it in historical context and theorizing its significance, we better understand the growing pains of social and cultural change, including backlash against such transitions. Mundane objects and texts—such as yogurt cups and soda cans, advertisements and Instagram posts—illuminate the dynamic tensions between low and high, resistance and containment. Consumer culture is richly meaningful and deeply political. It shapes and reflects society, who we are, and who we might become. These are the stakes of *Diners, Dudes, and Diets*.

Diners, Dudes, and Diets

Introduction

Gender, Consumption, and the Great Recession Era of Corporate Food Marketing

"Will eating Luna Bars turn me into a woman?" A (presumably male) member of a *Men's Health* online forum asked this question in 2007. Clif Bar & Company launched the Luna Bar brand in 1999 into a sports nutrition market far less crowded than today's, dubbing it "The Whole Nutrition Bar for Women." Clif Bar reported after the launch that they routinely fielded anxious queries from men, including if eating Luna Bars would cause them to grow breasts.[1] While this may sound like a joke with an unsatisfying punch line, men's hesitancy extended beyond Luna Bars. In fact, the concern gripped the food, media, and marketing industries at the turn of the twenty-first century. How could the Food Network get more men to watch food television, if men perceived cooking as feminine? How could food and beverage companies encourage more men to drink diet soda or to eat yogurt, if they were thought to be mostly for women? How could Weight Watchers grow their male membership, if, as the cultural refrain goes, real men don't diet?

This book tells the story of how such companies tried to answer these questions. They developed products like Dr. Pepper Ten, which the Dr. Pepper Snapple Group crowned "the manliest low-calorie soda in the history of mankind." Powerful Yogurt created Greek yogurt for men as a high-protein snack with six-pack abs molded onto the sides of every container. More subtly, Weight Watchers developed a program that they promised men was all online and designed just for them, so dieting could easily be kept secret.

Each of these developments reveal examples of "gender contamination," or what marketing scholar Jill Avery describes as "consumer resistance to brand gender-bending."[2] On one hand, market segmentation by gender is simply a strategy to expand market share and increase profits. On the other, the food products examined in this book are objects of American consumer culture in which we can read, interpret, resist, and reimagine gender.

Malleable and distinct from biological sex, gender is a social and cultural construct. Power relations and repetition define (and can redefine) its meaning in everyday life.[3] Concepts like gender contamination reveal how power is organized and controlled in society, particularly within patriarchal

1

cultures like the United States, where power consolidates around masculinity, whiteness, and affluence. This idea of gender contamination can work in multiple directions. For example, a woman drinking a brand of whiskey marketed to men can create perceptions of empowerment. But for male consumers, eating a Luna Bar or sipping Diet Coke can lead to a perception of social stigma because the brand is feminine. Since we eat food, gender contamination stretches beyond social concerns that a man might be considered feminine to the perceived risk of actually *becoming* a woman. In a patriarchal society, such a transformation represents a decline in status and power, a fear to be avoided at all costs.

And yet food-based gender stereotypes—for example, diet sodas are "lady drinks"—are not natural facts.[4] They are culturally constructed notions, articulated through gender scripts or codes.[5] Dominant food gender scripts are often singular, fixed, heteronormative, and prescriptive. Food is also a realm where gender scripts are especially easy to recognize: meat is masculine; salad is feminine. Men have big appetites, while women have (or should have) small restrained ones.[6] These static and stereotypical definitions of gender appear in advertisements, television, magazines, and social media accounts. Through this repetition, day after day, all around us, these gender definitions become all-encompassing, or hegemonic, norms— so seemingly natural, so taken for granted, that we may no longer observe their constructed presence, let alone question or resist them.

In this way, food is a battleground, one that intimately and uniquely shapes gender. Because food is consumed—literally taken into our bodies— and experienced on multiple levels of taste, emotion, and memory, its power is distinct when compared to other consumer objects and habits. Specific foods, flavors, appetites, and health beliefs perform gender just as food activities like cooking and dieting are all ways to "do gender."[7] Many cultures associate meat with strength, power, and virility and code it as a quintessential and archetypal masculine food, one that overtly performs and symbolizes masculinity, as its expense marks class status as well.[8] Though times supposedly change—we've been stuck in such change for decades—domestic food labor, such as planning meals, shopping for food, cooking, feeding, and cleaning up, continues to be considered a distinctly feminine form of daily drudgery; yet cooking in professional settings remains entrenched as masculine.[9]

While these daily acts of life define gender, they also pose opportunities to challenge and reimagine it. Food's physiological intimacy, visceral materiality, cultural salience, and presumed moral weight provide a window into the most pressing tensions in contemporary American life. Food poignantly illuminates fears of gender contamination.

Concerns about gender contamination are also historically specific. Such anxieties peak during cultural moments of extreme transition and conflict. The turn of the new millennium in 2000 posed such a moment. A host of social and cultural transitions emerged within gender roles; collectively they challenged the stability and prowess of white, middle-class masculinity. For example, the institution of marriage between men and women began to change considerably as the percentage of families with a married mother as breadwinner increased, just as married women's education surpassed that of married men.[10] At the same time, in 2000, George W. Bush was elected president, in part, because he was seen as the candidate voters would most want to have a beer with. After the terror attacks of 9/11 and the passage of the Homeland Security Act in 2002, American society turned extreme attention to the policing of U.S. borders and peoples, to U.S. safety and strength, to the militarized and muscular risk-taking of what some dubbed cowboy diplomacy.[11]

The aftereffects of this national traumatic experience and subsequent acts of defense collided with the global economic collapse of 2007–2008 that stretched into 2009. The recession—called the "he-cession" and "mancession" by economists and cultural critics alike—purportedly challenged conventional masculinity.[12] With job loss more pronounced among men than women, some men ventured into traditionally female employment sectors, such as nursing, while others performed more work at home while un- or underemployed. These gendered aspects of the recession reverberated in popular culture, though feminist media scholars assert that mancession narratives reinforced and deepened not only the existing labor inequalities women face but also those inequalities driven by social class and citizenship status.[13] Masculinizing job loss during the recession was less about men and masculinity, they argue, than a media strategy that sought to humanize an otherwise abstract financial crisis.[14] Nevertheless, the mancession narrative took root throughout American culture.

With Barack Obama's election in 2008, national discussions of race collided with already rising concerns about financial stability and breadwinning, border control, and terrorism. Additional legislation passed during the Obama presidency further shifted social boundaries, such as the repeal of Don't Ask, Don't Tell in 2010, the repeal of the Defense of Marriage Act in 2013, and Obama's DREAM executive action on U.S. immigration in 2014. This confluence of factors notably challenged the status of white, middle-class, heterosexual, cisgender masculinity, resulting in waves of anxiety and resistance. Post-2000 America proved a tumultuous place for the ongoing negotiation of gender, which significantly impacted our consumer culture.

Recognizing and capitalizing upon this moment of changing gender norms, the Chicago market research group Midan Marketing coined the term "manfluencer" in 2012 to indicate a man responsible for at least 50 percent of a household's food shopping and preparation.[15] The firm argued manfluence would redefine how marketers thought about men. Indeed, branding and advertising play significant cultural roles as they construct and negotiate gender as they sell products. The food, marketing, and media industries had long sought strategies to create socially acceptable routes into and through the feminized terrain of home cooking. Even with women's increasing educational and professional attainment and gender equity increasing somewhat in the home and workplace, foodwork continued (and continues) to be viewed as women's responsibility. Furthermore, given gay men's historically more open embrace of food and body practices, engaging with food and the body broached perceived risks of not only gender contamination but also encroachment upon male heterosexuality.

The 2000s and 2010s provided a particularly ripe social and cultural moment to renegotiate these perspectives. During these years, a number of companies sought expanded markets for products typically considered feminine. To engage more male consumers in cooking, food, and dieting, marketers deployed a specific gender discourse, one marked by a cool and playful appeal: the dude.

Defining the Dude

While social definitions of masculinity require that "a real man" works, competes, triumphs, and provides, the dude abides — a phrase turned mantra made famous by Joel and Ethan Coen's 1998 film *The Big Lebowksi*. Resisting the demands of manhood like competitiveness and breadwinning, the dude relaxes. He celebrates the slacker and the average (or even below average) guy.[16] Despite his lackadaisical demeanor, the dude remains complicit in masculinity's overall structure of power and inequality. He retains his spot atop a gender hierarchy that subordinates women and femininities, as well as marginalized masculinities and sexualities. The dude simply opts out of the struggle.

The twenty-first-century dude communicates a cool, unserious nonchalance, but he has a longer history. In the nineteenth century, the word "dude" referred to fastidiously well-dressed, urban men. It later described the dudes of dude ranches, men of means seeking to escape modernity and recapture the supposedly natural masculinity of the West.[17] In the late 1930s and 1940s, urban African American and Mexican American men began using dude to refer to one another. These dudes were fashion conscious, but they used the dude to mark their collective masculinity in contrast to the white affluent dandy. By the 1950s, dude became essentially synonymous with "guy," as white culture appropriated the term from African American culture along with words like "groovy" and "cool."[18]

With remnants of these histories attached to it, the meaning of dude today originated as a countercultural form of resistance within "surfer" and "druggie" subcultures. In the 1980s, the dude rebelled against yuppie consumerism and careerism. In the 1990s, he slacked even further, embracing nihilistic views.[19] A series of films from the 1980s through the 2000s, such as *Fast Times at Ridgemont High* (1982), *Bill and Ted's Excellent Adventure* (1989), *Wayne's World* (1992), *Clerks* (1994), *The Big Lebowski* (1998), and *Dude, Where's My Car?* (2000), exemplify today's use and meaning of the dude. Through slacking, these films depict the relationship between masculinity and youthfulness, achievement and failure.[20] Whether tasked with passing a high school history course, saving the world from aliens, or just making it through the workday, the dudes in these popular films achieve their goal before the credits roll, but they remain disengaged and unenthused.

As an identity reinforced by a wide range of popular media, the dude straddles lines of gender and sexuality. The dude provides a stance that allows men to navigate the balance between masculine solidarity and homosociality (closeness between men) on the one hand and strict heterosexuality and hierarchy (distance between men) on the other.[21] While U.S. culture considers the dude's cool solidarity a masculine attribute, women can and do enact it as well, indicating a degree of female masculinity.[22] For example, in the web-series-turned-television-show *Broad City*, actresses Abbi Jacobson and Ilana Glazer depict the relatively rare occurrence of female dudes, women with the freedom to slack off and do whatever they want.[23] It is not a coincidence that the show's dialogue used dude more than 200 times in its first three seasons, which aired from 2014 to 2016.[24] The women sometimes use dude to refer to men. Most often, they use dude between themselves to mark their close friendship and the ways that they defy the norms of conventional femininity.

With regard to race, not all dudes are white but the dude's social privilege often depends on the power of whiteness.[25] The risks of defying definitions of "real manhood" are far lower for straight white men of a certain class standing. In that way, the dude also connotes an implicit whiteness; his investment in the overall social power of his masculinity is ambivalent, but the dude remains fully enmeshed in existing racial hierarchies.[26] Ironically, the coolness so central to the dude's identity originated in and was appropriated from Black culture. While the dude's subordination of femininity might seem more visible, the dude's dominance also rests in historical processes of cultural appropriation across racial lines and the social power afforded by whiteness.

The dude also thwarts expectations and responsibilities that come with age and adult status.[27] He is no longer just a way for young white men to hail one another, as is often depicted in dude films. Instead, men of various ages adopt a dude identity to resist the demands of conventional masculinity that come with maturity. Contemporary examples of the dude coincided with the rise of "adulting," that is, "the practice of behaving in a way characteristic of a responsible adult, especially the accomplishment of mundane but necessary tasks."[28] Adulting is now a verb, cultural phenomenon, and meme. Adulting social media posts address adulthood's demands around routine and responsibilities, such as doing laundry, filing taxes, and running errands, particularly with hashtags such as #adultingishard and #adultingsucks. For some millennials, including dudes, the recession made the possibility of effectively or "successfully" adulting more difficult. For others, it delayed adulthood altogether. But in the midst of this, the dude retains the power and authority afforded by masculinity. While applicable to multiple identities, the dude continues primarily to connote a sense of masculinity that is inherently white, straight, cisgender, and youthful.

In popular culture and in everyday life, the dude positions himself both alongside and against hegemonic masculinity.[29] As a culture's dominant form of masculinity, hegemonic masculinity secures some men's principal position in a society at a specific moment. It subordinates and marginalizes women, as well as men who are not white, middle class, or heterosexual. The theory of hegemonic masculinity does not intend to list a set of discrete ideals that make up a society's definition of what it means to be a man. And yet, he is often represented in media in prescribed ways. When I ask my students for examples of "real men" from American media, they list well-muscled Hollywood celebrities and sports stars like Chris Hemsworth and Dwayne "The Rock" Johnson. In the United States the idealized masculine character is typically defined as a white, middle-class man, who is strong, competent, in control, competitive, assertive (even aggressive), and, because he is oriented toward the public sphere rather than the home, a breadwinner.[30] Hegemonic masculinity also shapes notions of health, as "real men" supposedly value independence, take risks, and are relatively unconcerned with well-being, as they eschew "healthy" behaviors and disease prevention as feminizing.[31] The dude resists the breadwinning, professional achievement, and competitive spirit of hegemonic masculinity, made all the more difficult to achieve during the recession. At the same time, the dude continues to share in the patriarchal dividend, the general advantage most men gain through patriarchy's subordination of women.[32]

The twenty-first-century dude mirrored broader trends in white male fragility, which boiled over during the recession years.[33] The dude proliferated in a moment characterized by seemingly destabilizing social changes, such as somewhat increasing gender equality, same-sex marriage legislation, border control, immigration, terrorism, and the enduring economic effects of the recession. In his cookbook *DudeFood*, Dan Churchill directly addresses this last point, writing that he "noticed that more and more people around my age stay at their parents' house after graduation," as many millennials faced delayed starts to their careers. Particularly for the millennial generation, the dude expresses purposefully arrested development, as a desire to withdraw rather than fail. As a result, the dude is relatively anti-careerist and anti-intellectual. However ironic or unenthused, the dude's opting out is self-protective against the potential risk of not achieving hegemonic masculinity. Always a relative impossibility, achieving such norms became more difficult to attain in the post-recession employment and housing markets. The dude rebelliously refused to step out into a future far less bright than expected.

Though the dude was never a dominant form of masculinity, he provided a way for marketers to thwart gender contamination, while generally upholding the power of whiteness and heteronormative masculinity. The food, media, and marketing industries manipulated and sustained the dude as they sought to convince men to engage in supposedly femininized activities—but with so little enthusiasm or investment that it still protected the power and boundaries of conventional masculinity.

U.S. Consumer Culture and Gender Crisis: A Short History

Although the dude trope proves useful as a food marketing strategy, it presents a challenge: the dude is ambivalent toward consumerism. Since a modern consumer culture became firmly established in the United States in the late nineteenth century, it has expressed and at times reinforced the idea that production is masculine, while consumption is feminine. Race and class also limit one's access to consumption. What's more, consumers form meaningful relationships with even the most mass produced of goods and can experience consumption as both empowering and oppressive.[34] Nevertheless this understanding of consumption itself as gendered and subjugated influenced the post-2000 dude. Given the perception that the recession rendered "masculine" production and productivity out of reach for some men, the dude provided a way to resist these expectations as a defensive measure. While the dude's openness to consumption brought the threat of gender contamination, it also posed a pathway to success within a capitalist system fueled by fevered consumption. Indeed, advertising has played a significant role in positioning consumerism as a remedy to masculinity crisis.[35]

The gendering of consumption has also shaped previous historical moments of "gender crisis." I place gender crisis in quotes to acknowledge scholarly discussions that theorize gender as an unstable social and cultural process; that is, a performative set of actions and meanings that are culturally and historically specific. Following Judith Butler, historian Gail Bederman argues gender is continuous and dynamic rather than a collection of traits, attributes, or roles; it is this historical and ideological process that links the anatomical body with cultural identity and social authority.[36] Bederman argues against the framing of gender as crisis, asserting gender instead as a process that "implies constant contradiction, change, and renegotiation" rather than undulating moments of triumph and failure.[37]

My examination of gender anxiety builds from an understanding of gender as a dynamic and contradictory process, but I see value in discussions of gender crisis, including the assertion that gender, especially masculinity, is perhaps *always* in crisis—constantly in flux. To be sure, masculinity and femininity are not stagnant collections of characteristics. They do not cohere into gender roles nor are they associated with only men's or women's bodies. Definitions and expressions of gender do not move intact through time. Gender does not stand alone, as it is coproduced with other categories of identity, such as race, class, and sexuality, and within systems of oppression.[38] Masculinities and femininities are plural, various, and shifting.

A culture's dominant understanding of what masculinity is, however, exerts a prowess and authority that constricts and expands at particular historical moments and in response to specific social and cultural conditions. Furthermore, representations of masculinity in mass media very often capture and preserve dominant forms of masculinity. These representations depict the shape and meaning of masculinity at a particular time, even if such representations do not reflect actual men's gender experiences, identities, and conflicts. Normative masculinity need not be common in reality in order to be culturally dominant.[39] Exemplars of masculinity, such as sports stars, Hollywood actors, and, in the case of food, celebrity chefs, function as authoritative symbols of how to be men. The authority of normative masculinity—that is, a white, heterosexual, cisgender, middle-class or affluent masculinity—undulated throughout the twentieth century. Peaks of reaction and resistance occurred during moments of intense social change. In each case, cultural ideas about food and the body transmitted concerns about the potentially feminizing effects of consumer culture. While I do not offer here a complete history of white masculinity crisis in the United States, I share a few key examples that reveal the enduring relationship between consumer culture, food, and the body in these moments.

One peak moment of gender anxiety and white masculinity crisis transpired in the United States between 1880 and 1910.[40] As the industrial market economy developed, it destabilized previous notions of white manhood. New forms of employment and wage-earning required men to prove themselves in the public sphere by ascribing to the impossible ideal of the self-made man.[41] Tensions grew between urban and rural interests. Working-class men, influxes of immigrants, worker unrest, and women seeking the right to vote all challenged middle-class white male authority. These changes brought about the words "masculine" and "masculinity," which marked a cultural shift from respectable, civilized manliness to virile, primitive masculinity.[42] Notions of "passionate manhood" emerged in the late nineteenth century, which more prominently emphasized ambition, combativeness, competitiveness, aggression, toughness, and sexual desire as admirable and virtuous qualities, often attached to a strong, athletic body.[43] Manhood transformed from an opposite of womanhood and boyhood to an opposite of femininity, which stigmatized feminine attributes and gay men.[44]

It was during this period that the relationships between gender, food, and the body grew increasingly moralized and socially salient. The shift to industrial capitalism and its paradoxical tensions between hedonism and restraint incited more widespread dieting and increased anxiety about the body: concerns that still shape us.[45] The white male body figured heavily in nineteenth-century gender anxiety. Doctors medicalized threats to masculinity as they criminalized homosexuality and diagnosed neurasthenia, a nervous disorder supposedly caused by brainwork, professional strain, and the increased pace of modern life.[46] Within this sociocultural and economic context, the controlled white male body marked proper, balanced, and moral consumption, as well as middle-class status, democratic citizenship, and nation building. The mid-nineteenth-century shift toward dieting and the thin body at first targeted men, operationalizing notions of masculine strength, as well as imperialist desire.[47]

As a result, ideal male body types changed from a plump and prosperous body to a thin and wiry frame. Body ideals emphasized muscularity near the end of the nineteenth century, embodied by the boxing heavyweight, bodybuilders, strongmen, and a new national craze: football. Muscular Christianity and the physical culture movement both reached peak popularity during this period, endorsing strength and assertiveness through literal muscle building and dietary control. Muscular Christianity was a reaction, in part, to the feminization and "weightlessness" of culture brought on by mass consumption.[48] Period bodybuilding expressed anxieties about living in a consumer culture, as "the white male body became a powerful symbol by which to dramatize modernity's impact and how to resist it."[49] These movements mobilized the fear that civilization spoiled male bodies, while white women were immune given their supposedly natural soft form.[50] Framed in such terms, dieting was primarily the concern of middle-class, white men until near the end of the nineteenth century.[51] Weight loss diets narrowed their gendered focus after 1920, predominantly enlisting women in a constant form of self-surveillance.[52] In subsequent decades, dieting itself became essentially coded as feminine in American culture. The fat male body was no longer a symbol of affluence and success, as social norms revised it as derisively feminine.[53]

Coupled with these ideas about the male body, the male gourmand spoke from the pages of men's cookbooks as a wholly masculine figure, one whose gastronomic knowledge was superior to his female counterpart's domestic cookery.[54] These men's cookbooks possessed subversive potential, as they blurred the gendered division of labor within the home and the kitchen. Nevertheless, their cookery advice simply endorsed male supremacy and upheld already accepted gender norms.[55]

These turn-of-the-century transitions in masculinity were reactions to a host of social shifts, including the perceived feminization of culture and the feminine character of modernity itself, most especially its consumerist aspects. Consumption and leisure provided new sites for men to communicate who they were, but in ways that notably conflicted with nineteenth-century notions of manliness. At the same time, consumption's role expanded in the American economy, national identity, and rituals of everyday life.

Consumption achieved the status of democratic contribution, recognized as a form of citizenship unto itself.[56]

As the language of the consumer culture, modern advertising depicted how to be an ideal consumer and by extension how to be an ideal woman or man.[57] The consumer culture and gender became intertwined in the average figure of consumption and the eventual target of much advertising, Mrs. Consumer. She was a white, middle-class, Anglo-Saxon, Protestant woman living in the suburbs, whose life revolved around shopping.[58] Advertisers—from the "most modern of men" to the savviest of female copywriters—routinely found Mrs. Consumer fickle and frustrating, but nonetheless powerful because she made the majority of her family's purchasing decisions.[59] In order to grow, however, the consumer economy needed to set its sights beyond Mrs. Consumer alone. But how could advertisers engage Mr. Consumer without encroaching upon his masculinity?

Men's magazines reveal a piece of this puzzle. Within their pages, Victorian masculinity—based on notions of property ownership, hard work, and character—shifted toward modern masculinity, a gender type that emerged between 1910 and 1935, emphasizing personality, appearance, success, sexuality, leisure, and consumption.[60] Emblematic of this modern masculinity, *Esquire* began publication in 1933 and was one of the first successful men's consumer magazines. At a time when consumption was culturally coded as feminine, *Esquire* employed misogyny and gender stereotypes to create a straight male consumer within the pages of the magazine.[61] This was especially the case when it came to food and other domestic activities. *Esquire* columns on cooking, cocktails, and interior decorating derided women's abilities and lack of sensuality. For example, Iles Brody's regular column "Man in the Kitchenette" constantly ridiculed women not only for poor and unimaginative cooking but also for lacking good taste and a gourmet appetite.[62] With overtly misogynistic-titled articles like William Powell's "Cocktail Party, Masculine" in the September 1936 issue and Dick Pine's "Women Can't Cook" in the September 1939 issue, *Esquire* claimed fine food, drink, and enlightened tastes as masculine terrain and massaged lingering anxieties about manly consumption habits.[63]

White masculinity fell into marked crisis again in the mid-twentieth century.[64] Popular culture memorialized the 1950s and 1960s with homemaking white women dressed in pearls and aprons alongside men in gray flannel suits, but the context of the Cold War, rapid suburban development, class politics, women's activism, race relations, and the Civil Rights Movement shaped gender norms in complex ways.[65] Midcentury concerns about masculinity also resurfaced the worry that mass culture had weakened and feminized American culture, and American men along with it, rendering the nation potentially unable to defend itself against threats looming large, from nuclear fallout to communism.

Voiced during a time of political and social uncertainty, gender crisis shaped midcentury food culture and bodily concerns. Food advertising and cookbooks, as well as kitchen interior design, appliances, and gadgets, each communicated a strict femininity. At the same time, barbequing, the grill, and home DIY projects carved out specific spaces for masculine domesticity.[66] Blurring such divisions, cookbooks published for a male audience between 1946 and 1960 sold well, though it cannot be known if men actually cooked from them.[67] Indeed, during these years *Esquire*'s food coverage, initiated in the 1930s, proved popular enough to support the publication of the *Esquire Cook-Book* in 1955, which was intended "for the pioneering male with a taste for fine food."[68] Like other cookbooks published at the time, the *Esquire Cook-Book* defended food and beverage as domains for superior masculine tastes, disparaging women and femininity along the way. Even as midcentury men may have read cookbooks and spent time in the kitchen, however, cooking itself was not gendered as a male responsibility but rather an expected daily duty for women.

Voracious consumption fueled suburban fantasies, but the midcentury culture of containment mandated that women balance it with the restraint of their own desires, appetites, and physical bodies.[69] Although diet programs primarily targeted women, men's dieting did not disappear. While turn-of-the-century physical culture promoted a hefty, muscular form, midcentury trends primarily endorsed a trim male body, a measured response to the period's growing consumerism.[70] Whether promoting muscularity or leanness, male dieting in the 1950s and 1960s continued to combat what were perceived to be the softening and feminizing aspects of modern American life, namely the consumer culture.

The impact of late capitalism, globalization, transnational corporations, and ongoing concerns about consumption compounded these concerns throughout the latter half of the twentieth century. The 1980s "new man" was more sensitive, emotionally aware, and gender egalitarian.[71] At the same time, the AIDS crisis significantly impacted gay masculinities, as it also inspired activism.[72] Interwoven with "yuppie" trends and popular health movements, some men in the 1980s engaged in fitness activities, gym culture, and "healthy" eating, inspired by increasing national conversations about nutrition, diet-related diseases, and body weight.[73] These shifts inspired backlash in popular culture, some expressed through the language of food and the body. Bruce Feirstein's *Real Men Don't Eat Quiche: A Guidebook to All That Is Truly Masculine* (1982) communicated the gender anxiety of the decade, complete with a crust to contain all its contradictions.[74] Resisting change, Feirstein's real men lifted weights, but they did not "work out." They ate meat and potatoes, but not vegetables.

Bringing satire to life, backlash to the new man inspired the "new lad" of the 1990s, a masculinity discourse that comprised a British subculture, but one with bearing for the American dude. The new lad was "depicted as hedonistic, post- (if not anti) feminist, preeminently concerned with beer, football, and shagging women, and anti-aspirational with an ironic relationship to the world of serious adult concerns," such as marriage, breadwinning, and fatherhood.[75] The new lad was a gender discourse rather than an expression of lived experience, one with strong roots in consumer culture, such as men's lifestyle magazines, shock jock radio shows, and "lad lit" publishing.[76] Despite the tensions between the new man and the new lad, 1980s and 1990s popular culture shared a focus on the muscular male body. With stars such as Sylvester Stallone and Arnold Schwarzenegger in roles like Rambo and the Terminator, the "hard body" action movie hero emerged as a muscular masculine icon of the time.[77]

The early 2000s inspired a novel form of masculinity that directly engaged the perceived feminization and sexual ambiguity of consumption: the metrosexual. Fully integrating consumption into masculine identity, the metrosexual "was identified as the urbane, successful, sophisticated, and well-groomed modern heterosexual man."[78] Defined in part by a fit and muscular body, metrosexuality also incorporated dieting, cooking, and knowledge about food. Relatedly, the "gastrosexual" is a food persona that builds on the metrosexual identity as it embraces the supposedly feminizing aspects of food, cooking, and feeding, while maintaining a solidly masculine stance.[79] Some aspects of metrosexuality have become more socially accepted and mainstream, such as enthusiasm for food and dining out. Overall, however, the metrosexual was somewhat faddish. Its prominence in popular culture peaked in the United States between 2003 and 2005, especially during the original primetime TV run of *Queer Eye for the Straight Guy*.

Twenty-First-Century Gender Crisis and the Dude

The twenty-first-century dude exists within this longer gender history. While a distinct gender discourse, the dude echoes aspects of other masculinities.

He bears most similarity to the British new lad, combining boy-like resistance with a touch of anti-feminist sentiment, while retaining conventional masculinity's social privileges and power. Although the metrosexual embraces fashion and grooming, the dude takes a different approach, eschewing such fastidiousness. And yet, both masculinities provide unassailable routes into and through the world of food.

The dude also emerged specifically within the social upheaval of the millennium, as he engaged the long-standing tension between masculinity and consumption's perceived feminization, particularly with regard to food. The dude navigates the demands of consumer culture, however, within a media environment significantly saturated with food and a cultural zeal for it. Today we don't just consume food media, we also produce and share it. We now engage with (or are bombarded by) cooking shows on not just public television or Food Network but also on Netflix and YouTube. Food media envelopes us at every turn with food magazines, coffee-table cookbooks, blogs, websites, podcasts, and social media platforms with advertising and branded content interspersed throughout. While gastrosexual "foodies" express great enthusiasm for all things food, the dude's relationship to food remains ambivalent.[80] The dude's food interests must remain unenthused, or at least appear as such.

Dudes are also generally ambivalent about their relationship to their bodies. They are aware of cultural ideals for six-pack abs and bulging biceps, but they resist these norms even as muscular examples occupy popular media. Take for example Marvel superhero characters, who have dominated popular film culture for the better part of two decades and endorse muscular heroism. The 2002 reboot of *Spider-Man* placed a muscularly transformed Tobey Maguire front and center in a tight-fitting costume.[81] Later films and stars—such as Chris Evans's super-soldier-serum-enhanced physique in *Captain America* (2011) or my students' aforementioned beautiful and brawny Chris Hemsworth in *Thor* (2011)—took the superhero body to a new level. In the Marvel Cinematic Universe, even dudes have god-like bodies. Chris Pratt's rumpled Peter Quill from 2014's *Guardians of the Galaxy* represents a dude superhero if ever there was one, though he still sports a ripped physique. Pratt's physical transformation was so noticeable, it required explanation when he returned to his role of Andy Dwyer on the television show *Parks and Recreation*. (Andy simply comments that he stopped drinking beer and lost fifty pounds.) In *Ant-Man* (2015), Paul Rudd's character Scott Lang transmutes from an everyman to an ant-sized Adonis in a flash thanks to his super-suit. One writer called him "the latest bro-next-door to transform into a man of steel."[82]

These superhero films presented muscular models of empowered masculinity, all the more meaningful, and contradictory, during the recession years and its attending gender crisis.[83] But they paralleled a cultural trend; multiple studies have found that men experience similar rates of body dissatisfaction as women and in similarly commonplace ways.[84] These concerns have yielded new concepts, terms, and areas of study that examine men and their relationship to their bodies, such as the Adonis Complex, muscle dysmorphia, and orthorexia nervosa.[85]

Muscular body ideals also reveal cultural norms about health. This is particularly the case under neoliberalism, which places responsibility for health squarely on the shoulders of individuals rather than on social institutions, public policies, or histories of racism. As a desired state of being, health expresses cultural aspirations, but it also endorses assumptions and expectations about morality and values.[86] Health creates hierarchies rooted in power and privilege. Furthermore, "healthism" exalts health as "a super value, a metaphor for all that is good in life," as it frames ill health as an individual concern rather than the result of political action or inaction.[87] In contemporary food media, the "clean eating" trend (orthorexia's supposedly harmless cousin) populates Instagram with colorful images of kale smoothies and acai bowls as visual representations of rational consumption and good health. Clean eating combines the raced and classed edicts of healthism with anxieties regarding modernity, impurity, and control.[88] Health comprises a culturally meaningful and socially charged part of identity, one intimately intertwined with the histories and contemporary experiences of gender, race, and class.

Men's media, particularly magazines like *Men's Health*, have strongly endorsed healthist messaging to men, making the dude's resistance to such ideas all the more noteworthy, though highly ambivalent. Despite broad cultural emphasis on health as a moral good with classed and raced value, masculine norms eschew health as a feminizing concern. Idealized masculinity represents an impossibility, as it requires the maintenance of a strong, vital, muscular, disciplined body but simultaneously considers health consciousness and actions to be negatively feminine.[89] I call this dynamic "ambivalent masculine body discipline," that is, the irreconcilable tension between performing masculinity as socially prescribed and caring for the male body and self. As examined in chapters 3 and 4, the marketing of diet sodas, yogurts, and weight loss programs actively communicated this ambivalence. Focusing on health and changing behavior require destabilizing the masculine self. Men must concede space for improvement. They must admit vulnerability and relinquish power. These are all actions in conflict with normative masculinity as currently crystalized. Efforts to influence the male body encroach upon such understandings. Rather than address masculine body discipline head on, the products discussed in this book and their marketing presence instead adhered to the dude, so that male consumers' masculinity remained intact while eating yogurt or following a diet.

Much scholarship on dieting and bodies has focused primarily on women and femininities, exploring how dieting enforces patriarchal power, exerts control, and conducts Foucauldian surveillance over women's bodies.[90] By examining men and masculinities, I find that men's experiences with dieting and ideal body types approach those of women, though women's bodies and selves remain disproportionately oppressed and the dominance of normative masculinity remains unchecked. In a neoliberal age, both men and women are expected to control their bodies through daily diet, weight loss, or wellness trends as part of productive and responsible citizenship.[91] These expectations increase further as everything from dietary advice to advertisements present consumption as a pathway to civic engagement, personal fulfillment, self-expression, and communal belonging.[92] The dude provided a complicated and highly ambivalent way to negotiate men's relationship to consumption, health, and bodies through food.

IN THIS BOOK, I examine foods and food figures in the United States since the year 2000 that deployed the dude to thwart gender contamination. From chapter to chapter, I consider cases that posed escalating challenges for marketers, starting with men's cookbooks and progressing to food TV shows and stars like Guy Fieri, food and beverage products, and commercial weight loss programs. More than an account of marketing strategies and their effectiveness, however, *Diners, Dudes, and Diets* tells a complicated story about contemporary American life. Food remains one of the most fraught spaces within consumer culture for shaping and reflecting identity, who we are and who we want to be, how others see us and how we wish to be seen.

Given my focus on consumer culture and on advertising as its language of choice, I examine the dude by analyzing advertising campaigns and marketing trade press.[93] To assess how the dude was reinforced across a host of food media forms, I draw from cookbooks, diet books, menus, magazines, food blogs and websites, podcasts, social media platforms, newspapers, food industry reports, restaurants, food criticism, food company histories, and food television. The words within these sources resonate in space, in time, in culture, and within dynamic hierarchies, especially as these texts and their producers sought to communicate with men about food, cooking, dieting, health, the body, and the self. To complete the holistic triangle that links cultural texts, producers, and audiences, I have sought to address men's perceptions of and experiences with these messages wherever possible. In the post-2000 United States, the food, media, and marketing industries approached male consumers at a time when men were again wrapped up in a moment of gender crisis. Studying how such audiences engaged with the dude reveals anxious and ongoing discussions of how to be "a real man."

I have wrestled with how to study masculinity without putting men at the center of my research. While this book tells the story of the dude, white men are not the unit of my analysis. Feminism and feminist theory do not take aim at white men, and neither do I, in my work or in my life. As I remind my students new to these topics, I am married to a straight white man who I love more than anything. What I *am* invested in is to show how the power of masculinity and whiteness works, to show how the oppression of a patriarchal system functions, flows, and replicates, so that it can be reconfigured. Patriarchy oppresses all of us—not all of us equally, not by a long shot—but all of us to varying degrees, compounded by gender, sexuality, race, and class. Gender contamination is the product of a patriarchal society and system that upholds the power of men and masculinity, whiteness, and affluence. Examining gender in food media provides an opportunity to unpack and challenge these structures of power.

Understanding the dude—how the discourse was constructed, deployed, and sustained, as well as how it was resisted and at times rejected—reveals one example of how these flows of power function in consumer culture and how they can be reworked. Indeed, studying how industries construct masculinities and approach men has greatly informed my understanding of femininities and women's experiences with food, our bodies, and our media lives. The dude reveals a specific case where culture and identity merged with the marketplace and its capitalistic aims. Food media depicts the ideal masculine citizen in relation to gustatory pleasure and taste, bodily control, health, nutrition, and cultural values, such as freedom and abundance. The dude embraced some of these aspects (like pleasure and freedom), while he resisted others (like bodily control and nutritional moderation), as the dude provided food makers and marketers a configuration of masculinity that could withstand feminization.

This book does not address every example of the dude in consumer culture. I could fill another book with how the dude has been used to sell soap, body wash, and tobacco-scented candles. Nor does this book include every food-based example. But those examined here demonstrate how and why the food media landscape forms a key site for analyzing gender and for understanding the drivers, mechanics, and logics of gender anxiety. These cultural texts do not just describe gender. They culturally reproduce gender binaries that uphold ideology and inequality.[94] In the chapters to come, I explore a series of interconnected binaries: masculine/feminine, public/private, production/consumption, real/unreal, rational/irrational, and satisfaction/restraint. The food, media, and marketing industries employed such binaries to their benefit when they sought more male consumers for products like cookbooks and yogurt. These binaries circulated as food's cultural capital exerted greater influence in American life and as food media expanded its reach. They formed a backdrop as men experienced the social shifts of the twenty-first century, including the recession and the ongoing question of how to be "a real man" in an ever-changing consumer society. The dude provided an answer.

Crafting Dude Food Media

From Advertising to Men's Cookbooks

Birthed from the historical context of the new millennium and amplified by the recession, the dude provided a solution for the food and media industries as they sought more male consumers for feminized products. They built these strategies upon the wholly masculine precedents set by a specific food genre: dude food. But what *is* dude food?

A Google Images search for "dude food" provides visual clues, as it returns thousands of photos of burgers, pizza, and hot dogs. On Instagram, posters use the hashtag #dudefood alongside the far more popular #foodporn, as well as derivatives like #meatporn and #burgerporn.[1] Unlike stylized food Instagram shots, often taken from directly overhead, these photos capture dude food on a slight angle or head-on so to display the full girth and height of immense sandwiches and bulging burgers. As is typical of food porn images, cheese and sauces ooze seductively as visible fat glistens and beckons.[2] In these photos, dude food often involves meat: beef burgers, fried chicken and wings, and barbecue favorites including brisket, ribs, sausages, and pulled pork. Although meat—a food perceived as masculine in cultures around the world—figures heavily, defining dude food proves more complicated than just a list of meat-laden dishes.[3]

Food writing and blogs describe a set of gastronomic qualities that typically define dude food. By and large, dude food's flavors and ingredients align with conventional notions of masculine foods and food attributes, but with a dude twist. Conventional (and often binary) definitions of gender create hierarchies that feminize certain flavors, foods, and appetites, marking dainty, light, and sweet flavors and foods, eaten in small portions with restraint.[4] Conversely, masculinity typically translates to spicy, hearty, and savory flavors, and hefty portions consumed with gusto; all characteristics of dude food. In the *Washington Post*, editor Bonnie Benwick defined dude food, with input from a number of food experts, by its emphatic and substantial flavors and textures: "salty, fatty, and crisp," "hearty, smoky, grilled," "heavy on the grease," and "tasty simplicity," "with bro-tastic sweetness and wicked heat."[5] Stated more bluntly, the *New York Times* food editor, Sam Sifton, defined dude food as "a cuisine that sits at the intersection of stoner and tailgate."[6] Devoured within moments of leisure, relaxation, and informality, dude food transcends ingredients and flavors, as it indexes the dude's anti-professionalism and slacker-friendly ease.

A look at recent food writing in print and online also delineates dude food as a broader culinary and social phenomenon with a number of underlying contradictions, particularly with regard to social class.[7] On a short-lived blog titled "Dude Food: Culinary Survival Guide for the Modern Man," Brooklyn-based chef Erik (no last name) wrote in 2011, "I'm all about 'guy food' and, well . . . the pursuit of whatever the hell *that* means" (italics in original).[8] Dude food possesses an inherent ambivalence, making it difficult to define the type of eater who cooks and consumes it, even among those who willingly adopt its label. Despite his admitted uncertainty, Erik wrote that the food on his blog "isn't going to be 'chefy' or pretentious. It'll be straightforward guy food with an everyday accessibility." Erik's characterizations of dude food as unpretentious, straightforward, and accessible reinforce the classed connotations of dude food as antithetical (or at least resistant) to the perceived pretension of fine dining. Like the dude himself, dude food indexes a particular type of anti-elitist masculinity, but one that even dudes themselves engage from a wary distance.

Infused with class politics, dude food embodies notions of lowbrow food and eaters, fast food value menu quantity, and the enthusiastic pursuit of exaggerated eating experiences. "Junk" food, a culinary category that includes dude food, can provide an alternate route to food knowledge and social status through "an ironic embrace of culinary capital by those who seem, on the surface at least, uninterested in it or the status it can confer."[9] The dude resists professional accomplishment and endorses slacking off, while maintaining masculine social power. Similarly, dude food plays around as it resists the typical standards of haute cuisine, even as it finds its way onto the menus at fine dining restaurants, where dinner menus offer burgers alongside continental classics and modern American creations.

Indeed, gastropubs are the dudes of contemporary American dining. With kitchens run by talented chefs, U.S. gastropubs offer top quality but relatively affordable food and drink in a relaxed and casual atmosphere that bucks some of the aesthetic and etiquette traditions of fine dining. These upscale urban eateries often combine the techniques and sensibilities of modern American cuisine with dude food. Early gastropubs in the United States built their reputations on excellently executed dude food, such as the now iconic burgers on the menu at Father's Office in Santa Monica in 2000 and the (now #MeToo infamous) Spotted Pig in 2004.[10]

Although gastropubs typically populate cosmopolitan cities, dude food codifies an inclusive sense of place and regionality beyond what are often framed as "elite" coasts and "hot" food cities. Dude food somehow manages to include regional or local specialties from sea to shining sea, whether a food's origins are specific or more diffuse. Chicago deep dish pizza is dude food. So is a Philly cheesesteak and Cincinnati chili. So are cheesy tater tot delights from the Midwest, chicken fried steak beloved in Texas and Oklahoma, and barbecue specialties from Kansas City, Memphis, and Austin, to name just a few. Dude food playfully resists classed understandings of high and low, junk and haute in a way that also claims people and places as its own.

Dude food also embodies the confidence, fearless freedom, and privilege of the dude to eat—and by extension do and be—whatever he wants, as well as the anxieties, risks, and consequences that come with eating and living like a dude. Concern for health tops the list of such anxieties. Defined by massive portions and full-throttle flavor, dude food enthusiastically endorses excess, as it thwarts nutritional advice that emphasizes restraint or even balance. Dude food serves as a site of resistance against dominant dietary advice, such as the healthy eating and anti-obesity mandates endorsed by government recommendations and policy.[11] For example, the description of the dude food Instagram account "Fat Fucks Unite" once read: "Make America Fat Again."[12] The account's description referenced Donald Trump's 2016 presidential campaign, which has inspired memes throughout U.S. popular culture, as well as significant social conflict. It also resists federal nutrition policy, such as that endorsed by former first lady Michelle Obama, which promoted healthier school food and a vegetable garden on the White House's south lawn. Later, the account's description changed to "It's a lifestyle. Join the movement," ironically rewriting dude food in the language of health and wellness trends.

Resisting healthy eating mandates, dude food is comfort food but with an edge of competitive destruction. Emphasizing such qualities, Sarah Lawson of *First We Feast* defined dude food as, "over-the-top, in-your-face culinary creations with no concern for moderation or decency."[13] Dude food demonstrates the contradictions inherent to ambivalent masculine body discipline, which devalues and discourages "healthy" eating as feminine.[14] Writer David Sax similarly asserts that food advertising to men "presents a cleverly crafted challenge to our manhood: Are you man enough to eat this shit?"[15] Dude food's propensity toward hyperbolic flavor and massive portion sizes yields potential overeating, health consequences, and food waste as eaters accept the challenge of being "man enough" to clean their plates. The Zagat-rated Triple Coronary Bypass burger at the Vortex Bar & Grill in Atlanta and the Quadruple Bypass Burger on the menu at Heart Attack Grill in Las Vegas ironically pose dude food consumption as a serious health risk. Articles on dude food address this contradiction with titles like "Dude Food That Is Actually Good for You," "7 Healthy Dude Foods," and "Diabetic Dude Food: Six Healthy Recipes Guys Will Love."[16] Chef, restaurateur, and *Top Chef* judge, Hugh Acheson, similarly critiqued dude food's unhealthy qualities, asserting that "dude needs balance. Maybe a salad? Hopefully we can lose the gender stereotypes of the '80s, when real men didn't eat quiche, 'cause often real men are morons."[17] Taken together, such messages create a paradoxical feedback loop between definitions of masculinity, dude food, and health.

These paradoxes of dude food grow more complicated when viewed through the more feminized gaze of Pinterest, a social media platform where women make up 70 percent of users and pin 93 percent of the platform's content.[18] Within Pinterest, one still finds recipes for bacon-wrapped meatballs oozing cheese out of their centers, but dude food's meaning shifts toward men as subjects to be fed and cared for by female cooks.[19] A number of pins link to Father's Day meals and menus. Recipe roundups such as "Dude Food: 18 Foods Dad Will Love" promise "man-approved" recipes, echoing the language that has appeared in cookbooks for many decades that reinforces traditional gender roles. Such pins prescribe dude food with a domesticated and feminized air, even as they offer recipes for baked buffalo wings, pizza dip, and meatloaf. The commercial media context of Pinterest also blurs the meaning of dude food. Some of the interspersed ads sponsor typical dude food, such as Old El Paso's promoted post for grilled steak bowls or Crown Royal's ad that asserts itself as "a better complement than fries." Other posts incongruously endorse dude food alongside products, such as RXBAR with its purportedly simple healthy ingredients and Daily Harvest's made-for-Instagram smoothies. Whether on websites, blogs, Instagram, or Pinterest, dude food connotes an unassailable sense of masculinity through its embrace of culinary excess, at the same time that it navigates contradictions surrounding power, access, waste, and health.

What's more, dude food saturated food media at a moment when men were increasingly engaging with food as part of their lifestyle and identity. The *Men's Health* website began running a "Guy Gourmet" column as a twice weekly blog in the mid-2000s, which primarily published recipes and cooking tips. In September 2012, Guy Gourmet had just surpassed 37,000 followers on Twitter.[20] Near its peak popularity in July 2017 it had more than

160,000 followers. In a 2012 article, "In Defense of Dude Food," *Men's Health* writer Paul Kita argued that the magazine's food readership had expanded dramatically to the point that food articles were among the most popular content they published online. Kita cited the increasing number of male-centric cookbooks, memoirs, food blogs, Twitter accounts, and Pinterest boards as evidence of "guys everywhere putting food at the center of their lives more than ever before," which he argued was "fueling a progression of gender equality in the home kitchen and a point of celebration when it comes to dining out."[21] Despite some men's increasing interest in food media and a supposed progression toward gender equality, dude food promotes a strict heteronormativity. Everything about dude food endeavors to heterosexualize food as a way to distinguish straight male interest in food and cooking from perceptions of femininity or gayness.

These paradoxical dude food relationships also guide the treatment of the male body, particularly with regard to a chiseled, muscular ideal.[22] Contemporary fat stigma frames fatness as a social problem, one with a corporeal and ideological force that obscures gender.[23] This results in what are perceived as out-of-control women and failed, effeminate men.[24] Even within the food features that Kita mentions, *Men's Health* framed dude food alongside health and social status. *Men's Health* magazine covers and articles, both in print and online, assert men's right to dude food, that is, to celebrate and satisfy supposedly manly appetites. At the same time, *Men's Health* demands of its readers personal responsibility for fitness and health, continuing to uphold the strong, muscled but lean, male body as central to straight white masculinity.

The cultural phenomenon of "the dad bod," which first made media waves in 2015, poses a different path altogether. While societal expectations predominantly hold a woman's body to the beauty standard of the thin ideal at every stage of her life, the dad bod celebrates "a nice balance between a beer gut and working out," as a male body of any age that "says I go to the gym occasionally, but I also drink heavily on the weekends and enjoy eating eight slices of pizza at a time."[25] In short, the dad bod is the dude (and dude food) body. Representing in physical form the laidback ethos of dudeness, the dad bod dispassionately resists unreasonable, male, ideal body types.

At the same time, the dad bod (just like the dude) remains complicit in overall structures of power impacting gender, sexuality, social class, and race. These power structures produce dad bods and dude food for men without dismantling the thin ideal for women or broader diet culture. Press stories routinely framed the dad bod as a straight phenomenon, mentioning heterosexual female desire as part of the impetus for the trend with titles such as "Why Girls Love the Dad Bod" and "Dad Bods Are More Attractive to Women Than Rock Hard Abs."[26] But the dad bod is permissible only for some men, demonstrating how the dude's social privilege functions through race and class. The dad bod exemplifies how white, straight, cisgender, middle-class, or more affluent men can resist social norms without consequence, while men of color, for example, do so with greater social risks. A Google Images search for dad bod returns photos of predominantly white men. When the popular press and gossip industry wrote stories in 2015 on dad bods, they focused on white celebrities, such as Leonardo DiCaprio, Seth Rogan, Vince Vaughan, Jason Segel, and Adam Sandler.

Some writers and viewers have interpreted the dad bod phenomenon as a sign of male body positivity. But as culture writer Pier Dominguez argues, defending the dad bod "merely promotes mainstream standards of desirability under the guise of subversiveness, repackaging thirst for the same conventionally hot bodies with a supposedly new twist."[27] In these ways, the dad bod and dude food exemplify the dude as a cultural figure and privileged social role defined by cool, unconcerned, and decidedly-not-earnest qualities.

The Dude in Food Advertising

The culinary contradictions of dude food and the privileged slacking of the dude represented an intriguing tension in the 2010s that multiple food brands sought to exploit. Around 2010, Kraft endeavored to target more than just working moms in their advertising.[28] At that time, Tiphanie Maronta, senior brand manager for Kraft's Velveeta meals, admitted, "We found a segment of men already making and cooking Shells & Cheese that we frankly weren't talking to. They are not a chef. They are not a foodie. It's somebody who is starting to cook."[29] They were dudes.

In August 2012, ad agency Wieden + Kennedy created a quintessentially dude campaign for Kraft's Velveeta Shells & Cheese: "Eat Like That Guy You Know." The television spots featured men in careers perceived as lower prestige, such as a mall kiosk salesman and a limo driver. The campaign brief described "that guy" as "getting paid an hourly wage to fly around remote control helicopters," that is, getting paid to play.[30] Defending dudes, the brief goes on to say, "What kind of guy eats Velveeta Shells & Cheese? That Guy. Because That Guy eats the way he lives his sweet life—effortlessly and awesomely. . . . That Guy just has living an inexplicably awesome life figured out." Despite "That Guy's" more modest professional accolades, or perhaps because of them, the advertisements depicted each of these men as a self-satisfied dude laborer, a man who goofs around and slacks off. He is coolly pleased in his work, not because it is prestigious, fulfilling, or well-paid, but because it is easy and effortless.

Further resisting the aspirational model of the businessman who eats power lunches at expensive restaurants, the dude eats microwave fare affordably and happily enough. Through such anti-careerism, the dude who eats cheesy microwave pasta resists traditionally aspirational male careers and masculinity's typical requirements for professional success, assertive and competitive achievement, and breadwinning—expectations all the more difficult to achieve during the recession. The dude opts out from the potential failure the nation's economic downturn brought. Instead, he triumphs as a slacker hero, celebrated for his lackadaisical work life and for eating whatever he wants. Working to forge safe pathways for men from eating toward cooking, these commercials made no mention of food preparation, just the act of boiling water.[31] At the same time, Velveeta's cheesy pasta options echo dude food's resistance to "healthy" eating, as they embrace convenient, comfort-food-type preparations.

Other food brands employed the dude to attract male consumers. The Minute Rice website once featured a recipe section titled "dude food" with the cooking directions, "Heat for 60 seconds, Mix with Whatever," endeavoring to communicate not just unlimited options, but the uninvested, non-committal attitude of "whatever, man."[32] In 2012, Kentucky Fried Chicken embraced the ethos of dude food with a Dude Food Rules survey. It included such findings as "46 percent of people think it would be more offensive to double dip than skinny dip at a party" and 26 percent "think it's okay to eat food that has fallen on the ground when no one else is around."[33] The survey framed food-related party fouls as part of casual, rule-breaking dude masculinity. Introduced in 2014, Oscar Mayer's P3 line of Portable Protein Packs combined the dude with high-protein food trends, offering eleven to fifteen grams of protein per serving. Served up via childlike, finger-food amounts of meat, cheese, and nuts, the snack combined the playful aspects of the dude (and Lunchables) with protein's promise to satisfy and settle appetites.[34]

Pivoting from their Weight Watchers frozen meal line, Kraft Heinz launched Devour frozen meals in 2016 for men in their twenties and thirties with marketing that emphasized dudeness.[35] The launch campaign created by ad agency Publicis Seattle extended the dude's casual and irreverent humor in ways that sexually objectified dude food's hyperbolic flavor. Devour meals included dude food offerings, such as loaded nacho fries or bacon-topped meatloaf with spicy ketchup. The brand presented frozen meals as feminine but not feminizing dishes to be sensuously consumed. In the "Lunch Spank" commercial, a man who works in an auto body shop ate a Devour meal standing up in the work break room, while in "Pool Boy" a well-muscled man in swim trunks ate a meal standing in a well-appointed kitchen as his female employer watched.[36] Like the men depicted in the "That Guy You Know" campaign, these men worked jobs perceived as lower prestige that require eating lunch quickly, while standing up, during a short break. After this set up, the man in "Lunch Spank" talked dirty to his macaroni and cheese as he ate it, like he might to a sexual partner. He said, "Say my name," "You like that don't you," and "You naughty little . . ." before he swatted the macaroni with his fork, acting out the product tagline "Food You Want to Fork."

While easy to dismiss as trivial, this campaign demonstrates how the dude upholds social arrangements of power through food and the body. Even as the dude spoke to the ongoing precarity of the post-recession years in the United States, even as the dude provided some men space to resist aspects of hegemonic masculinity, he continued to uphold gender hierarchies that subordinate and marginalize femininities, as well as other masculinities and nonbinary expressions of gender. Devour's marketing indexes dynamics of power that construct men as subjects who define and enact sex, women as objects who must receive sex, at times in violent ways.[37] Devour performed these power relations through macaroni and cheese in their initial ad launch, and again in a Super Bowl commercial in 2019. Created by ad agency DAVID Miami, the commercial blurred the concept of food porn and actual pornography to depict a disheveled man who was addicted to food porn; that is, he ate Devour meals so often that it interrupted his life, particularly with his girlfriend. With more than 15 million views on YouTube in June 2019, the ad intertwined the dude's cheeky irony with the real power dynamics of sex, gender, and food.

From Devour frozen meals to Velveeta's cheesy pasta, these brands deployed dude food and the gender discourse of the dude to sell their products to men. In most cases, however, these brands used dudeness to sell products only minimally affected (or even unaffected) by gender contamination. Building from this dude food foundation, the rest of this book documents and analyzes examples of food and media that are gender coded in

American culture as feminine and feminizing. Starting with men's cookbooks, these examples document how the dude has been deployed to combat gender contamination and to uphold the current status of straight white masculinity.

The Dude in Contemporary Men's Cookbooks

By crafting an overtly masculine food genre, dude food charts socially acceptable pathways into the kitchen for men to cook for themselves and others, spaces and actions conventionally gendered feminine — negotiations laid bare within the pages of men's cookbooks. As novel cultural texts for analyzing food and media, cookbooks provide far more than just recipes as instructions for cooking. Cookbooks are elements of popular culture, valuable historical evidence, and prescriptive literature that shape and reflect notions of gender. Cookbooks speak volumes even in today's increasingly digital and highly saturated food media moment. Despite fears that "print is dead," cookbook publishing has continued to thrive in the twenty-first century.[38] Cookbooks specifically for men are not a new phenomenon, though they comprise a smaller subset of the cookbook market.

In her history of American cookbooks, Jessamyn Neuhaus cited at least thirteen men's cookbooks published in the United States between 1946 and 1960, manuals that provided a complicated answer to the postwar crisis of white masculinity.[39] I have collected an approximate number of cookbooks published specifically for a male audience in the last twenty years, from 1999 to 2019. They similarly communicate the gender anxiety and backlash of the time through the language of recipes. Cooking at home is not a naturally gendered activity, but in American society it is a domestic labor still disproportionality performed by women. Even as more men, particularly dads, take on these duties, cookbooks reveal how we are still combatting the notion that home cooking is culturally considered feminine and feminizing.

As a result, my sample of men's cookbooks demonstrates the techniques that cookbook authors and publishers employed as they attempted to masculinize home cooking. My sample of men's cookbooks does not include those whose specific aim was muscle building or fitness, such as Michael Matthews's *The Shredded Chef* from 2016, *Bobby Flay Fit* from 2017, or Kevin Curry's *Fit Men Cook* from 2018. I also didn't examine cookbooks dedicated specifically to meat or grilling, such as Meathead Goldwyn and Greg Blonder's *Meathead: The Science of Great Barbecue and Grilling* from 2016 or Steven

Lee's *The Grilling Bible* from 2019. These themes pose less risk of gender contamination than more general home cooking. Of the men's cookbooks I analyzed, some embraced the ambivalence and contradictions of the dude and dude food. Others clung more closely to conventional renderings of gender, food, and cooking, in some cases repeating the tropes of the enlightened male gourmand and the campfire adventurer common in men's cookbooks published between 1890 and 1970.[40] Overall, contemporary cookbooks for men mix the classically manly with the millennial dude-ish in their recipes, organizational structures, visuals, and commentary, all in an effort to masculinize home cooking.

Some of these cookbooks adopt simple and traditional strategies, as they depict cooking alongside conventionally masculine concepts and symbols. Using a common trope from men's cookbooks over the past century, David Bowers frames men's cooking in *Bake It Like a Man: A Real Man's Cookbook*, published in 1999, as different from (and better than) women's cooking. He writes, "What sets man apart from woman in the kitchen is that for him, cooking is not a humdrum everyday event. Women cook merely to put supper on the table; men cook for nobler purposes, shrouded in mystery and smoke, high priests of self-sufficiency."[41]

Bake It Like a Man's cover reinforces this gendered difference with an image of a man in a loose-fitting white T-shirt and jeans with a tool belt around his hips, filled with kitchen utensils: a whisk, baster, spatula, tongs, and timer. W. J. Rayment's *The Real Man's Cookbook* from 2000 similarly depicts a man in a dirty leather apron more fitting for a welder than a home cook.[42] It is not uncommon for the opening section of a cookbook to outline recommended items for a home cook, but "tools" signify something different within a men's cookbook. Esquire's *Eat Like a Man: The Only Cookbook a Man Will Ever Need* from 2011 lists with a dude-ish cool air "Some Tools You'll Need" to "get you through most recipes." Later in the cookbook, the headnote for Chef Frank Crispo's Spaghetti Carbonara continues this focus, as he writes, "My dad was a plumber so I grew up with a wrench in my hand, learning how to fix things. Recipes are no different. You have to tinker with a dish until it works for you." *Guy Gourmet*, published by *Men's Health* editors in 2013, goes a step further as it frames kitchen utensils as "The Kitchen Toolbox," complete with an image of a red toolbox and translations between "shopspeak" and "chefspeak." For example, saw means chef's knife, drill press equals mixer, and pliers are tongs. These nonculinary accessories strive to masculinize and heterosexualize cooking for men, while also aligning culinary endeavors with brawny, working-class masculinity.

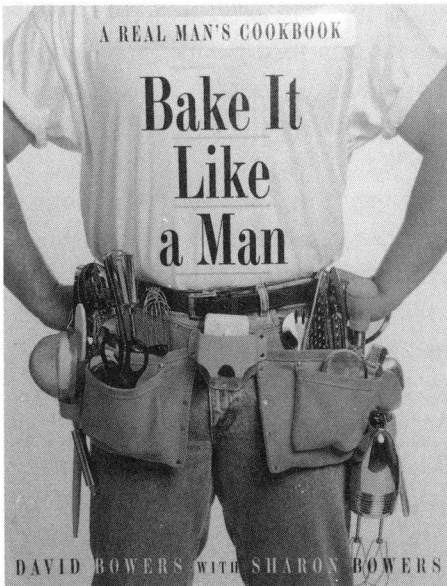

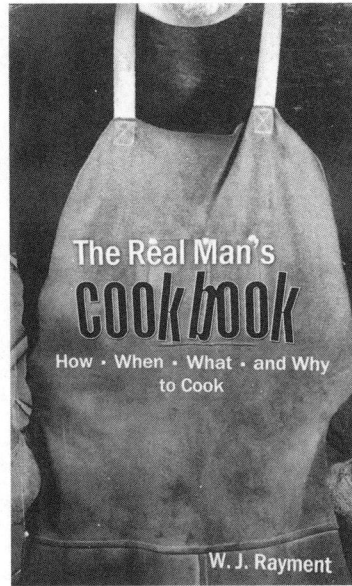

The cover images of the cookbooks *Bake It Like a Man* (1999) and *The Real Man's Cookbook* (2000) evoke working-class masculinity as they depict nonculinary accessories, such as a tool belt and a dirty leather apron, all in an effort to masculinize men's cooking.

A number of other cookbooks similarly employ masculine conventions to protect the status of men's home cooking. Building on their decades of men's cookery advice, Esquire pitches *Eat Like a Man* for "the new vanguard of men who consider cooking one of the manly arts."[43] In the cookbook's cover image, a steak suggestively peeks out from beneath torn brown paper, invoking both the packaging of the butcher shop and the vintage appearance of erotic magazines on newsstands, obscured yet clearly in view. In *Dude Food: Recipes for the Modern Guy*, published in 2000, Karen Brooks, Gideon Bosker, and Reed Darmon define dude food through masculine conventions such as car culture, speed, competition, and victory. Zach Golden's 2011 cookbook, *What the F*@# Should I Make for Dinner?: The Answers to Life's Everyday Question (in 50 F*@#ing Recipes)*, employs rule-breaking profanity to bring hesitant cooks into the kitchen, a strategy taken to a new level in the white-authored *Thug Kitchen* cookbooks.[44] Just as the dude provides men a gender strategy to combat recession-era financial insecurity and employment frustrations, Golden's cookbook asserts that "Life is tough, but dinner doesn't have to be." This culinary promise appeals to cooks of all sorts and of every gender, but it also speaks to the specific challenges and anxieties of the millennial dude.

Following such gendered logics, the sections in contemporary men's cookbooks are not organized around meals or food groups, as one might expect. Instead authors and editors orient the recipes around purportedly masculine desires and efforts to thwart feminizing food anxieties. *A Man, a Can, a Plan*, published by *Men's Health* in 2002, offers up the categories: Ham, Chicken, Fish, Chili, Beans, Veggies, Fruit, and Beer.[45] A confounding section dedicated solely to SpaghettiOs communicates the boyishness of dudes, straddling childhood meals and the responsibilities of cooking for oneself. Dan Churchill's *DudeFood: A Guy's Guide to Cooking Kick-Ass Food*, published in 2015, includes sections dedicated to Sandwiching the Gym, The Hangover Cure, and Foods That Last, offering recipes not so much for meals as to fuel a dude's lifestyle made up of workout routines, partying, and insatiable appetites.[46] Brooks, Bosker, and Darmon's *Dude Food* organizes recipes by men's roles rather than food categories with titles like Master of Ceremonies, Patio Daddy-O, Mr. Mom, The Lone Ranger, and Sweet Talkin' Guy.

The organization of men's cookbooks also isolates some foods as unmasculine. *Bake It Like a Man* offers chapters on "Men and . . ." meat, flame, big food, fat, hot foods, and fermentation, along with the admonishment that "real men rarely make sweets," which the author deems feminine and feminizing. *The Real Man's Cookbook* includes a single page for desserts, blank except for the words, "Real men don't make desserts. However, we will eat them on special occasions." Desserts aren't the only food deemed too feminine to make the cut. Mario Batali's NASCAR tailgating cookbook includes a section titled, "Chicken and (don't say it too loudly) Fish," belying the idea that marine creatures sit below white meats on the gender hierarchy of protein.[47] Apparently, fish isn't masculine enough to earn a spot on a tailgating menu.

These odd tables of contents, simple recipes, meaty ingredients, and bold flavors adhere to stereotypically masculine conventions, but the tone of dude cooking instruction is oppositional, suggestive, casual, and joking. In the *Washington Post*, Benwick describes the audience for dude cookbooks as "a guy who's up for spending time in the kitchen who will find the dishes relatively unfussy and meat-centric, with atta-boy recipe language."[48] With friendly, self-denigrating dude humor, *A Man, a Can, a Plan* offers "50 great guy meals even you can make!" Organized in simple, mathematical terms (ingredient A + ingredient B + ingredient C = dude meal), the cookbook aims to address men's potential lack of culinary skill and comfort in the kitchen. This novice approach extends to the book's design, which called for recipes to be printed on forty-three thick, cardboard pages set in the style of a baby book. With recipes like "Border-Patrol Casserole," "Cowboy Stew," and "Homeboy Homefries," recipe instructions further emphasize the dude with verb choices such as dump, smother, stab, nuke, and plop. Of his own cookbook, Australian personal trainer Dan Churchill concedes, "I wrote *DudeFood* in a language I like to call 'colloquial dude.' Cheers, brah!" To this end *DudeFood* includes recipe titles such as "Spag Bol" (short for Spaghetti Bolognese), which "serves 3 or 4 hungry blokes," and "Basic Bro Burger."

Beyond recipes, *DudeFood* also represents the dude visually. Images throughout the cookbook feature groups of young men together eating, drinking, cooking, surfing, and laughing. Shot in a candid style, these images communicate the carefree homosociality, but strict heterosexuality, of dudes. A particularly striking photograph shows two tanned men in baseball caps, shot from behind as they stand shirtless on the beach, looking toward the open ocean. Unlike Churchill, whose lean and toned body adheres to ideals of masculinity, these men's bodies read as youthful and powerful, but rounder, softer, and less sleek than ideal body types—more dad bod than bodybuilder. These men physically embody the easy, comfortable, and relaxed qualities of the dude, particularly the countercultural surfer cultures that inspired today's use of the term. By including such images, Churchill's *DudeFood* provides a unique distillation of the relationship between dude masculinity, food, cooking, and the body. The cookbook defines what dude food is alongside how dudes should act during the recession-era moment when the conventions of how to be a real man were destabilized.

Health also remains a key theme in twenty-first-century men's cookbooks. In *Man Made Meals: The Essential Cookbook for Guys*, published in 2014, Steven Raichlen includes health and environmental sustainability in his "The Men Who Cook Manifesto." As in *Men's Health* magazine, *A Man, a Can, a Plan* seeks to masculinize food and cooking through connections to nutrition science and health. It decrees, "This food does everything from prevent heart disease and prostate cancer to boost your immune system and energy levels." The *Guy Gourmet* cookbook endorses a message that paradoxically blends dude food and moderation: "Man does not live on steel-cut oatmeal and sockeye salmon alone. He needs . . . chili and steak, chicken soup and jambalaya. He must, on occasion, have barbecued ribs. And hot dogs, upgraded with gourmet toppings. Yeah, even hot dogs."[49] While health-focused cookbooks typically encourage women to exist in a near constant state of deprivation and restriction, men within *Guy Gourmet* "need" and "must have" indulgent foods to properly satisfy male appetites and fuel masculinity. This relationship between an appetite for dude food and health inspired Serena Wolf of the *Domesticate Me* food blog to create "The Dude Diet" in 2012 for her then boyfriend, who had developed a dad bod. Published as a cookbook in 2016 (followed by a second cookbook in 2019), Wolf's recipes balance the bombastic flavor profile of dude food with nutritional moderation in the pursuit of a disciplined, healthy, male body.[50]

In their cookbooks, *Men's Health* also broached dieting and weight loss in ways that reveal the ambivalence inherent to caring for the male body. Recipes throughout the cookbook feature symbols representing specific health benefits rather than a typical diet mentality of restraint. A flexed bicep marks recipes with high protein content, a heart denotes heart-healthy ingredients such as whole grains or "healthy" fats, and a stick figure with arrows pointing to its waist identifies "gut shrinkers." What might be marked as light or diet-friendly recipes in a cookbook for women are described for men as "all the flavor for fewer calories — these dishes will help you stay lean or lose the weight you want." Such a description reinforces assumptions about masculine appetites that demand satisfying flavors, even when dieting.

In such ways, many of these cookbooks demonstrate an ongoing tension between traditionally masculine food conventions and the dude's more flexible interpretations. In *Dude Food*, Brooks, Bosker, and Darmon defined dude food broadly as a sort of ethos: "a way of life, freely interpreted, a life in which confidence, fearlessness, and fun metamorphose into truth and soul, guy-style."[51] In a para-textual twist, however, the book design uses solely vintage images from midcentury. The cookbook visually depicts the ambivalence surrounding questions about how, where, and when food and cooking figure into masculinity today.

This contradiction between conventional masculinity and the dude remains strong in *Guy Gourmet*, which explicitly targeted dudes interested in food. Despite this, the foreword from acclaimed chef Thomas Keller hails everyday men to cook through the all-too-conventional imagery of cavemen, the invention of fire, and the overused trope of seducing women through culinary skill and gastronomic care.[52] While *Men's Health* intended for *Guy Gourmet* to update cultural ideas about men cooking, including gender equality, it actually reinforced the caveman tropes it used eleven years prior in *A Man, a Can, a Plan*, which asserted that men do indeed cook and have been "since we discovered fire."[53] References to conventional masculinity appear throughout *Guy Gourmet* from a section on Breakfast that cries, "Wake up and smell the protein!" to a section on Muscle Snacks and another on

Eating Outside, which promises, "From grilling to barbecuing to camp cookery, here's how to make yourself the lord of the fires." Shopping tips blare out, "Gentleman, Stock Your Pantry." Such language serves to maintain masculine status even as the dude encourages men to cook more often.

Other cookbooks also ambivalently combine conventional masculinity with the dude. In *Man Made Meals*, Raichlen refers to esteemed celebrity chefs like Thomas Keller and Nathan Myhrvold as "Food Dudes" and he asserts, "Repeat after me: Grilling is not gender specific."[54] Despite this attempt to recode the gender of grilling, Raichlen reverts back to convention a sentence later, writing, "Grilling taps into the primeval male urge to make and manage fire, and it generally involves two other beloved guy entities, sharp knives and alcohol." Recipes feature contradictory mixtures of ironic dudeness and hard-nosed manliness, as Raichlen refers to both "righteous brunch dishes" and "high-testosterone grilled cheese." Similarly, the front cover design of Fritz Brand's 2017 cookbook, *Cook Like a Man: Master Your Own Kitchen with 78 Simple and Delicious Recipes*, evokes traditional masculinity with a dark chalkboard background and a burger stabbed with a knife. The back cover, however, speaks to gender stereotypes and men's anxieties about cooking, as it encourages men to "beat down [the] stereotype" that men grill but do not cook, as well as to "confront their fears, drop the excuses, get their hands dirty, and cook like a man!"[55] These cookbooks engage the ambivalence of the dude, as he resists some masculine conventions, while maintaining others.

Cookbooks can serve subversive purposes, providing a platform for the too-often-silenced voices of women and people of color.[56] Contemporary men's cookbooks do not. Just as the dude continues to marginalize women and femininities, these cookbooks reinforce female subordination as they encourage men to cook. Some men's cookbooks frame cooking as an act of reclamation. They present men asserting their right to dominance in spheres public and domestic, both of which women (especially feminists) have purportedly curtailed. In *Bake It Like a Man*, Bowers bellows, "All real human drama takes place in the kitchen. And for too long, it's been the sole domain of woman. But man has an equal right to the place, and it's time he asserted himself domestically. . . . Tell your significant other to step back and let a real man handle the job." With such words, Bowers transforms masculine domesticity from a gendered risk into an ordained right. Speaking to an audience of "real" and "average" men, Rayment similarly complains in *The Real Man's Cookbook* that "the domestic culinary arts have been closed to the typical American male," citing this as an "urgent need" to rectify in "these trying times of feminism." Rayment reconfigures men's well-documented avoidance of daily cooking into a set of denied experiences to which men deserve access.

The language of rights also appears in cookbooks dedicated to conventionally masculine culinary endeavors like grilling. *Marlboro's Cook Like a Man Cookbook* asserts, "BBQ is a right not a privilege. Bigger is better. No apologies. Man is at the top of the food chain."[57] Similar to *Eat Like a Man's* cover, this final sentence demonstrates Carol Adams's ecofeminist critique of the sexual politics of meat. She asserts that patriarchal culture subjugates women and animals in interrelated ways, as "an attitude and action that animalizes women and sexualizes and feminizes animals."[58] Through such arrangements of power, both are subordinated and treated as pieces of meat.

Some men's cookbooks gesture to gender parity and equality as part of men cooking at home, but despite such messaging these cookbooks reinforce gendered conventions and inequality. For example, Greg Ford's cookbook was inspired by recipes that he gave his son when he got married, a gift intended to promote sharing domestic duties. And yet the 2013 cookbook is juvenilely titled *No Girls Allowed: Cookbook for Men*, excluding women as it encourages men to cook. In the foreword to Esquire's *Eat Like a Man*, chef Tom Colicchio also encourages men to expand their culinary purview beyond the backyard grill. He asserts that the division between men dominating professional kitchens and women home kitchens "is beginning to break down."[59] The cookbook nevertheless walks the tightrope between feminine home cooking and masculine chef work, as it includes recipes only "from chefs we respect."[60] Whether from women or men, the recipe authors' professional status further masculinizes and legitimates cookery advice for the male home cook. Unsurprisingly, these recipes come from mostly male chefs (such as Colicchio's "Steak with Potatoes" and Michael Symon's "Meat Loaf"), including chefs with long histories of sexual harassment and assault revealed by the revitalized #MeToo movement, such as Mario Batali's "Pork Shoulder Alla Porchetta" and John Besh's "Braised Beef Short Ribs." In *DudeFood*, Churchill contends that he wrote the cookbook "to educate, motivate, and inspire an intimidated male audience," especially since "gone are the days of the stereotypical housewife, when the men earned the bread and the women would slave away cooking." Although Churchill aspires to help men learn how to cook, he still frames cooking for men as either a masculine challenge or "an unforeseen expectation," in either case, not as domestic drudgery, the gendered and expected work of women.[61]

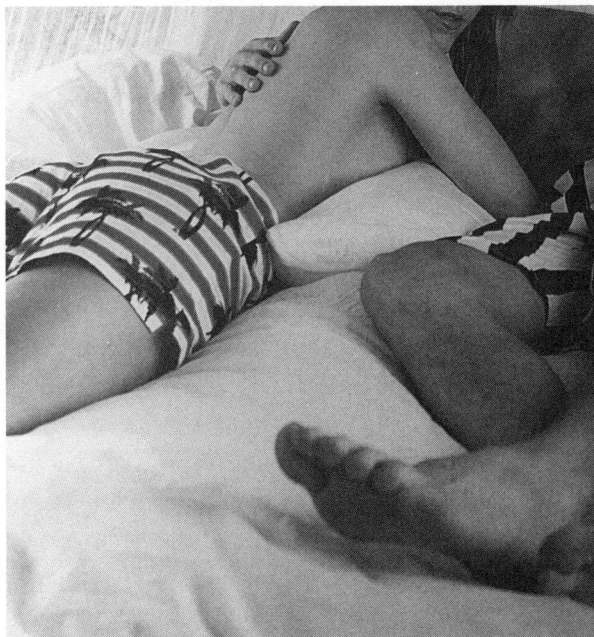

This image from the "How to Impress a Girl" section in *DudeFood* (2015) is highly unusual for a cookbook, as it depicts for men the erotic spoils of cooking: the seduced and bedded woman.

Furthermore, Churchill leans hard on the men's cookbook trope of using food to seduce women. One one hand, women's cookbooks that endorse traditional gender roles—much like the dude food Pinterest pins mentioned previously—offer advice to use food to please, nurture, and hold onto men's attentions. On the other hand, men's cookbooks disclose instructions for how to entice women into bed and perhaps discard them afterward. Jim Madden and Thomas Jacques center this trope in their self-published 2012 "comedy cookbook," *Man Meets Stove: A Cookbook for Men Who've Never Cooked Anything without a Microwave*, which offered recipes, such as "Nachos without Artificial Implants," "Apricot Chicken, or, How to Get Laid," and "The Morning-After Chilaquiles," in order to "make a girl gasp with ecstasy with nothing more than a spoon."[62] *Guy Gourmet* includes a more tame and respectful "Date Night" section with recipes for a "sexy-as-hell" "Chipotle Sweet Potato Fondue" and a "sensual" "Chocolate pot de crème." Esquire's *Eat Like a Man* is full of stories about feeding brothers, but the headnote for chef Daniel Boulud's "Scrambled Eggs with Smoked Salmon, Caviar, and Potatoes" considers the dish only as part of breakfast in bed: "You want your woman to stay lazy while you bring it to her. . . . And if you serve it to her unexpectedly, there might be, shall we say, compensation."[63]

In *Man Made Meals*, Steven Raichlen assures his readers, "When a guy does breakfast, it becomes an event. You'll know what I mean—if you don't already—the first time you cook breakfast for a date that began the previous evening."[64]

Churchill's *DudeFood* takes culinary seduction to another level by visually depicting such results. Not inconsequentially, the "How to Impress a Girl" section features the only photo of a woman in the cookbook, which is, rather unusually, full of photos of people.[65] A thin, white-skinned, and blonde-haired woman—resting topless in bed on her stomach as a man embraces her—appears before recipes for "Peri-Peri Roast Chicken," "Poached Salmon with a Walnut Apple Salad and Honey Mustard," and a cake titled "Getting Out of the Doghouse." In a dude cookbook, recipes come with a side of partially visible breasts. My personal copy of *DudeFood*, which I purchased used, further reveals Churchill's focus on seducing women and defending cooking on heterosexual terms, as it bears his signature and the handwritten message, "To the girls who got my shirt off without having to say anything." Such examples sustain the erotic precedent set within the pages of men's cookbooks over the last century, revealing the limits of the dude to encourage men to cook in ways that actually promote gender equality.

As this discussion of men's cookbooks reinforces, the dude upholds many aspects of hegemonic masculinity. Some of these cookbooks reinforce conventional notions of masculine flavors and appetites. Some employ misogynistic and anti-feminist messaging. Many of these cookbooks frame men cooking within the context of seducing women or of cavemen, primal fire, and hunks of meat. These cookbooks also reveal how the dude differs from conventional norms of masculinity. Given the dude's ironic sense of humor, dudes can make fun of themselves and their lack of culinary skills. Dude cookbooks navigate the perceived feminization of health. Dude cookbooks sometimes consider the dude body, which does not mirror the well-muscled covers of men's fitness magazines.

Beyond the pages of cookbooks and the dude food content found on blogs, social media accounts, and food websites, dudes also learned it was okay to cook and to feed others from food television. Like cookbook publishers, however, the Food Network sought to gain more male viewers to a feminized genre. They did so through a particular food television star, promoted not as a masculine culinary expert, but as a dude chef: Guy Fieri, the focus of the next chapter.

CHAPTER TWO

Creating a Dude Chef

Food Network's Guy Fieri

Food journalists and cultural critics have flexed their muscles of description to capture Guy Fieri, ardently seeking the words and metaphors to make sense of his polarizing potential. They call him "a supernova of kitsch" and "the so-called rock-n-roll comfort food king—but more accurately the extremely unhealthy-looking, ear-splitting maniac who thinks he's fronting a college garage band circa 1995." They label him a "rebel, clown, frat boy, chef" and "a flaming-skull decal brought to life." They draw attention to his "rocker-meets-dad image." They assert, "Fieri's entire essence, from the glasses to the hair to the jewelry to the beard, is a catchphrase."[1]

Guy Fieri entered the public eye in 2006 when he won the second season of the reality show cooking competition, *Next Food Network Star*.[2] On this program, chefs of varying amateur status compete against one another to win their own Food Network television show. From the start, Fieri did not fit the norms, practices, and appearances of a chef, a food celebrity, or a twenty-first-century TV star. Unconventional, he wore his hair bleached and spiked. Boisterously energetic, he yelled into the camera at top volume. Purposefully unprofessional, he cooked dishes that broke the rules of any established cuisine and were in his own words "off the hook." Fieri connected with audiences, who responded to his populist appeal.[3] Audiences and critics love and hate Guy Fieri specifically for his dudeness, for the numerous ways that he thwarts the expectations of normative masculinity.

Guy Fieri within the History of Food Television

Guy Fieri's critics accuse him of destroying the Food Network. They blame him for the over-commercialized, competition-oriented, and sensationalized state of today's food television. Nevertheless, despite significant changes in how viewers now experience television—streaming any show, anytime, anywhere—television still functions as a "cultural hearth."[4] This is particularly true of food television's cultural role. Food and cooking engage the hearth—and its contemporary manifestation, the kitchen—materially, spatially, and ideologically, as a space for making meaning, defining community, and, in the case of the Food Network, creating stars.[5] Guy Fieri is just a single point in long-standing historical debates about the social position of broadcast media itself.

The tension between education and entertainment plagued radio and television, its producers, and its critics, from the beginning of each medium's history.[6] Early television critics in the 1960s bemoaned the transition from the Golden Age of live anthology dramas filmed in New York and based on traditional theater to a "vast wasteland" of Hollywood-preproduced, genre-based series with recurring characters, devoid of cultural prestige and artistic merit.[7] Some voiced this same concern for food television's shift from culinary education and food as high art toward gastronomic entertainment with programs focused on competitive spectacle like *Top Chef* (2006–), *Chopped* (2007–), and *MasterChef* (2010–).[8]

These concerns specifically index gender. Watching television is framed as domestic, feminine, and femininizing compared to the public, masculine, and dominant position of cinema.[9] Pushing gender boundaries, Julia Child in some ways initiated food television's recombination of instruction and spectacle, content and audience engagement.[10] On *The French Chef*, which aired from 1963 to 1973, she taught challenging and exacting French cooking techniques through her genuine larger-than-life personality, including broadcasting her own kitchen mishaps. Male TV chefs also pushed the culinary boundaries of edutainment long before Fieri made waves. The first to cook before a live in-studio audience on *The Galloping Gourmet* from 1969 to 1971, Graham Kerr emphasized personality, humor, and showmanship as much as he did gourmet cuisine. In his cookbooks, which are in tone and content quite serious, Kerr presented himself as "a source of entertainment, enjoyment, and information."[11] Laying precedent for Fieri's antics, Kerr embodied the show's title at the beginning of each episode as he literally galloped into the studio, leaping over a chair and up onto the stage set, all with a nearly full glass of wine in his hand. He never spilled a drop and grinned with every step.

Starting in 1993, the Food Network inserted cooking shows and celebrity chefs into the daily lives of a significant number of viewers, though largely women.[12] Erica Gruen began her term as Food Network president and CEO in 1996, as only the second woman to perform such a role in cable television history. Due to previous arrangements regarding cable subscriptions, advertising comprised the network's sole revenue source. As a result, Gruen needed a larger audience, so she shifted "the programming emphasis from people who like to cook to people who love to eat."[13] With stars like

Emeril Lagasse, who cooked with masculine bravado, Gruen sought to re-gender cooking programming in a strategic move to expand the network's audience.

Masculinity and male viewers proved key players in the Food Network that Gruen built around Emeril. It mattered that men watched Emeril in significant numbers, as "the largest segment of his viewership was men over 30 — including firehouse crews watching his show en masse — and thus he was [the Food Network's] ticket to not becoming Lifetime Network II" — that is, a network intended for a female demographic.[14] Furthermore, Emeril originated key features of the Food Network persona Fieri would adopt and expand. He predated Fieri in being hailed as a "dude chef."[15] Network co-founder, Reese Schonfeld said, "Sociologically I think the biggest thing we did was Emeril. I think it's Emeril who made it possible for men to cook."[16] Food Network marketing and branding executive Susie Fogelson, later made the same case for Fieri, saying that he "really resonates with men," and that his prime-time shows garnered more male viewers than any other show on the network.[17] Lagasse would also directly intersect Fieri's food TV origins. In the penultimate episode of season 2 of *Next Food Network Star*, Fieri filmed the pilot episode for his proposed show, *Cooking Off the Hook*, which Fieri aptly described as "a cross between *Jack Ass*, *American Chopper*, and *Emeril*." Paula Deen concurred, gushing, "Guy reminds me of a cross between Emeril and Mario [Batali]." It was fitting that Lagasse himself was live on set to announce Guy Fieri the winner and Food Network's next star, though no one could have predicted how large of a star he would become.

Beyond his Lagasse lineage, Guy Fieri is further nestled within the history of the Food Network and its programming trends. When Fieri competed on the second season of *Next Food Network Star* in 2006, the network had begun shifting their prime-time programming from stars cooking to stars competing, though these shows still retained elements of pedagogical intent. Compared to more recent seasons of *Next Food Network Star*, early seasons of the program endeavored to teach viewers not how to cook, but how to produce food television. Alongside culinary challenges and elimination ceremonies, these early episodes included interview clips with producers, directors, technicians, stage managers, and food stylists, each explaining the work they did behind the scenes. On the final episode of season 2 of *Next Food Network Star*, Brooke Johnson — who began as president of the Food Network in 2004 and retired at the end of 2016 — marched on stage herself with a contract in hand for the winner.[18] Her presence made tangible and visible details of the Food Network production process that have become far less evident since then, at least to viewers. More recent seasons of the program promote the budding stars themselves rather than the mechanics of food TV production.

Furthermore, all seasons of *Next Food Network Star* serve as intra-network promotion, each episode a twenty-one-minute advertisement. Episodes feature a main challenge that brings other Food Network stars onto the show, serving as both inspiration for contestants and cross-promotion for the network. On Fieri's season of *Next Food Network Star*, Iron Chefs Masaharu Morimoto, Mario Batali, and Bobby Flay tested contestants' knife skills and presentation chops, as they demonstrated their own technical prowess. Rachael Ray taught the aspiring food stars how to cook on camera, while sharing her trademark style, which in 2006 had already led to four TV shows, dozens of cookbooks, and a magazine. Sandra Lee guided the contestants in developing their culinary point of view while she explained her convenience approach on *Semi-Homemade Cooking*. Giada De Laurentiis tested contestants with a two-dish multitasking challenge, while providing tips and examples from her show, *Everyday Italian*. Dave Lieberman shared his laid-back style; Alton Brown supported the contestants as they filmed a field report from Chelsea Market; and Paula Deen coached the final two contestants as they filmed their test pilot episodes—all while promoting their own shows and personas. It is within this Food Network media mix, which emphasized entertainment more than cooking instruction so to gain more male viewers, that Guy Fieri and his unusual, dude approach to food and gender took root.

Guy Fieri: The Dude Chef People Love to Hate

Who is Guy Fieri? In his program audition tape, Fieri greeted viewers at top volume, "Hi, I'm Guy Fieri. I like to live big, laugh hard, and cook wild!"[19] He conceded, "When people first meet me, I think that they're a little . . . stand back," acknowledging his destabilizing presence. From his first minutes of food TV fame, Fieri directly discussed his unusual sense of style and dress, as he said, "I sit on the board of directors for the California Restaurant Association and everybody's suit and tie. I was done wearing suits and ties a long time ago." As he made this comment, the camera cut multiple times to Fieri's clothes and body; one shot scanned him from toe to head. His food industry colleague (dressed in modest business casual with a blue, long-sleeved dress shirt, khaki pants, and a brown belt) contrasted strongly with Fieri's dude uniform: a short-sleeved, bright orange shirt, tucked into long black shorts with a studded belt and a silver star buckle, along with

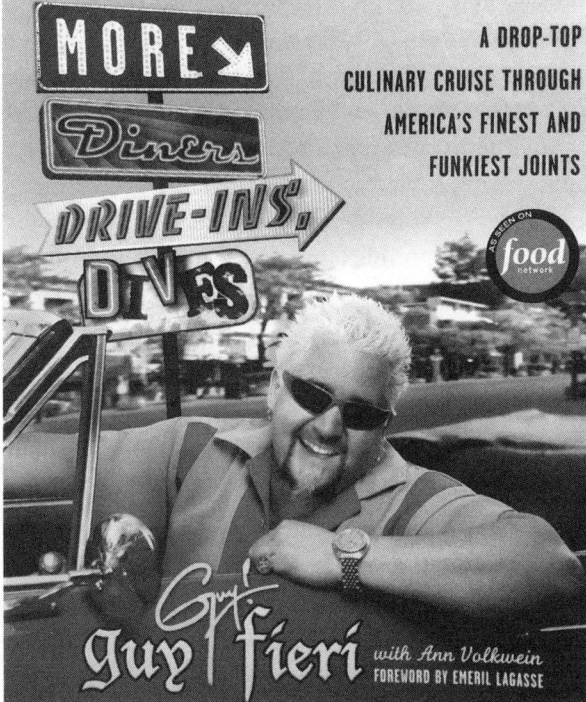

The cover image for *More Diners, Drive-Ins and Dives* (2009) depicts Guy Fieri and his typical style—bleached and spiked hair, goatee, sizeable and noticeable jewelry, sunglasses, loud shirts, and an open-mouthed grin—which audiences embrace and celebrate, as well as deride and parody.

sneakers, a black arm band, a clunky watch, silver hoop earrings, and sunglasses. Fieri presented his sense of self as quirky but actualized, further demonstrated through a food metaphor: "If I was a food, I think I'd be lasagna: multilayered, meaty, a little cheesy, a little spicy, and I'd feed everyone." Importantly, it is Fieri's privileged social status—as a white, cisgender, heterosexual man who began his career as a middle-class, college-educated restaurateur and now owns and operates a food empire—that makes his rule-thwarting dude approach possible.

Despite the ways Fieri transgressed food celebrity—or perhaps because of it—he catapulted to Food Network success within three years of winning a reality competition that for most contestants has yielded only a brief blip of notoriety.[20] Since his first Food Network show, *Guy's Big Bite*—which completed its nineteenth season in 2016—he has had a slew of popular programs. These included dozens of seasons of *Diners, Drive-Ins and Dives*, as well as *Ultimate Recipe Showdown* (2008–2010), *Rachael vs. Guy: Celebrity Cook-Off* (2012–2014), and *Guy's Grocery Games* (2013–), among others. His food empire also boasts multiple restaurants, cookbooks, "rock 'n' roll" gastro-tours, food products, and kitchen equipment. His estimated net worth is as much as $10 million, and he is routinely listed among top-earning chefs, alongside culinary figures like Thomas Keller and Rick Bayless and fellow Food Network stars like Bobby Flay and Ina Garten.[21] In May 2019, Fieri became the third chef ever to receive a star on the Hollywood Walk of Fame, joining chefs Bobby Flay and Wolfgang Puck.[22]

Different from these culinary stars, however, dude chef Guy Fieri established his public expertise and achieved his fame on reality TV, a genre "on the cusp of developments in media convergence, interactivity, user-generated content, and greater viewer involvement in television."[23] In this vein, Food Network viewers' votes supposedly determined the outcome of *Next Food Network Star*, affording audiences agency to create Guy Fieri as a star and site of fandom. Despite his popular appeal, Fieri did not progress through the regimented hierarchy of George Auguste Escoffier's traditional brigade de cuisine in a professional kitchen.[24] Instead, he studied abroad in France during high school and earned a college degree in hospitality management from the University of Nevada, Las Vegas.

A uniquely polarizing figure, widely adored by fans and vehemently disdained by critics, Fieri garners significant media attention. By my count in spring 2020, the Vox Media food website Eater had published more feature articles and entries on Guy Fieri than culinary figures like David Chang, Anthony Bourdain, or Julia Child. Indicating Fieri fervor, both positive and negative, these Fieri entries generated more than double the user comments than any other chef.

More than anything else, critics attack Fieri for his unique appearance. From his first seconds on *Next Food Network Star*, Fieri's presentation of self boldly resisted standards of professionalism as it embodied the boy-like resistance of the dude. On a panel at the 2009 New York Wine and Food Festival, Bourdain and Chang both identified Fieri as an enemy of the food world.[25] Chang reportedly remarked upon "Fieri's 'douche glasses,' and 'stupid f***ing armband,' and he asked Bourdain to 'catch me and kick me in the ass' if he ever took on the look."[26] While he eventually changed his tune, Bourdain lobbed negative comments at Fieri over a period of years. He included derogatory remarks in his 2015 *Close to the Bone* speaking tour, saying, "I sort of feel in a heartfelt way for Guy [Fieri]. I wonder about him. He's 52 years old and still rolling around in the flame outfit. . . . What does he do? How does Guy Fieri de-douche?"[27] In *Salon*, Farsh Askari similarly derided Fieri's choice of dress, ridiculing him as "a grown man with a penchant for Billabong clothing."[28] Such comments belie an underlying disdain, an indictment that Fieri is not a real man particularly for the boy-like aspects of the dude that he strongly embodies. Fieri's critics deride him for not adhering to the rules of how masculine and middle-class men dress and present themselves, particularly TV celebrity chefs. Critics similarly attack Fieri's presentation style and use of catch phrases, describing him as "ear-splitting," "shouting," and a "loudmouth," in short, not adhering to white middle-class notions of decorum, speech, and gastronomic authority.[29]

Christening Guy Fieri a junk food TV star, critics also lambast him for cooking and promoting dude food and its nutritional excess. An *Observer* article asserted, "Mr. Fieri has built his career valorizing deeply unhealthy eating habits, rhapsodizing about all that is fried, caloric and meaty in his cookbooks and on his Food Network shows."[30] In *Salon* Askari decrees, "Guy is trying to kill us."[31] A Fieri profile titled, "The Trailer Park Gourmet," concurred, describing *Diners, Drive-Ins and Dives* as "spirited gluttony as entertainment."[32] But Fieri is far from an outlier on the Food Network in this regard. Paula Deen built a career atop butter and oil. Chefs on *Chopped* routinely use the deep fryer. Meat is the central feature of multiple shows, including *Bobby Flay's Barbecue Addiction* (2011–) and Michael Symon's *Burgers, Brew & 'Que* (2015–). High-calorie fare is a staple across the network. Sometimes it's even the main focus. On the short-lived *Guilty Pleasures* (2015–2016) various Food Network stars revealed "their best-kept, most-intimate, guilty-pleasure secrets for the first time ever!"[33]

The "unhealthfulness" of the foods Guy Fieri cooks, eats, and promotes is only part of the fury behind these critiques, leveled in the name of good health. Rachel Syme in *The Daily Beast* gets it quite right as she argues, "This may be the crux of Fieri's controversial image—in a time when a majority of the food world (and Michelle Obama) has turned to organic, locavore obsessions, Fieri not only acknowledges the way that many Americans really eat—burgers, tacos, coladas—but enjoys it with relish."[34] Fieri's food views also resonate today within the political context of the Trump administration. The United States shifted from Barack Obama, a president once criticized for elitism for mentioning arugula and shopping at Whole Foods, to a president who not only enjoys and frequently consumes fast food but even serves it to White House guests. Health-based critiques of Fieri's cuisine and media empire are strongly rooted in class- and gender-based understandings of taste, consumption, and pleasure. The neoliberal politics of healthism allow critics of "unhealthy" food to accuse Fieri of lacking not only taste but also a sense of morality and public decency.[35]

These threads of criticism demonstrate how Fieri transcends the bounds of the celebrity chef and culinary authority, which appeals to his viewers. As Julia Moskin wrote in the *New York Times*, Fieri "has a Sarah Palin–like ability to reach Americans who feel left behind by the nation's cultural (or, in his case, culinary) elite."[36] Moskin interviewed New Jersey residents who attended Fieri's 2010 culinary tour, who made such comments as, "You feel like he has that same background just like you do, never pretentious, nothing fancy" and "He's the only one who never talks down to anybody." These viewers felt recognized by Fieri, in the same way that they felt ignored and disrespected by other food celebrities. For example, after Fieri opened Guy's American Kitchen and Bar in New York City, Bourdain called the restaurant a "terror-dome" and derided the diners who eat there as "all of these poor diners, drives and whatever, douchebags waddle in there . . . all of these poor bastards see him eating cheap food on TV, they go in there."[37] Fieri's core audience are food enthusiasts, but ones who resist and reject the perceived pretention and aspirational focus of foodies, who foster cultural capital through their culinary knowledge and (often expensive) food experiences.[38]

Analyzing the critiques lodged against dude chef Guy Fieri reveals social fractures along the lines of gender, sexuality, race, ethnicity, and most particularly social class. These divisions grew stronger during the Great Recession era's economic crisis. Fieri's polarity communicates a broader classist disdain toward particular types of foods, ways of eating, eaters, and bodies.

Creating Guy Fieri on the Food Network:
Reading Relational Masculinities

Next Food Network Star created Guy Fieri's dude masculinity in part by fashioning it relationally through and against the gender identities of those around him. My relational analysis of Fieri's dude masculinity takes its inspiration from Jack Halberstam's reading in *Female Masculinities* of James Bond in *Golden Eye*.[39] As Halberstam demonstrates, without the female masculinity of M, the gay masculinity of Agent Q, the hyperfemininity of the Bond babes, and the hypermasculinity of the villain, Bond himself would not be legible as epically or heroically masculine. It is within these relational arrangements that gender is created, that it is made meaningful and observable. In this way, Guy Fieri's dude masculinity was produced within multiple relationships, contexts, and scales: on *Next Food Network*

Star with his fellow contestants and the judges, within the celebrity chef lineup that preceded him on the Food Network, within the Guy Fieri empire he created (where he is largely adored), and within the broader food media world, where he is a uniquely polarizing figure.

Fieri's dudeness and his culinary point of view were made meaningful on *Next Food Network Star* between the final four contestants who lasted the longest in the competition. Carissa Seward, the only woman in the final four, trained at Le Cordon Bleu and cooked French dishes for an American audience. Despite her expertise, her culinary point of view endorsed sensual food and her own sex appeal. Thin with long hair and a carefully made-up face, she performed a conventional femininity with a flirtatious style. Her sexualized femininity served to bolster the masculinity of the three remaining male contestants: Fieri, Nathan Lyon, and Reggie Southerland.

The most hegemonically masculine, Lyon was a culinary school trained chef who also worked at farmer's markets, at which colleagues reported, "women flock to him."[40] As the camera zoomed in on his bulging, veiny biceps in one shot, Lyon reported that he was also a personal trainer and "fitness nut." Lyon boasted that he loved competing, attention, and the camera, as he oozed confidence that he was sure to win *Next Food Network Star*. In addition to professional prowess and a fit body, Lyon was conventionally good looking (and knew it), speaking often of women in sexualized ways. Compared to Lyon, Fieri appeared family friendly despite his rock 'n' roll aspirations. The differences between Lyon and Fieri were also made apparent through their food. Compared to Fieri's commercialized and hybrid style of cooking and Seward's more traditional French cuisine, Lyon's cooking was the most technically sophisticated. While Fieri turned to commonly known and easily accessible ingredients like onions and tequila, Lyon used more esoteric options like pomegranate molasses and makrut lime leaves. While Lyon might appeal to a foodie viewer's sense of taste today, the program portrayed Lyon's style as overly complicated, showy, and misaligned with the Food Network's audience in 2006. Compared to Lyon, Fieri appeared less hegemonically masculine, but conventionally manly nonetheless.

Fieri made it to the final round with Reggie Southerland, who worked at a café and bakery where the owner described him as "very unique" and "big, in every sense of the word." A tall, large-bodied, and flamboyantly gay Black man, Southerland dressed in colorful dress shirts beneath sweaters, paired with dress pants or khakis, and described his food as "sassy." As a pastry chef, his culinary specialty was narrower than other contestants,

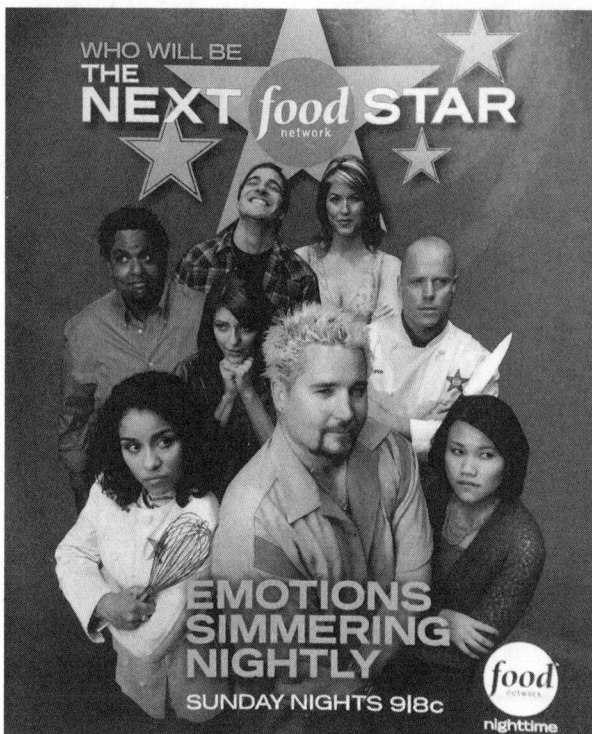

This promotion for season 2 of *Next Food Network Star* depicts Guy Fieri front and center. The program defined Fieri's dude masculinity relationally against the gender identities of Reggie Southerland (second row, left, in a blue button-down shirt) and Nathan Lyon (right, in a white chef coat), with Carissa Seward, in the back dressed in a pink sleeveless top.

limiting his professional reach and relegating him to a culinary track dominated by women, derisively called "the pink ghetto" of the professional kitchen.[41] His culinary brand emphasized hosting and entertaining in ways that invoked the traditionally feminine character of domestic food work.[42]

The differences in gender and sexuality between Fieri and Southerland grew more apparent as they each pitched their show ideas to the judges and filmed their test pilot episodes. Southerland proposed a show called *Simply Spectacular*, which featured simple dishes prepared and presented with flair. Conversely, Fieri's pilot was for *Cooking off the Hook*, evoking the rebelliousness of the dude from the show title on out. Fieri pitched the show idea to the judges as, "I believe there's an opportunity to reach a demographic in food entertainment that maybe we're not hitting yet. I like to call it the 'Generation X / Generation Y.' I think that we can get a show that speaks to them in music, in enthusiasm. . . . [T]he show's called *Off the Hook*. Let's make food that's off the hook, unbridled, not held back, not controlled."[43] From the program's initial conception, Fieri built *Cooking Off the Hook* from the characteristics and privileges of dudes: enduring youthfulness and not playing by the rules.

As they filmed their pilot episodes, Fieri's dude masculinity stood out against Southerland's domestic queerness. After a title sequence full of guitar riffs, Fieri started his pilot by confidently walking in from stage right, announcing in simple sentences, "I'm here to rock your kitchen. My food is fun. It's fearless. And it's fundamental." In contrast, Southerland began his show gesticulating with his hands as he said, "It's time to take the simple and make it spectacular. Remember the flavor always tastes better when your food is served up with a little bit of style." Southerland cooked for the camera roasted balsamic glazed chicken with sweet fennel, which he described as healthy, sweet, crispy, and juicy. For dessert—or what Southerland called "an encore"—he prepared a raspberry lemon curd tart drizzled with chocolate, calling it an "all grown up" take on a Pop Tart.

Conversely, Fieri cooked tequila turkey fettuccine, describing it as "off the hook," and a breath mint pie "guaranteed to push your taste buds into uncharted territory." Even as he performed "off the hook" dude masculinity, however, Fieri invoked fatherhood when he sliced a turkey breast, mentioning that his son Hunter loves turkey. Throughout the episode, Southerland spoke to a straight female (as well as gay male) audience, as he repeatedly addressed the camera as "girl" and "girls." He also made multiple references to romance and boyfriends. Alternately, Fieri spoke to a gender-neutral audience that skewed masculine in tone, addressing the audience as "amigo" and "all you garlic lovers." At the end of his pilot episode, Fieri closed with, "Thanks for hanging with me," invoking the cool homosociality of dudes hanging out together, while Southerland adopted a more TV traditional, "Thanks for watching. Be well."

In these ways, *Next Food Network Star* fashioned Guy Fieri's gender identity and food footprint within the context of his fellow contestants and their attending culinary points of view. The program constructed Fieri's dude masculinity and broadly appealing food in contradistinction to Carissa Seward's conventional femininity and classic French cooking and to Reggie Southerland's performance of queerness and "simply spectacular" cuisine. Nathan Lyon's hegemonic masculinity, fit body, womanizing comments, and highly technical New American cuisine further rendered Guy Fieri approachably masculine and family-friendly, while making Fieri's food appear relatable and unpretentious.

In addition to his fellow contestants, *Next Food Network Star* constructed Fieri's television gender identity in relation to the host, Marc Summers, and two Food Network executive judges: Bob Tuschman, who at the time was senior vice president of programming, and marketing and branding executive

Susie Fogelson. To the delight of contestants, chef Bobby Flay was the third judge, challenging the contestants not only from the judge's seat but also on the kitchen floor.[44]

While Bobby Flay is a successful Food Network chef, scholars and food writers alike read him differently than Guy Fieri despite the similarities the two food stars share. Like Fieri, Flay describes his culinary point of view as big and bold. Both chefs prefer spicy flavors, invoking a conventionally masculine flavor profile in what they cook and eat. Flay also traveled around the country and cooked regional specialty dishes with restaurant owners and chefs on his show *Throwdown with Bobby Flay* (2006–2011). But in a media analysis of "culinary personas," the authors categorize Flay as a chefartisan, while they consider Fieri "the working-class champion of diner food and greasy-spoons."[45] They categorize Fieri's persona as a "self-made man" who "upholds traditional notions of masculinity and family but crosses class boundaries by emphasizing an upward class mobility trajectory." Such characterizations reveal how starkly class differentiates Fieri's and Flay's food. While both possess culinary technique, albeit earned through different processes of professionalization, Flay's food reads as haute, while Fieri's dishes could most always fit on the menus of chain restaurants like TGI Friday's or Applebee's. Moreover, Fieri and Flay differ in their presentations of self. Flay is cool and restrained, while Fieri is too hot and purposefully over the top.

Comparing Fieri to Flay reveals some of the ways in which Fieri's food and dude identity transgress the boundaries that outline hegemonic masculinity, more affluent tastes, and the typical celebrity chef. These points of difference and rebellion remain remarkably constant throughout Fieri's career on the Food Network. Unlike celebrities who constantly reinvent themselves, Fieri's brand was forged on his first episode of *Next Food Network Star*. It has exhibited significant staying power. As a result, Fieri's destabilizing presence steadily approaches critical mass, resulting in both celebration from fans and disgust from those immune to his brand of culinary transgression.

Guy Fieri and Fatherhood

Despite the persona and food views that make Guy Fieri a polarizing dude chef, his repeated references to heteronormative fatherhood render him acceptable and legible as a masculine persona. After establishing his edgy but institutionalized culinary authority as a board member of the California

Restaurant Association who wears shorts and an armband, Fieri's opening clip on *Next Food Network Star* cut to him at home in his living room with his child and pregnant wife as he said, "I have a son. I have another son coming." The next clip showed him cooking with his son, Hunter, who said, "I love cooking with my dad. I make him proud and it's fun." From his first moments on screen, Fieri presented fatherhood as a central element of his culinary persona, emphasizing the evolving role of parenthood within conventional masculinity.

Born in 1968, Guy Fieri first became a father at the age of twenty-eight in 1996, a time when fatherhood's role within American masculinity continued to expand, following trends begun earlier in the twentieth century.[46] The term "domestic masculinities" describes the "ways in which men's increasing engagement with homemaking practices shapes masculine identities."[47] Domestic masculinity created a male sphere within the home, transforming the role of fatherhood from distant to engaged, which shifted the structure of modern families. These changes continued throughout the course of the twentieth century, as more actively involved fatherhood increasingly became a responsibility of ideal American manhood.[48] Today, fathers are by and large more involved in their children's daily lives, and traditional parenting gender roles have also shifted.[49] While most stay-at-home parents continue to be mothers, the number of families with a stay-at-home dad and a working mom has doubled in the last twenty-five years.[50] Particularly within the context of the Great Recession, more men expanded their parenting and domestic work while under- or unemployed. Contemporary popular culture has also captured these shifts in American fatherhood, such as the 2015 Super Bowl, which prominently featured "dad-vertising" in multiple spots.[51]

While the boundaries of hegemonic masculinity have flexed to incorporate notions of engaged fatherhood, it still upholds the traditional connections between food, care work, and femininity.[52] Even as more men actively partake in domestic duties like food shopping and cooking, these domestic practices continue to be coded as feminine, and women still perform more of them.[53] Some food media continue to frame men's cooking as a hobby or leisure activity, a refined skill or talent, or even as entertainment.[54] Women's home cooking remains a quotidian and expected duty, while men's cooking is still often presented as a special and praiseworthy contribution to the family. Within this history and social context, Guy Fieri's emphasis upon fatherhood and men's cooking contributed a novel food TV persona.

The discourse of fatherhood and family also infiltrated Fieri's cookbooks. The first words of *More Diners, Drive-Ins and Dives*, published in 2009, puts

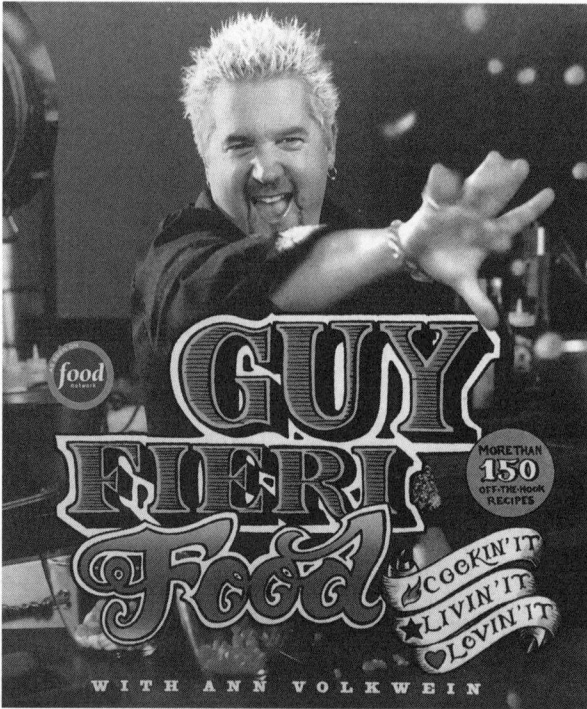

The cover image for *Guy Fieri Food: Cookin' It, Livin' It, Lovin' It* (2011) reveals the consistency of Fieri's style, years into his career as a successful Food Network star. This image also depicts how his hallmark gestures typically burst out of the frame and toward the viewer, an aspect of his visual persona that fans, genuine and ironic, often mimic themselves.

restaurants and recipes within Fieri's life story and his dedication to fatherhood as it read, "All I wanted was to be a great dad and a chef—to own a restaurant, cook what I want, feed people, make them happy—okay, maybe I wanted to be a rock star, but I can't play a thing, so that wasn't going to happen."[55] Fieri's three *Diners, Drive-Ins and Dives* cookbooks also visually communicate the discourse of family, as publishers designed them in the scrapbook style of a family album. Notions of family also include his show crew. The introductions to the *Diners, Drive-Ins and Dives* cookbooks and *Guy Fieri Food* each begin with several pages that list the names, titles, and photographs of the entire crew for the show, laid out like a yearbook. Across his food media empire, Fieri and his co-authors, producers, and editors promote the narrative of a rockin' dude chef, who is first and foremost a loving, engaging, and involved father to his sons and a benevolent patriarch to his food media team.

Establishing his culinary persona outside of *Diners, Drive-Ins and Dives*, Guy Fieri's subsequent cookbooks reinforced his family focused brand. Published in May 2011, *Guy Fieri Food: Cookin' It, Livin' It, Lovin' It* told Fieri's life story from childhood to his first restaurant to *Next Food Network Star* and all that came after. It even included photos of Fieri without his hall-mark bleached, spiked hair![56] Along with recipes, the book featured many family photos and even essays from Fieri's mother and father. Fieri dedicated the cookbook to his sister, Morgan, who died from cancer the year the book was published. This text reinforced fatherhood in overt and subtle ways. For example, a page listing the items in Fieri's pantry included a photograph of his home kitchen, which featured a framed photograph with his son Hunter on the counter and Hunter's report card on the refrigerator.[57]

Fieri dedicated his fifth cookbook, *Guy on Fire: 130 Recipes for Adventures in Outdoor Cooking*, published in 2014, to his sons Hunter and Ryder, calling them the next generation of outdoor cooks, after Fieri's own dad and father-in-law. Throughout the cookbook, photographs depict grilled dishes as well as Fieri with family and friends grilling, tailgating, camping, and vacationing outdoors. Fieri's 2016 cookbook, *Guy Fieri Family Food*, elevated this focus on family with nothing but recipes for family meals throughout the week along with tips for involving children in the cooking process. Fieri further centered family and fatherhood in shows such as *Guy & Hunter's European Vacation*, which aired in February and March 2016, and *Guy's Family Road Trip* in 2017.

The set spaces of Guy Fieri's shows also emphasize family. After winning *Next Food Network Star*, Fieri filmed his first TV show, *Guy's Big Bite*, where he exhibited a more stereotypical form of masculinity than he does on subsequent programs. The set featured overtly dude spaces and symbols: "the road, the bar, the arcade, and the indie band stage."[58] The masculine character of the *Big Bite* kitchen flexed as Fieri welcomed family members and friends into the space to cook with him. Rebooted during later seasons, *Guy's Big Bite* moved from the stage set to an outdoor barbeque and grill in Fieri's home backyard in Santa Rosa, California. Although intended to connote an aura of authenticity, this "real" backyard grill is nonetheless a stage set, a site for the performance of Fieri's dude masculinity, though one that prominently figures fatherhood and family. The "backyard bite" reboot of the show also employed the gendered character of backyard grilling and meat, forged in the postwar period as unquestionably masculine with links to camp cooking and adventure.[59] And yet Fieri tempers the grill by emphasizing that he barbeques not to master beast and flame but to feed his family and friends, who are prominently featured on show episodes and in his cookbooks.

In these ways, Guy Fieri's emphasis on fatherhood and family demonstrates how the dude functions and sustains social position. On the one hand, these various invocations of fatherhood render Fieri's identity as the rocker dude chef socially acceptable. They place him within the boundaries of more normative masculinity. On the other hand, Fieri's prominent focus upon fatherhood and feeding his family progressively transgresses the conventional links between femininity and foodwork. When he cooks on television, Fieri plays less the role of celebrity chef feeding a crowd, than a Food Network star who is a father feeding his family and friends.[60] Fieri's role as a dude dad resonated strongly during the Great Recession era when some men unexpectedly found themselves at home, perhaps newly tasked with cooking and full-time fathering. As a result, some of these men may have had to renegotiate their own sense of masculinity. Dude chef Guy Fieri proved an unorthodox model. Fieri's unique style of fatherhood provides an example of how parenting, food, and masculinity continue to evolve, engaging circuits between private and public, home kitchens and food TV set spaces, daily life and food media.

Defining Guy Fieri Cuisine

Beyond his dude chef persona, the food that Guy Fieri cooks and promotes exemplifies the dude with a unique approach that constitutes its own cuisine. By definition, a cuisine is categorical. It has identifiable boundaries, whether based on geography, ethnic identity, institutional purview, culinary technique, or celebrity status. Cuisine engages notions of hierarchy, establishing "high" versus "low" cuisines, mirroring concerns over the social status of high versus low culture.[61] "Middling" cuisines bridge such distinctions, as they make tasty, pleasurable, and specialized foods widely available to all eaters in society, in part, thanks to industrialized food processes.[62] Interpretations and perceptions of cuisine include and exclude not just particular ingredients and ways of cooking, but also people and identities. Fieri's cuisine doesn't follow traditional rules. From the beginning of his culinary career, Guy Fieri promoted a rebellious approach to food. He describes the menu at Johnny Garlic's, his first restaurant opened with a business partner in 1996, as "fresh, contemporary, and a no-holds-barred attitude."[63] As this description reveals, Fieri cuisine endorses unbridled enthusiasm and limitlessness.

Embracing a fusion approach, Fieri readily and frequently appropriates ingredients, flavors, and techniques from a variety of ethnic traditions. In *Guy Fieri Food* he asks, "Why not have eleven different things at one sitting, with no boundaries and no set ethnicity? You can move all over the board to different countries and be as eclectic as you like."[64] Fieri cuisine imagines a culinary world in which rules and boundaries do not exist, including those that mark ethnicity and race, a conceptualization that depends upon the considerable privilege that Fieri marshals. It is from *his* standpoint that he can craft a food space that unmarks marked categories and seats them all at the same table. Only a dude of such significant social privilege could make such culinary and cultural claims.

A cuisine typically includes five main elements: (1) core ingredients or dishes, (2) particular techniques for preparing food, (3) a set of flavor principles, (4) a code of manners and etiquette, and (5) a food chain through which food travels from farm to fork.[65] These elements demonstrate how cuisine functions in and as culture. Cuisine forms a language and medium of communication, as well as a means for verbalizing and amplifying resistance.[66] Applying this framework to "Guy Fieri cuisine" reveals it to be an anti-cuisine of sorts, as its dude-ish center resists codification and rules. Throughout his career, Fieri's conception of cuisine has remained consistent, if difficult to understand and define as it mirrors the unusual quality of his high-energy presentation style and unique sartorial aesthetics. With flexible (or nonexistent) boundaries and following few rules, Fieri cuisine transgresses the norms of cuisine codification and culinary expression as it embraces the dude and the privilege it registers.

To start, the core ingredients and hallmark techniques of Fieri cuisine tend to purposefully break convention and embrace hybridity. An episode of *Diners, Drive-Ins and Dives* featuring Johnny Garlic's makes this approach clear.[67] Customers explain the restaurant's cuisine with phrases like "It's a very unique menu," and "They always have something different from the norm." One diner said, "It's a mixture of so many different cuisines," further elucidated as "Asian blended with Mexican blended with Italian blended with Cajun." In the episode, Fieri described Johnny Garlic's himself as "a diverse approach." On *Next Food Network Star*, Fieri originally defined his culinary point of view as, "The gauntlet of food. My culinary point of view is kinda off the hook and out of bounds," exemplified by the dishes he cooked for show challenges, such as Full-Flavored Bird, Waka Waka Salad, and Guido's Artichokes, titled after his nickname.[68] While the *Next Food Network Star* judges nearly always applauded Fieri's food for its flavor and endorsed his culinary skills, his food noticeably differed from the fare prepared by his fellow contestants, which fell into more categorical styles, such as traditional French, modern American, and American Southern.

Fieri's approach to a set of flavor principles is arguably big, bold, and (for better or worse) decidedly inclusive. Rather than aiming to balance or

In 2018, Guy Fieri prepared trash can nachos on *LIVE with Kelly and Ryan*, during which the hosts shared in Fieri's exuberant and rowdy culinary manners.

harmonize flavors, Fieri seeks equitable representation and a sense-stunning experience. For example, Fieri prepares the wasabi cream sauce that accompanies his Sashimi Wonton Tacos with heavy cream, salt, sugar, lemon juice, rice vinegar, wasabi powder, and sour cream. Fieri describes it as, "A little acid component, a little sugar component, salt component. Getting all the flavor profiles, and this right here is the heat component." This all-flavor, all-the-time formula guides Fieri cuisine, forming the inspiration for one of his best-known catch phrases: "Welcome to Flavortown."

Beyond how he builds flavor in the kitchen, Fieri also endorses a rowdy set of culinary manners in his food spaces that thwarts middle-class notions of respectability, distinction, and good taste.[69] From tater tot pizza to mac daddy mac 'n' cheese, Fieri's recipes afford primarily exaggerated flavor and portion size, equally divided between finger foods and dishes requiring a knife and fork. No dish transgresses the norms of middle-class decorum and fine dining more than Fieri's trash can nachos. With trash in the name, the nachos flirt with the ludicrous and monstrous. They tease the eater's sense of disgust, push the sensory limits of edibility, and directly engage the classed and raced politics of "trash" people and tastes. In April 2018 Fieri prepared the dish on *LIVE with Kelly and Ryan*, coaching the hosts to gently shake the can and pull upward to set loose a tower of desperately cheese-laden nachos that slowly tumble and ooze onto the plate. This gorgeously grotesque food porn moment is made all the more real through the recipe and its nutrient tally, as the cheese sauce — what Fieri calls on his menu

SMC (Super Melty Cheese)—calls for 2 cups half & half, ½ pound Velveeta cheese (cubed), ½ pound smoked gouda (shredded), ½ pound white cheddar (shredded), 1 tsp Worcestershire, and ½ tsp Tabasco.

Similarly pushing typical limits of culinary decorum, Guy Fieri's set of culinary manners concludes with a boisterous verbal exclamation of one's delight and satisfaction. Fieri models this in every episode of *Diners, Drive-Ins and Dives* as he enthusiastically tastes a restaurant's hallmark dish and then assures chefs and cooks that their food is rockin', killer, gangster, off the hook, and funkalicious, as well as the more originally superlative: "That's a hot Frisbee of fun," "That puts the shama lama in ding dong," "Mmm dude it's winner winner hot dog dinner," "I'd go round 6 and 7 with that one. It's a knock out," and, of course, "That's a rocket ship to Flavortown."[70] Such exclamations noticeably diverge from the words, phrases, and levels of enthusiasm typically used to critically assess food, such as "My compliments to the chef."

Finally, despite the criticism Fieri receives and the middling character of the food he cooks and promotes, his food system knowledge approaches that of many respected chefs. Fieri describes his firsthand knowledge of livestock production, as he discusses growing up in small town northern California and helping to raise, feed, and butcher hogs as a child.[71] Furthermore, he describes Flavortown in the language of recent food trends, using markers of food quality such as local, from-scratch, and mindfulness. While critics lambast Fieri for serving corporate fare in his restaurants, he is not the only food celebrity to see something worthwhile in the commercial. Famed French chef Jacques Pépin describes his culinary experience at Howard Johnson's restaurants as "revolutionary." Furthermore, Pépin writes: "The most important thing I learned at HoJo's was that Americans had extremely open palates compared to French diners. They were willing to try items that lay outside their normal range of tastes. If they liked the food, that was all that mattered."[72] Echoing such sentiments, Guy Fieri embraces the tastes of mainstream American eaters and commercial food without judgment.

Fieri cuisine possesses gendered character as well, as it enthusiastically endorses dude food in its ingredients, flavors, nutritional profiles, presentation style, portion size, and overall attitude. On his cooking shows and in the food he features on *Diners, Drive-Ins and Dives*, Fieri heavily promotes meat, invoking its masculine coding. Fieri's food appeals to men, which may inspire not only more men to watch food television, but also more men to cook. As one Las Vegas food critic put it, "If adding pepperoni to lasagna is what it takes to get men to pick up pots and pans, so be it."[73] In short, more men watched Guy Fieri on Food Network not only for how his gender performance matched the dude but also for how his cuisine endorsed dude food.

The accessibility and approachability of dude food reveals how populist taste forms a cornerstone of Fieri cuisine, or as Julia Moskin put it in the *New York Times*: "Mr. Fieri's cheerful embrace of taste at the expense of tradition is an example of what makes him so popular, and of why other chefs tend to dismiss him."[74] Indeed, Fieri chooses to celebrate the public's tastes rather than endeavor to elevate, educate, or mold it, as do other chefs, such as Alice Waters or Jamie Oliver. Fieri's take on sushi purposefully suits the taste preferences of a segment of American eaters who would never identify as foodies. They are eaters who food writers rarely celebrate or even discuss. Unlike chefs who derisively judge what they consider uninformed taste, Fieri says, "A lot of people who like sushi don't really like raw fish or seaweed. So I make what they do like."[75] For the sushi uninitiated, he makes "The Jack Ass Roll" using tapioca paper instead of seaweed nori, BBQ chicken instead of raw fish, and adds in avocado and spicy chili mayo for a California twist on a Japanese tradition.

The mainstreaming of sushi consumption in the United States post-1970 has been considered an indicator of America developing a more robust culinary culture.[76] In "How Sushi Went Global," Theodore Bestor writes, "From an exotic, almost unpalatable ethnic specialty, then to haute cuisine of the most rarefied sort, sushi has become not just cool, but popular."[77] Speaking of our current food moment, *Food & Wine* further declares, "America has become a sushi nation . . . a nation of sushi connoisseurs, able to discuss the difference between o-toro and chu-toro."[78] *Food & Wine* assumes a nation of foodies, which Fieri's popularity proves is not necessarily the case.

Fieri gives voice to eaters for whom sushi is not a norm. He addresses the eaters who view raw fish as a culinary exoticism or even a taboo that they do not desire to experience or one that they purposefully resist. While sashimi-loving foodies might not be able to imagine that there are consumers disinterested or disgusted by raw fish, anti-foodies are a viable audience.[79] For example, in 2014, *BuzzFeed* published a YouTube video, "Americans Try Sushi for the First Time," which has attracted more than 8 million views.[80] While some of the first-timers enjoyed the sushi they tasted, others described it as slimy, disgusting, and gross. In 2015 *TIME* published a feature titled "Should I Eat Sushi?" which addressed consumers' sushi-related concerns about if sushi was healthy, safe, and sustainable to eat.[81] By speaking to and for an anti-foodie audience in direct contradiction to culinary experts, food writers, and foodies, Fieri exerts his populist power. Critics may judge Fieri's cooking and restaurant promotion as lowbrow, but his fans are more likely to view it as middling: that is, a tasty, accessible, pleasurable way of eating made possible by an industrial food system. This populist focus forms a cornerstone of his cuisine, served up at his various restaurants, including one of his largest ventures: Guy's American Kitchen and Bar, which opened in New York City's Times Square in September 2012.

The Rise, Fall, and Rise of Guy Fieri

After visiting Guy's American Kitchen and Bar four times, *New York Times* food critic Pete Wells gave the restaurant a zero-star poor review in November 2012. It was the lowest rating in the history of the column, since the rating system was instated in 1963.[82] In a moment when food knowledge pointedly expressed cultural capital, Wells's lowest of the low review wielded considerable force. Readers across the country read restaurant criticism in the *Times*, but the Fieri review—described as "the restaurant slam read 'round the world"—became a pop culture phenomenon unto itself. Even though the review was published late in the year in November, it was still the newspaper's fifth-most-emailed article of the year, a viral status that changed the cultural landscape of Wells's writing and food criticism at the *Times*.[83] Notable not only for the low ranking it awarded and its massive readership, the review broke the standard rhetorical structure of restaurant reviews. Composed solely as questions, Wells's critique ruptured convention and style, but the content was not novel. It merely repeated the intersecting and overlapping reasons for which Fieri had been adored and reviled since his first minutes on food television.

Now a historic pop culture phenomenon unto itself, Wells's review demonstrates both the power and the limits of food criticism, as Fieri's status has only continued to grow in its wake. Wells's scathing comments remade Fieri as a prominent, populist voice in food media. Fans of *Diners, Drive-Ins and Dives* are not the only ones to avidly support Fieri. Fellow Food Network star, chef Robert Irvine said of Fieri criticism, "For every snooty critic, there's a dad, grandma, kid, biker, dentist, or garbageman who'll tell you Guy's the man," reinforcing Fieri's populist appeal, particularly among viewers likely considered anti-elitist food enthusiasts.[84] Furthermore, since the 2012 *Times* review, Fieri has been the subject of multiple laudatory features, particularly in men's magazines. In 2015, *GQ* defended Fieri, writing, "[I]f you close your eyes and listen to Fieri speak, he doesn't sound so different from the chefs and the foodies who so gleefully despise him."[85] A 2016 feature in *Esquire* fully endorsed Fieri with the glowing title, "The Unrecognizable Genius of Guy Fieri."[86] In 2015, *Playboy* decreed, "Guy Fieri Is the Hero We Need."[87] While the title heralded him as a hero, the article's image invoked religious iconography, depicting Fieri as a sacred figure or a martyr. Styled like stained glass, Fieri appeared haloed and dressed in flame-decorated robes with his right hand raised in a gesture of blessing. His left hand holds a small stainless-steel diner against his chest, where a religious icon would clutch a holy text.

Journalists further reframed Guy Fieri as a good dude savior in the wake of the 2017 and 2018 California wildfires, during which he voluntarily cooked for and fed displaced residents and fire-fighting crews. Emblematic of this recuperative journalism, Jelisa Castrodale wrote for *Munchies*, "If you just know Guy Fieri for his trademark wraparound sunglasses, frosted tips, and embroidered flame shirt, then it sounds like you don't know the real Guy Fieri."[88] *Esquire* decreed, "We need more Guys in the world."[89] *The Daily Meal* wrote, "Readers who mostly associate Fieri with high-volume detours to Flavortown might be surprised to find out how much time and energy the big-hearted chef has spent helping people from *actual* towns."[90] Myriad publications — news outlets like CNN, CBS, ABC, and NBC's *The Today Show*; food writing websites like Eater and Grubstreet; and celebrity gossip sites like *People* — each ran such stories, heralding Fieri and his actions.

This post-fire coverage re-emphasized how Fieri uniquely bridges the divide between the professional food world and the realm of home and family. The *Huffington Post* mentioned how Fieri served home-style, comfort food such as pulled pork. Fieri addressed this himself, saying, "We're going to make people happy. We're going to give them a little moment. I think food is always — we call it comfort food because it makes you feel good."[91] Reinforcing the role of fatherhood within his brand, Fieri brought his sons with him to cook and mentioned them in interviews, such as "In these times that we're facing as a country, it's so trying. But that's the example I set for my sons: You stand up; you face it; and you go after it. You don't back down from it."[92]

These stories and their accompanying images also tell an ambivalent tale of how Guy Fieri's persona transformed from a Flavortown flop in the *New York Times* to an emblematic good dude. Some journalists framed this conversion as incomplete. *CBS News* sneered, "When you hear the words 'Guy Fieri' and 'fire' in the same sentence, your mind probably goes to one of two places: spicy food or his famous shirt covered in yellow and red flames."[93] While Eater's coverage credits Fieri's actions as civil service, they still frame him and his expertise as "the longtime incumbent mayor of Flavortown."[94] Stories communicated this state of partial transformation visually as well. Some stories featured photos of Fieri cooking at the volunteer site and posing for photos with first responders. Other stories included older photos of Fieri, smiling wide and cooking over a blazing grill, connecting Fieri and flames on the level of photo keywords and metadata more than the actual context of the California wildfires.

Fieri's social media presence also played a role in his brand and persona transformation at this key moment. Many of the news stories applauding his charitable cooking included Twitter posts from the Butte County Sheriff, the Auburn Police Department, and Fieri himself. Presented as if authentic evidence, these posts circulated across and between digital platforms like Fieri's own account and news websites, both national and local. These stories often included Fieri's November 12, 2018, tweet, which breaks from his normal presence on Twitter. His account typically features short posts of thanks that mention sponsors and collaborators. More polished tweets promote his various shows and appearances. The account retweets and responds to fans and cracks jokes. Made up of far more words than most tweets from his account, this earnest post expresses something different, as it reads, "In today's tumultuous world, it's amazing to see our fire fighters, military, law enforcement, and first responders come together to rescue our communities devastated by fire. So many great people stepping up to take care of one another #ProudAmerican #CampFire."

Despite such a statement and Fieri's recuperated good dude brand during the fires, his actions and persona remain decidedly apolitical, especially in comparison to chef José Andrés, who also volunteered during and after the fires. A Michelin-starred chef, Andrés founded World Central Kitchen in 2010 to serve meals when natural disasters strike, in many cases filling in gaps caused by insufficient government aid. Journalists applauded Fieri's charitable acts along such lines, writing, "You might not expect Fieri, host of *Diners, Drive-Ins and Dives*, to be the natural heir to humanitarian José Andrés, but the Food Network star has proven himself to be a philanthropist in his own right."[95] That said, Fieri's contributions bear a conservative and safely patriotic veneer. Fieri's actions are far removed from Andrés's pointed critiques, for example, of the Trump administration's positions on immigrants and immigration reform, racism and racial violence in the United States, and the lack of needed aid for Puerto Rico after Hurricane

Maria. By cooking during the fires, Fieri acted charitably and admirably, but true to the laidback ethos of the dude, he engaged no further.

Despite its limitations, Fieri's easy dudeness has resonated with various audiences. For every critique fired at Fieri, there are fervent fans and overt supporters, constituting Guy Fieri fandom. Media fandom is "the recognition of a positive, personal, relatively deep, emotional connection with a mediated element of popular culture."[96] Audiences, whether made up of fans or less enthused viewers, are far from passive observers of a static, mass culture. They construct their own identities and communities through the media that they consume. They can also be agentive, enthusiastic, and creative producers themselves, viewers who transform media through their engagement with it.[97] Some Fieri fans engage in this sort of relationship with his food media empire. In 2008, Minnesota-based fan Rick (no last name) started the website Flavortown USA, which he promotes as a *Diners, Drive-Ins and Dives* restaurant guide maintained for loyal fans of the show. He describes the website's origins saying, "I love the show and decided to build a site devoted to Guy Fieri, the Food Network and the show, *Diners, Drive-Ins and Dives*."[98] In 2010, he had visited more than fifty restaurants featured on the show and designed an app to help other fans do the same. The website today maps more than a thousand restaurants and features reviews and images authored by Rick and other fan contributors.

Other fan websites abound. The "Fans of Guy Fieri" blogspot site was maintained from 2006 to 2011, featured more than 800 posts, and described itself as "We Google 'Guy Fieri' so you don't have to."[99] Although not updated for years, the site still reports robust monthly blog traffic. Bill Grella of Leesburg, Virginia, a ramp service and safety advocate at Washington Dulles International Airport, has been visiting restaurants featured on *Diners, Drive-Ins and Dives* since 2008. He began blogging in 2011 to track his cross-country adventures to dine at all of them.[100] The *Syracuse Times* wrote a story on Grella when he made his five hundredth restaurant visit to Pastabilities. Restaurant owner, Karyn Korteling, said, "What I've discovered is that Guy Fieri has such a fan base that people literally put pins in a map to follow his selections. The show has really put us and put Syracuse on the map."[101] Revealing how and why some fans connect with Guy Fieri, Grella remarked, "I started watching the show shortly after it premiered in 2007. I not only enjoyed seeing cool places to eat but loved Guy's persona and wanted to try the different places."[102] In 2017, Grella visited his six hundredth restaurant featured on *Diners, Drive-Ins and Dives*. Even as he approached a decade of following Fieri's restaurant recommendations he remarked, "Every time I get to a milestone, I say I'll slow down, but something always pulls me back."[103]

While these fans of *Diners, Drive-Ins and Dives* follow Guy Fieri's road map to visit the restaurants he endorses and consume the foods he recommends, another fan segment more ambivalently applauds Fieri's persona. These fans celebrate Fieri, but blend fandom with a degree of anti-fandom: that is, getting pleasure from disliking or hating a media text or figure.[104] Fanning over Fieri from a cool, dude-ish distance, these fans do not deny the critiques often lodged against Fieri for his fashion choices, culinary exaggeration, and loud-mouth style. Instead, these fans simultaneously celebrate and mock, impersonate and deride Guy Fieri. Like the dude, this fandom is playful and ironic. It adds a touch of ridicule and snark to fan activities that in some cases become phenoms unto themselves.

Take for example "FieriCon," a gathering akin to SantaCon, which first began in 2016. At the annual event, fans dress up like Fieri—complete with spiked blond wigs, visors and bandana headwraps, facial hair, bowling shirts, and sunglasses—as they trade his over-the-top catch phrases and participate in a daytime bar crawl in New York City. In event photos, FieriCon attendees impersonate energetic Fieri gestures like the hand-horns rock 'n' roll salute, a finger-gun with pointed index finger, or a knuckle sandwich. Most iconic, they pose with their feet apart and knees bent, one arm bent with an index finger pointed to the camera, the other arm jutting straight forward. At the 2018 FieriCon, an attendee jokingly quipped, "You know Guy's one of those guys you want to emulate. He really embodies flavor."[105] In 2019, the event organizer, David Gold, wrote on the FieriCon website that it began when he was twenty-three years old "as something that I thought would be a funny thing to do with some family and friends. Since then, it has grown into an event that has spanned 5 cities, 2 continents, raised money for charity, became the subject of local news stories and got featured in a Vice Munchies video that has over 2 million views."[106]

FieriCon events have taken place in cities as far afield as Milwaukee, Wisconsin, and Buffalo, New York. According to coverage of the FieriCon in Austin, Texas, the organizers felt a more endearing fan connection to Fieri. They had purportedly eaten an anniversary meal at Mac & Ernie's Roadside Eatery, the only restaurant in Tarpley, Texas, and one of the first restaurants to be featured on *Diners, Drive-Ins and Dives* in 2007. And yet, Austin FieriCon fans still expressed a combination of affection and loathing for Guy Fieri. One asserted that Guy Fieri "may be a douchebag, but at least Fieri is America's douchebag," while another boasted, "Fieri *is* America."[107] This ambivalent celebration of Guy Fieri captures the complicated ways that *Diners, Drive-Ins and Dives* defines American food and America through populist roadside eateries that critics often deride as low class and unhealthy.[108]

Outside of official FieriCon events, dressing up as Guy Fieri also takes hold at Halloween, which celebrity Chrissy Teigen famously did in 2015. Guy Fieri is now a popular enough costume that entering his name into Amazon's search bar returns numerous options for the now iconic fashion Fieri sported early in his career: bowling shirts adorned in flames, sunglasses, chain necklaces, and an astounding number of black visors with bleached spiked hair sprouting out the top. The food website Delish offers a step-by-step guide to dressing like Guy Fieri for Halloween, a topic so pressing the article was published in the month of July.[109] Guy Fieri actually embraces fans who dress up as him. For Halloween 2019, he created a Twitter thread for fans to share their Guy Fieri costumes. It reached more than 750 replies, garnering stories on a number of news and food sites, including the *Washington Post* and *Food & Wine*.[110]

Whether intended to endorse or deride Fieri, these costumes make up only a small part of the Fieri ephemera found online. Themed T-shirt designs read "Welcome to Flavortown" and "Guy Fieri is my Patronus," linking Fieri and Harry Potter fandom. As part of the ever-growing ugly Christmas sweaters tradition, another design sprawls "Have a Merry Fieri Christmas" around Fieri's floating head, thronged by spatulas and flames.[111] While Fieri's own website sells his cookbooks and T-shirts, eclectic merchandise sporting Fieri's likeness is widely available online: slippers, ties, mugs, stickers, posters, throw pillows, bed spreads, clocks, and even wall tapestries.

The space where Guy Fieri fandom and anti-fandom meet also spawned erotic Fieri fan fiction. *Guy Fieri and the Fieri in My Heart* has garnered more than 50,000 reads on Wattpad, an online storytelling platform. Published in 2016 on Tumblr, *Frosted Tips* imagined Fieri in a romance with Texas senator Ted Cruz.[112] The premise alone earned media attention on multiple sites, including *Eater*, *First We Feast*, and *AV Club*. Fans and anti-fans have made innumerable Guy Fieri memes, but Fieri's PR team also creates such memes themselves and posts them to the Guy Fieri Instagram account. As if speaking directly to the regeneration of his star persona since Pete Wells's zero-star poor review, Fieri remarks, "Man, you've got to be able to laugh at yourself."[113] Through such events, products, and memes—however ironic or ambivalent—Guy Fieri's persona continues to expand beyond the purview of simply a Food Network celebrity. Guy Fieri's fans engage with and transform who and what he is in popular culture.

Bombastically conjured as the patron saint of greasy spoons, Guy Fieri encapsulates the possibilities, contradictions, and ongoing power structures of the dude, including if and how to be a father who cooks and cares. While the Food Network leveraged dude chef Guy Fieri to garner more male viewers, food and beverage companies deployed the dude to combat a larger gender contamination challenge: selling diet sodas and yogurts to men, which we'll explore in the next chapter.

CHAPTER THREE

Producing Foods for Dudes

The Masculinization of Diet Soda and Yogurt

Searching online for ads that represent food and gender returns dozens of lists full of examples "so sexist you'll lose your burger craving" and "that will make your jaw drop."[1] Such countdowns chronicle how women's bodies have been used to sell beer, burgers, and just about everything in between. Although advertising campaigns for gender neutral foods have depicted identity more inclusively, such as Cheerios TV spots featuring biracial and gay families, ads for strongly gender-coded foods continue to reinforce more rigid social patterns.[2] Products, such as diet sodas and yogurts, are not naturally gendered but they are perceived as feminine in U.S. culture, and advertising has repeatedly coded them as such. Company executives specifically cited feminization as the reason for developing diet soda and yogurt options for men. In the *Atlanta Journal-Constitution*, an unidentified Coke executive declared that diet is a "four-letter word" for men aged 16–24. Similarly, Dr. Pepper's director of marketing, Dave Fleming, cited focus group findings that "men don't like the taste or imagery of diet sodas." Powerful Yogurt chief executive Carlos Ramirez characterized the grocery store yogurt shelf as, "Everyone's talking to women and their digestive health . . . *this* stuff was created for guys."[3]

As food brands jockeyed for market share, advertising and subsequent press employed the dude to masculinize each of these products. In 2005, Coca-Cola Company launched Coke Zero, which was soon after dubbed "bloke Coke" in Australia and the United Kingdom for its overt target marketing.[4] In 2011, Dr. Pepper Snapple Group launched Dr. Pepper Ten with the tagline, "It's Not for Women," drawing significant media attention, both positive and negative. Powerful Men LLC (later renamed Powerful Foods) introduced Powerful Yogurt in February 2013 as "the first yogurt in the United States designed for a man's health and nutrition needs," followed by Oikos Triple Zero from Dannon in January 2015.[5] Journalists quickly christened both offerings "brogurt."[6] Examined through the cool aloofness of the dude, diet sodas and yogurts for men demonstrate how gender contamination functions, how brands manipulate it to their advantage, and how such actions may affect consumers' media lives and food experiences.

Diet Sodas and Yogurts in the Recession-Era Marketplace

When food companies deployed the dude, diet soda and yogurt's unstable sales mirrored the gender anxiety brought on by the recession's economic crisis. The food industry constantly negotiates a complicated and evolving web of quality standards, profit motives, marketing innovations, global expansions, consumer desires, and notions of health. In the cases of diet soda and yogurt, this contextual web also included gender. Since the first diet soda was introduced in the late 1950s, no- and low-calorie beverages have incited debates with gendered implications regarding sweetness and thinness. Carbonated soft drinks also provide a meaningful window into twenty-first-century food trends of decline and opportunity. During the Cola Wars between Coca-Cola and Pepsi, waged from the mid-1970s to the mid-1990s, U.S. soda consumption consistently increased, but then sales stagnated. Since 2000, U.S. soda sales have dropped, in part due to public health studies indicting "sugar sweetened beverages" for their potential role in weight gain and the "obesity epidemic."[7] Changing consumer tastes have also negatively affected soda sales.

Coke Zero was Coca-Cola's largest new product launch in twenty-two years. The company sought to regender diet soda by reconstituting the product itself.[8] Coca-Cola pitched Coke Zero not as a diet cola but a zero-calorie cola. Coke Zero's launch proved successful, as its U.S. sales consistently increased even as carbonated soft drink sales continued to shrink nationally. In 2009, when overall U.S. soda sales were down about 2 percent, Coke Zero sales jumped 20 percent, continuing its 17 straight quarters of double-digit sales growth.[9] In 2010, Coca-Cola celebrated Coke Zero as "the best-selling addition to its CSD [carbonated soft drink] portfolio since Diet Coke debuted in 1982."[10]

Aware of the market challenges and successes of Coke Zero, Dr. Pepper Ten launched nationally in October 2011 targeting men 25 to 34 years old, who purportedly preferred full-calorie Dr. Pepper but sought a lower calorie option for health and weight-related reasons. Like Coca-Cola, Dr. Pepper Snapple Group boasted about their men's low-calorie soda sales performance. Their 2012 Annual Report proclaimed, "In 2011, we launched the manliest low-calorie soda in the history of mankind—Dr. Pepper Ten—and it has underscored our ability to create news for CSDs."[11]

The report's pronouncement includes an image that can be read in a number of ways, including through the dude. Of all the representations I have reviewed and analyzed as part of this project, dudes are overwhelmingly depicted as white. This is one of the few instances that depict a Black dude. He is young, fit, smiling, and pictured outdoors, free from the confinement of the kitchen or domesticating forces. He wears a sleeveless white shirt under denim overalls, attire that connotes strength and virility in racialized ways, as well as the dude's boyish resistance to norms of professional dress. Invoking conventionally masculine symbols, he skewers a giant steak, still red and raw on a circular grill alight with small flames, while he holds in his other hand a bottle of Dr. Pepper Ten toward the camera.

While the soft drink industry deployed the dude amid falling sales, yogurt companies employed a dude approach as their sales grew. In the mid-2010s in the United States, yogurt was typically coded as a feminine food that brands marketed primarily to women. Yogurt's target market changed with the increasing availability and consumption of Greek yogurt, which is thicker and creamier than regular yogurt and affords more protein per serving. In 2007, Greek yogurt made up just 1 percent of refrigerated yogurt sales, but surged to nearly 50 percent by 2015. Even though Greek varieties commanded a higher price than other yogurts, sales grew throughout the years of the recession. Prior to 2015, men made up only 37 percent of Greek yogurt sales. Powerful Yogurt went so far as to claim that men were the "most neglected consumers in the category."[12] Just as diet sodas for men boasted strong initial sales, so did yogurts for male consumers. Dannon reported 22 percent growth for Oikos Triple Zero at the end of 2017. Powerful Yogurt sales reached $2.1 million in 2014 and, according to a 2018 *Inc.* profile, reported $9.6 million in revenue in 2017, representing a 482 percent growth over three years.[13]

Within these trends, brands sought to increase market share by regendering these supposedly feminized foods. While all of these brands employed the dude in their launch advertising campaigns, they first built up these products as conventionally masculine. At the product development stage for diet sodas, soft drink companies funded the research and development of new "real" tasting artificial sweeteners, which were developed based on the gendered assumption that men desire satisfying flavors more than women do. Yogurts posed less of a gender contamination challenge, as brands simply enhanced and promoted Greek yogurt's relatively high amounts of protein, which is culturally considered a masculine macronutrient. These companies designed food packaging that strongly connoted conventional masculinity through elements such as color, shape, size, material, typography, and graphics. As they endorsed more conventionally masculine qualities, product development and package design built a foundation to thwart gender contamination. These products' launch campaigns then pivoted from conventionally masculine strategies to dude tropes, as they advertised diet sodas and yogurts for men, providing a suitable pathway into feminized fare. Taken together, these various stages of food marketing and advertising reveal how the dude both reinforces and resists aspects of hegemonic masculinity. The dude continued to subordinate women and femininities as he slurped diet sodas and downed yogurts in the slacker pursuit of "real" flavor and "good" health.

Gendered Assumptions of Sweet Taste and Protein Power

Diet sodas remedy a central tension of consumer culture: how can we voraciously consume *and* piously restrain? Carolyn Thomas argues that artificial sweeteners find this balance through "indulgent restraint," a process in which "consumer pleasure can be stripped of its negative consequences."[14] Sweeteners without calories made it possible to have our cake and eat it too, but these saccharin solutions still needed to taste desirably sweet. Originally developed as medicinal products, drinks made with artificial sweeteners quickly became a popular grocery item. But this shift from pharmaceutical to consumer good incited new development challenges with regard to flavor. Creating a sugar substitute without an astringent aftertaste has proved an ongoing challenge for more than fifty years.

The quest for real sugar taste without the calories took on new urgency when companies endeavored to create diet sodas purposefully designed for men. From the earliest stages of product development, Coke Zero and Dr. Pepper Ten worked from the assumption that men desire and demand real flavor and satisfying taste more than women do. This assumption built upon definitions of good taste (following sociologist Pierre Bourdieu's writings on food, taste, class, and status), as well as gender scripts that crystalize overlapping stereotypes about masculine flavors, hearty appetites, and ways of being.[15] Particularly during the socially destabilized recession era, food companies endeavored to reinforce masculine attributes for men. Alternatively, women are scripted for dainty eating, light flavors, and restraint. Coupled with disproportionately insistent cultural demands for thinness, women have been the primary consumers of diet sodas, beverages concocted from an ever-shifting formula of artificial sweeteners with varyingly acrid flavor. For example, Coca-Cola's Tab boasts a loyal following of female consumers but even they describe the soda's flavor as "peppery," "metallic," and "diety."[16]

The perceived relationship between gender, taste, and flavor shaped the development of Coke Zero and Dr. Pepper Ten, as food scientists endeavored to devise sweeteners with no or few calories that tasted real so to appeal to masculine expectations. One senior Coca-Cola executive quipped, "The R&D team wanted to formulate a zero-calorie cola that punched up above its weight class," employing a stereotypically masculine boxing metaphor to describe the gendered nature of this research, which began as early as the 1990s.[17] As a result, Coca-Cola sweetens Diet Coke with aspartame and Coke Zero with a sweeter combination of aspartame and acesulfame potassium, referred to as "Ace-K," which together provide a more sugar-like flavor and mouthfeel than aspartame alone. At Dr. Pepper Snapple Group, David Thomas, executive vice president of research and development, spent three years developing the sweetener for Dr. Pepper Ten.[18] Made from both real ingredients and artificial sweeteners, Dr. Pepper Ten's sweet kick combined two grams of sugar with high fructose corn syrup and aspartame. Unlike Coke Zero's zero calories, Dr. Pepper Ten contains ten calories, making it a low-calorie beverage further removed from the tainted feminine character of drinks without calories. As was the case at Coca-Cola, researchers materialized in the lab food gender stereotypes that link masculinity with robust and satisfying flavors.

Male consumers are aware of these cultural associations between gender, flavor, and diet products. As but one example, in his enthusiastic Amazon reviews for Coke Zero, a customer identified as Christopher Foley asserted the product is "great soda and 10 times better than any 'diet' drinks out there, no after taste."[19] Echoing Coke Zero commercials, he describes the "real 'Coke' taste WITHOUT the sugar." This self-described "Coke junkie" reinforced the product's promise of real flavor, while distancing himself from diet drinks by placing the offending descriptor in quotation marks.

Armed with the flavor of a new real-tasting sweetener, Coke Zero's advertising to men explicitly addressed taste with the tagline "Real Coca-Cola Taste Plus Nothing." In addition, fifteen-second TV spots emphasized, "Real Coca-Cola Taste, Zero Calories, No Compromise," characterizing diet soda for men as real, tasty, and assertive. In 2007, ad agency Crispin Porter & Bogusky expanded on the concept of real Coca-Cola taste in the campaign, "Taste Infringement." Based on the premise that the zero-calorie soda had stolen the taste of Coke, the campaign featured lawyers hired by Coca-Cola to sue Coke Zero. The campaign positioned Coke Zero not as imitating the taste of sugar, as Diet Coke always had, but as assertively delivering calorie-free Coca-Cola flavor. The ad pitched Coke Zero's flavor so convincingly

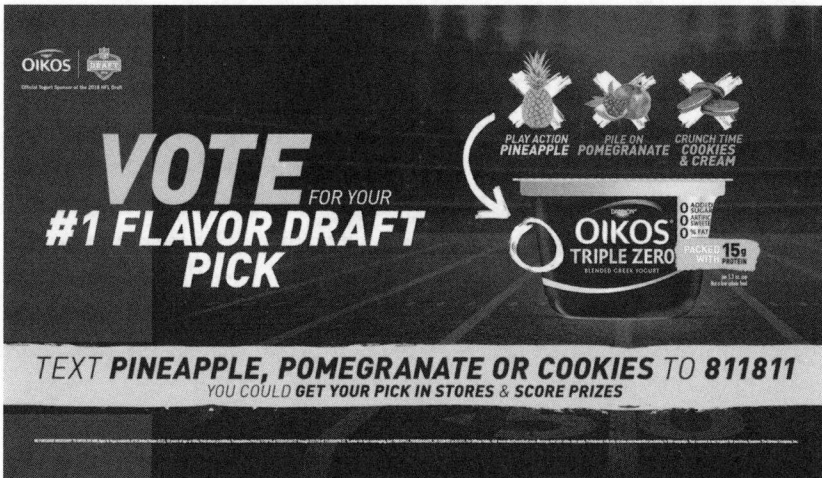

Dannon has promoted Oikos Triple Zero yogurt with a "Flavor Draft Pick" campaign. The 2018 promotion included choices like play action pineapple, as well as the brand's typical black packaging, nutricentric labeling, and the NFL logo.

that it not only could be mistaken for the real thing but could incite concern that it might replace the original. Notably, it was a zero-calorie soda intended for a male audience, rather than a diet soda for women, that marshalled such power in the world of food, business, and the law, even if in the imagined world of an advertising campaign. While diet sodas had for decades endeavored to develop and market beverages to consumers on the merit of their taste, Coke Zero's campaign reserved the right to real flavor for men alone. Dr. Pepper Ten also reinforced this point, prominently mentioning taste on every product label, proclaiming, "10 bold tasting calories," invoking food gender stereotypes, claiming bold flavors in the name of masculinity.

Yogurt flavor options also endorse gendered notions of taste. CEO Ramirez said Powerful Yogurt's initial testing sought to "man up" yogurt flavor, experimenting with bourbon and scotch, but the products didn't taste good enough to make it to market.[20] In 2018 and 2019, Dannon reinforced Oikos Triple Zero's connections to the NFL by promoting a "vote for your #1 flavor draft pick." Game-themed choices included "play action pineapple," "pile on pomegranate," "crunch time cookies & cream," "game-changing mint chocolate," and "can't-miss mango."

Outside of these competitions, Dannon names the flavors of its Triple Zero Greek yogurt with simple one-word descriptions compared to the more ornately named flavors of Oikos Traditional Greek yogurt, which is not targeted directly to men. Compare a flavor name like Coffee to Café Latte. Contrast Vanilla with Toasted Coconut Vanilla. Furthermore, while Oikos Triple Zero does come in sweet dessert-like flavors, such as Chocolate and Salted Caramel, Oikos Traditional Greek yogurt more directly substitutes for actual desserts with flavors like Apple Pie, Lemon Meringue, and Orange Cream. These flavor offerings relate to the diet culture of restraint routinely depicted in yogurt advertising for women.[21] These commercials frame yogurt as a "healthy" dessert—a small taste of sweetness allowed on strict diet plans, a tiny indulgence that will not spoil the thin female form. Yogurt for men provides a tasty, high-protein snack. Yogurts for women do not just taste like dessert, they *are* dessert.

Coke Zero ads endorsing real Coca-Cola taste also included overt misogynistic threads. A British Coke Zero ad starred a young white man. Blond-haired and conventionally attractive, he reacted in the commercial with surprise and delight in the beverage's "real Coke Taste and zero sugar." He then asked, "Why can't all things in life come without downsides? Like girlfriends without five-year plans," framing commitment to women as a downside of life.[22] Other examples of "life without downsides" further emphasized the dude, such as vacations without having to come home and work friends without work, all obstacles of masculinity's expectations of exertion, breadwinning, and achievement. The ad linked the concept of real taste to the dude in a way that downplayed the perceived femininity of its zero calories. At the same time, such ads marginalized women, who had for decades served as diet sodas' target demographic and loyal customer base—one who likely contributed to the sales success of Coke Zero and Dr. Pepper Ten as well. Indeed, numerous customer reviews from both men and women cite the "better" and "more real" taste and flavor of these beverages, especially when compared to other diet options on the market.

While diet sodas built upon gendered assumptions about masculine tastes and desires for "real" sweet flavor, Greek yogurts more straightforwardly built a masculine identity upon protein's perceived gender. Protein is considered masculine as it builds muscular tissues and controls appetite through increased satiety. A high-protein diet has traditionally been popular among body builders, strength athletes, and young men generally. Protein's coding as masculine creates clear gender legibility for high-protein fare marketed to men, including yogurt. Both Powerful Yogurt and Oikos Triple Zero emphasized protein in their product pitch, prominently posting on the product label Oikos Triple Zero's fifteen grams and Powerful Yogurt's twenty to twenty-five grams.

In the late 2010s, protein's status reached even higher heights, symbolizing not just masculine muscle-building potential, but totalized wellness in the eyes of many consumers. Global trend tracker, Euromonitor, wrote, "Few ingredients in recent memory have experienced protein's sustained and meteoric rise . . . as protein's health halo continues to shine brighter."[23] In 2016, ad agency JWT categorized this trend as the rise of "athleisure snacking," linking high-protein snacking with fitness trends and athleisure fashion.[24] Notably, Powerful Yogurt CEO Ramirez shared that the company did not design the product for athletes but for "regular guys. I thought about active men, but not necessarily Rocky Balboa, not necessarily a super fit guy, it's just regular dudes . . . who probably work out now and then, we take care of ourselves, but at the same times, you know, we drink our beers."[25] Ramirez's comments echo the ambivalent dudeness of the dad bod that straddles protein and fitness, beer and moderation while caring for the male body.

Despite this ambivalence, Ramirez explicitly argued that his product met men's protein goals, especially when compared to competitors. Speaking of Oikos Trip Zero, Ramirez asserted, "It's 15g of protein. If you look at Yoplait, the most feminine product, that is also 15g of protein. . . . Guys are all about protein, a satisfying meal or snack."[26] From Ramirez's comments, it was not just the presence of protein that made a product masculine but having more protein than the norm, such as Powerful Yogurt's substantial twenty grams (or more) per serving. Ramirez also positions protein's masculinity against a feminizing concern for fat. He again critiques his competitor, saying, "Danone, with all of the research capability it has, could have done better. All the research we have and feedback from consumers, especially male consumers, also shows they don't care about fat-free actually. Danone has a value proposition of triple zero and guys couldn't care less." Unspoken but alluded to is women's long-standing consumption of low and non-fat products, as part of the constant quest for socially mandated weight control and idealized thinness. In Ramirez's comments, large doses of protein and a dismissal of feminizing concerns for fat serve to bolster masculinity.

In fact, Dannon and Powerful Yogurt positioned their products not to compete in the dairy aisle alone, but with protein supplements like Muscle Milk, which are often saddled with additives that consumers seeking "natural" alternatives avoid. Brands positioned Greek yogurt products as not just high protein, but as "clean" and "natural," qualities of interest at the time. Consumers are often confused by nutritional advice, made all the more complicated by food industry health claims. In our anxious foodscape—

marked by decades of low-fat rules and more recent low-carb crazes—protein is a "good" nutrient, one that consumers feel free to eat more of rather than less.

American consumer obsession with protein may be shifting away from meat, but it is far from disappearing. High quality and high-protein yogurts pose significant potential for profit, as protein supplements are a $4.7 billion industry, while the global whey protein market was valued at $6.1 billion in 2016 and projected to potentially reach $14.5 billion by 2023.[27] This is in part due to the myriad ways protein indexes power, as it marks masculinity, social class, and status. Typically, only malnourished eaters suffer from the consequences of inadequate protein intake. In the United States, adequate protein consumption is of little concern, as most Americans eat enough or even too much.[28] Furthermore, high animal protein consumption in the United States in part drives our nation's disproportionate use of fossil fuels, water, and other resources, particularly in discussions of climate crisis and how to combat it.[29] Powerful Yogurt's positioning of specifically *men's* yogurt as a hyper-protein food indexes such broader dynamics of power. Eating like a dude means eating whatever and whenever you want, including ample amounts of protein—whether from animals, plants, algae, or the next source yet to be isolated and marketed—without much concern or thought. Such a privileged eating philosophy has real consequences within our global food system and its current inequalities when it comes to food waste, wealth, risk, security, and sovereignty.

Inventing Zero: Anti-Diet Food for Men

Food producers and advertisers further masculinized diet sodas and yogurts through the invention of "zero," a masculine, positive, and empowered opposite to the feminine, negative, and restrained connotations of diet. Diet foods for women market what they lack. Zero foods for men market what they contain. And yet, both promote a neoliberal perspective on health, wellness, and the individualized control of the body. Coke Zero and Oikos Triple Zero directly engage the concept of zero in their product names, but zero is distinct from the low-calorie and diet products that have traditionally been marketed to female consumers. By default, diet food is for women, but it often is not real food, not quite. Women like Jean Nidetch (one of Weight Watchers' founders, discussed in chapter 4) endorsed the view that artificially sweetened diet food was "a fundamentally positive—even required—practice for women attempting 'healthy' living in the modern age."[30] Such diets introduced food science concoctions into women's daily lives that still lurk in today's supermarket. Diet products signify and embody lack, restraint, and un-realness. These qualities, especially lack, have been used to derisively define femininity and female sexuality.[31] This is particularly the case in arrangements of power that oppress women and femininity, while they substantiate men and masculinity. To consume diet products is to purposefully seek out lack in the pursuit of an idealized, thin, controlled body, coded as supremely feminine.

The invention of zero for men depended upon the rationalizing and legitimizing influence of quantification and nutrition science, often displayed on product labels. These numeric, nutritional proclamations operationalize what Gyorgy Scrinis calls the ideology of nutritionism.[32] By narrowly focusing on nutrients, nutritionism obscures and overrides concerns about food's quality and production, as well as the sensual, practical, social, and cultural knowledge of food. Focusing solely on food's quantification has significant consequences.[33] It changes what food is and can be, what can be known about it, and what food can represent.

In complicated conversation with fashion's use of size zero in women's clothes, the concept of zero crystalized and masculinized this quantified system of food meaning. Powerful Yogurt and Oikos Triple Zero proudly proclaim their grams of protein, not buried in the nutrition facts but front and center on the label. Masculinized nutritionism encompasses the entire brand promise of Oikos Triple Zero as it spells out its "0 added sugars, 0 artificial sweeteners, 0 fat" on the front of the package. The brand frames these components not as lack, not as the pursuit of slimness and nothingness, but as high value characteristics that comprise a healthier, better product worth a premium price. Similarly, Dr. Pepper Ten's can declared the beverage's "10 bold tasting calories," while Coke Zero's packaging announced its "Real Coca-Cola taste and zero calories." Zero diet food masculinizes nutritionism's decontextualized and acultural rationality and system of quantification. It creates a way of seeing, feeling, thinking, and consuming food meant to read as masculine as it marginalizes femininity.

Extending the masculinizing power of nutritionism from quantification to nutritional components, Powerful Yogurt sought to describe and qualify each of its flavor offerings in scientific terms, a strategy men's fitness magazines have used as well.[34] The website masculinized and legitimized apples through their fiber and vitamin C content, blueberries and acai berries for their "high-octane" antioxidant content, and maple syrup for its thiamine, manganese, and zinc, which promote heart health, digestion, and immune response. Powerful Yogurt's descriptions of flavor also indexed notions of masculine appetites, realness, and power. The key lime yogurt "perfectly balances your craving for tangy and sweet," suiting masculine appetites and urges meant to be satisfied rather than controlled or restricted. The vanilla bean flavor was real, smooth, and pure. Sweet fruit flavors were masculinized through language, decreeing mango "The King of Asiatic Fruit."

Although these products limited zero to men, the concept of zero poses a more empowering potential than diet, though one still implicated in capitalist structures and aims. Diet foods embody the constraints of capitalism, as one can experience flavors and textures that approximate "the real thing" without the consequence of the calories. It is through these artificial, unreal foods that women have found ways to eat freely and to gain a sense of empowerment and control over their bodies and lives, despite patriarchal demands for thinness.[35] Eating for weight loss could also be liberating if it de-emphasized restriction, denial, and deprivation and did not depend upon unreasonable ideal standards.[36] Weight loss could be more feminist if it focused on collective politics rather than individual change, and if it were separated from capitalist gain. This inchoate feminist potential is depicted in zero products for men. Coke Zero imbues zero calories with masculine heft, rather than the feminine and decorative lack of Diet Coke. Similarly, Oikos Triple Zero's brand name celebrates what it lacks as central components of the product's appeal and value proposition. While Coke Zero and Oikos Triple Zero imbue diet soda and yogurt with the empowering character of zero rather than the restraint of dieting, these positive attributes were marketed primarily to *male* consumers.

Designing Gender: Masculinity and Food Packaging

As men navigated the gender anxiety of the recession era, food brands sought to strongly assure male consumers' status with diet sodas and yogurts packaged to undeniably signify masculinity. More than just a product's material container, food packaging communicates lively, important, and complex cultural messages, including notions of identity for brands and consumers. As Coke Zero, Dr. Pepper Ten, Oikos Triple Zero, and Powerful Yogurt navigated perceived gender contamination, their designs reinforced, repeated, and restructured masculinity through elements such as color, shape, size, material, typography, and imagery.

Coke Zero's masculine aesthetic evolved within the design family of the Coca-Cola line of products with its red, white, and silver colors; the nostal-

Coke Zero was commercially successful in the United States once repackaged in a black can. Situated within the Coca-Cola design family, Coke Zero's original white can shared too much visual similarity with Diet Coke and its perceived connotations of femininity.

gic serif font of the Coca-Cola logo and swoosh; and a uniformly shaped, aluminum can. Compared to the vibrancy, saturation, and bold sensuality of Coca-Cola's red can, Diet Coke's silver can visually represents diet and signifies lack. It symbolizes the absence of calories and the dearth of a real food ingredient (sugar) and of real Coca-Cola taste. It embodies the conventional expectations for restrained feminine appetites and thin female bodies. Coke Zero originally launched in the United States in a white and silver can with the traditional Coca-Cola logo in slightly muted red letters bearing a black shadow effect. Placed in a design spectrum between the bold red can of Coca-Cola classic and the silver can of Diet Coke, Coke Zero's original design too closely resembled that of Diet Coke, visually attaching Coke Zero to diet drinks and femininity.[37]

While Coke Zero initially drew meager sales in the United States, Coke Zero launched more successfully in Australia in a black can designed to appeal to fans of the All Blacks, New Zealand's popular national rugby team.[38] Coupled with an aggressive marketing presence, Coke Zero tripled its first year South Pacific sales goals.[39] Based on this success, Coca-Cola repackaged Coke Zero in the United States in 2007 in a black can. After the repackaging, Coke Zero sales soared, which Coca-Cola largely credited to the redesign. The revised color and style communicated a materially autonomous product, distinct from the light-colored femininity of Diet Coke. Caren Pasquale Seckler, Coca-Cola's group director of diet cola brands in North America, concurred, "We learned from other countries that the dark color connoted a stronger, bolder flavor," hinting at cultural beliefs linking masculinity, flavor, and design.[40] Coca-Cola extended this strategy in

Dr. Pepper Ten's can and box design feature a gunmetal gray color scheme and industrial rivets, intended to evoke notions of working-class masculinity, just as the cookbooks shown on page 29. The packaging prominently mentions calories but qualifies them as bold tasting in order to distance the brand from feminized notions of "diet."

2014 in the "Share a Coke" campaign, as it printed feminized nicknames on Diet Coke cans, such as BFF, Star, and Bestie, but masculinized ones with dude-ish qualities, such as Grillmaster, Wingman, Bros, and Buddy, on Coke Zero cans.[41]

Purposefully designed to connote masculinity, Dr. Pepper Ten's design boasted a gunmetal gray color scheme and industrial rivets in the packaging because, as Dr. Pepper's senior vice president of brand marketing, Jaxie Alt, asserted, "What's more manly than a guy and his tool belt?"[42] Such comments indicate the enduring perception of working-class masculinity as supremely masculine, as well as the gender anxiety that resonates between social classes and labor categories. Similar to the brand color spectrum of Coca-Cola, Dr. Pepper Ten's gray can was centrally positioned between maroon Dr. Pepper and white Diet Dr. Pepper. The labels on Dr. Pepper Ten cans and bottles declare in all capital white letters: "10 BOLD TASTING CALORIES." Such description legitimized and masculinized the perceived feminine character of calories and actions involving them, like calorie counting. A brand press release overtly stated that the product's packaging "complemented Dr. Pepper Ten's exclusive testosterone-driven marketing strategy."[43]

Gender also shaped the design of yogurt cup packaging. In the *Wall Street Journal*, Powerful Yogurt's chief executive Ramirez quipped, "The yogurt shelf is light blue, light pink, white."[44] At the time, he wasn't wrong. Take, for example, Dannon Light and Fit yogurt, which sells low-fat dairy products with feminine flair. The words "light" and "fit" describe not only the yogurt but also the bodily characteristics that female consumers desire to

POWERFUL
YOGURT

BLUEBERRY ACAI   STRAWBERRY   VANILLA BEAN

POWERFUL   POWERFUL   POWERFUL
YOGURT   YOGURT   YOGURT

BLUEBERRY ACAI YOGURT   STRAWBERRY YOGURT   VANILLA BEAN YOGURT

Powerful Yogurt packaging seeks to evoke masculinity in multiple ways, with black color, bold serif fonts, the horned bull logo, the more angular shape and larger size of the cup, grams of protein called out in large font, and the materiality of six-pack abs, which appear ribbed into the sides of each container.

acquire by eating it. The yogurt's purple and sometimes pink packaging along with curvy, serif fonts further reinforce yogurt as a product formulated for female customers. Not surprisingly, Powerful Yogurt and Oikos Triple Zero launched in black containers, evoking a masculine color scheme, particularly within the color palette of most other yogurt offerings.

Both brands also incorporated stereotypically masculine imagery. Powerful Yogurt's logo is the silhouetted head of a longhorn bull, appearing front and center on every product and visually communicating the power behind the brand's name. Oikos Triple Zero is affiliated with the NFL and features its shield on every package. Bringing symbolic packaging messages to life, Dannon also reported that all NFL training centers stocked Oikos Triple Zero.[45] Powerful Yogurt similarly endorsed sports on its website and social media platforms, which featured fitness tips and workout inspiration that reinforced personal responsibility for health. Images of men and women exercising intensely were captioned with phrases like "No excuses," "Bring it Monday," and "When you never skip leg day," with accompanying hashtags like #EatPowerfulBePowerful, #FuelthePowerWithin, and #HighProteinHighPower.[46]

Yogurt cup size also engaged notions of gender. Oikos Triple Zero comes in a 5.3-ounce container, the same size as Dannon Light and Fit.

Comparatively, Dannon's Activia measures 4 ounces and General Mills's Yoplait 6 ounces. Powerful Yogurt's CEO argued that "an 8 oz serving size, 33 percent larger than the standard 6 oz serving size" achieved the brand's promise as yogurt for men. Again critiquing the competition, he asserted, "Dannon has gone in the opposite direction, with a relatively puny 5.3-oz size."[47] Powerful Yogurt further emphasized package size by associating it with enhanced nutrition, particularly its higher protein content.

Powerful Yogurt also distinguished its brand through package shape, material, and weight. Joyce Wadler effectively described the packaging in the *New York Times* as "the triumph of muscular packaging. . . . If Darth Vader did his own grocery shopping, this is what he would toss into his cart."[48] In a comparatively massive eight-ounce size, the container features molded six-pack abs on the sides, materially embodying the brand tagline, "Find Your Inner Abs." Despite a brand promise to men who are not "Rocky Balboa," as Ramirez quipped, Powerful Yogurt still reinforces the elusive six pack as a cultural symbol of health and productive citizenship. Powerful Yogurt viscerally navigates ambivalent masculine body discipline, as it emphasizes the intersections of masculinity, protein, and body surveillance in the pursuit of six-pack abs on every package and in every ad. Furthermore, both brands packaged their products in a heavier weight plastic than that used to package Dannon's Light and Fit or Activia yogurts, whose packages flex concavely when held. Forged to literally feel weighty and substantial, these yogurt cups signify masculinity at every turn, as they both reflect and shape masculine stereotypes. While Powerful Yogurt provides a more exaggerated case study, all of these products' designs strongly endorsed conventional masculinity in an effort to regender their contents.

Launching Diet Sodas and Yogurts for Men by Embracing the Dude

The dude reinforces some aspects of hegemonic masculinity, while he resists others. The branding of diet sodas and yogurts for men similarly combined the hegemonically masculine alongside the dude-ish. These brands first built a strongly masculinized foundation for their products through assumptions about taste, flavor, calorie and protein content, and packaging design. They then launched their products with updated dude messages that emphasized slacker, boyish qualities alongside some of the dude's enduring allegiance to aspects of hegemonic masculinity.

Grounded in the dude, the initial Coke Zero launch campaign sought to advertise its "real Coca-Cola taste" with zero calories to a young demographic that included men. Ad agency Crispin Porter & Bogusky developed the TV spot "Chilltop" as a contemporary remake of Coca-Cola's well-known and regarded 1971 "Hilltop" commercial.[49] Created by ad agency McCann-Erickson, Hilltop depicted a diverse, multicultural group of young people happily singing about finding global peace and harmony. Chilltop updated the commercial based on the agency's study of beer ads—a key source of dude tropes—in order to reach a more male market.[50] In the ad, G. Love, a young white musician, strums an acoustic guitar, sings, and raps surrounded by a dozen or so young compatriots of various races who sing along. Rather than a verdant hilltop in Italy, they gather in a grittier, urban space: a Philadelphia rooftop with the cityscape in the distance. While the lyrics of the original Hilltop chorus read, "I'd like to teach the world to sing in perfect harmony," Chilltop wanted "to teach the world to chill" and to "take time to stop and smile." Both ads would "like to buy the world a Coke," but in 1971 the aim was to "keep it company," while the 2005 update wanted to "chill with it a while."[51]

Chill encapsulated the ethos of the dude, as it emphasized relaxation and opting out from stress, particularly with regard to work. Additional Chilltop lyrics emphasized resistance to the world of work and its anxieties, referring to "erase the stress from the rat race," "relax when things get rough," and "turn off your phone." Although Hilltop is known for its cooptation of the counterculture's values of love and harmony, which find their way into the lyrics, it began with a more market-driven premise: "to buy the world a home / and furnish it with love." While that love came from "apple trees and honey bees and snow-white turtle doves," the notion of purchasing a home is quite different in Chilltop, which begins, "I want to give the world a little break."

Consumers today might find in Chilltop an anthem for our now mainstream discussions of stress, anxiety, and post-recession burnout, particularly for the millennial generation that this ad targeted.[52] Too far ahead of the cultural curve, Chilltop did not resonate with audiences at the time, in part because it failed to explain what Coke Zero was. Chilltop counterintuitively changed Hilltop's "the real thing" to "the simple thing." This captured the chill ethos of dudes but missed the mark when it came to Coke Zero's value proposition of real taste without the calories. Although the Chilltop ad was ultimately unsuccessful in launching Coke Zero as a diet soda for dudes, its invocation of one of Coca-Cola's most well-known ad spots demonstrates how significant company executives hoped Coke Zero would be in the future of the company and how they centered the dude in that effort.[53]

After "Chilltop" and "Taste Infringement," subsequent Coke Zero ads and campaigns more directly engaged the dude through connections to professional sports, which continue to exude and validate masculinity even as popular culture embraces a number of highly successful female celebrity athletes.[54] Coke Zero's early TV ads ran during college basketball games and the NCAA tournament. Coke Zero ads also included tie-ins with NASCAR, such as the Coke Zero 400, and can redesigns for action and sci-fi movies expected to have significant male audiences, including *Avatar*, James Bond films, and *Tron: Legacy*.[55] The Coke Zero website also included game-like features intended to attract dudes, such as a Fantasy Football section where users could "design a championship ring, create a touchdown dance, upload their image to the grandstand of fans, and send 'smack talk' taunts to fellow fantasy players."[56] These games demonstrate the boy-like qualities of the dude, who embraces play and resists the adult responsibility that masculinity requires of men.

Coke Zero's advertising directly employed the dude when the New York agency Droga5 won the account from Crispin Porter & Bogusky in August 2012. Pio Schunker, head of Integrated Marketing Communications at Coca-Cola North America, conceded a shift in strategy, stating that in the new campaign, "We're talking to men more overtly."[57] The Droga5 website described the Coke Zero account in terms that explicitly emphasized dude masculinity: "Tasked with changing the Coke Zero conversation among a male target largely opposed to the idea of 'diet,' Droga5 repositioned the brand as a form of permission to enjoy the awesome — but sometimes frowned-upon — things that guys enjoy."[58]

Similar to Velveeta's "Eat Like That Guy You Know" campaign, these irreverent thirty-second TV commercials celebrated guys enjoying themselves, as H. Jon Benjamin's deep and emphatic voice assured male viewers, "it's not their fault" for a variety of slacker dude sins. It's not their fault that they played video games for ten straight hours. It's not their fault that they watched basketball or football all day instead of cleaning the gutters, doing their laundry, or studying for a midterm. It's not their fault that they overreacted when their team lost, even if their girlfriends dislike such outbursts.

The spots offered humorous rationalizations for these dude failures. One ad depicted two men in dress shirts and ties in a workplace cubicle, as the Benjamin voiceover proclaimed, "It's not your fault you're working on brackets instead of working on work. Picking sides has always been an American tradition. You're not slacking. You're just being patriotic."[59] Another ad assured men it was not their fault that they forget Mother's Day, described as "a random day in May that is borderline impossible to remember."[60] With a dude twist, Droga5 also ran a "Mother's Day Motherpieces" contest. Winners who posted the best excuses for forgetting Mother's Day on Twitter with the hashtag #motherpieces received artist-drawn portraits of themselves to give their mothers as pathetic, but humorous, apologies. Albeit in creative ways, these ads operationalized aspects of hegemonic masculinity's dominance, particularly over women and femininity, while embracing, forgiving, and legitimizing the slacker qualities of the dude.

At the same time that the 2013 Coke Zero campaign made overt connections between Coke Zero and dudes, Diet Coke (also a Droga5 account from 2013 to 2016) made more blatant connections to femininity. Such shifts reveal a relational dynamic when creating hypermasculine and hyperfeminine food brands. Taylor Swift served as Diet Coke brand ambassador in 2013 and 2014 with a series of girly ads. Diet Coke campaigns also emphasized high fashion with Karl Lagerfeld as Diet Coke's creative director in 2011 and Jean Paul Gaultier in 2012. Serving in the role in 2013, Marc Jacobs celebrated Diet Coke's thirtieth anniversary with the "Sparkling Together for 30 Years" campaign.[61] Jacobs described his designs as "whimsical, feminine, colorful, and fun," further defining Diet Coke as a feminine beverage for women.[62] In these ways, campaigns for Diet Coke emphasized hyperfemininity rising to match the increasingly masculinized campaigns for Coke Zero, which targeted men and emphasized the dude.[63] Coca-Cola managed to protect, and perhaps expand, their market by targeting both male and female consumers with clearly gendered diet soda options, but such tactics upheld the gender binary with every step.

While Coca-Cola took a more moderate approach, Dr. Pepper Ten's advertising directly endorsed the dude and excluded femininity with the tagline "It's Not for Women." Compared to all other diet sodas marketed to men, Dr. Pepper Ten was the most directly irreverent in its messaging regarding gender contamination. Dr. Pepper Ten's brand testing strategy reinforced dude masculinity as it rolled out a mobile "Man Cave" that traveled to test markets, setting up at what they called "testosterone zones," such as sporting events and car shows.[64]

The opening paragraph of the Dr. Pepper Snapple Group's product launch news brief exemplified Dr. Pepper Ten's approach, which packed the dude in a box of misogyny. It asked, "Have you ever had to suffer through a marathon of overly emotional chick flicks or wedding reality shows? Been forced to wait for hours at the nail salon, holding her purse while she gets pampered? Had to pretend to be an expert in women's fashion when she asks your opinion on an outfit?"[65] It then assured men that Dr. Pepper "is helping you reclaim your manhood in the form of 10 bold calories with Dr. Pepper Ten." While soft drink companies purportedly developed these sodas to provide beverage options for men seeking lower calorie options, Dr. Pepper also constructed its manly soda as a reaction to encroaching and emasculating femininity throughout a man's life. This campaign echoed the social circumstances that birthed the dude, in which men perceived greater losses, professionally and personally, following the recession. The opening lines of the news brief spoke to men not as guys or dudes—male roles that stand alone—but as brothers, husbands, and boyfriends, roles depicted as disdainfully and frustratingly connected to women. Although brushed off as "man-centric humor" by its creators, Dr. Pepper Ten's campaign spoke to the gender anxiety of the recession era, popular misogyny, and backlashes to twenty-first-century feminism.[66]

Created by ad agency Deutsch, Los Angeles, Dr. Pepper Ten's first TV commercial debuted on October 11, 2011, and strongly portrayed the hegemonic aspects of dude masculinity. In it a white man with bulging biceps runs through a jungle. He battles snakes, lasers, and villains with a massive weapon in tow. For a moment, he pauses and looks directly into the camera to say, "Hey ladies, enjoying the film?" He answers his own question, "'Course not. Because this is *our* movie," and as he fearlessly jumps off a cliff, he calls out, "And Dr. Pepper Ten is *our* soda." Employing the dude's sense of irony and playfulness alongside conventionally masculine stereotypes, the ad both coopted and seriously parodied the cinematic conventions of the action movie genre, reinforcing the perception that men like such films, while women do not.[67] In doing so, the commercial attempted to reconfigure the gender coding of diet soda as well.

The ad sought to masculinize low-calorie soda in other ways too. A typical drink commercial showcases the food porn adjacent "pour shot." The camera zooms in as an often invisible hand smoothly pours the beverage over ice into a cup, which seductively condensates. The dispensed soda makes its trademark groan, as it churns in the cup and breathes a stimulating mist of effervescent bubbles out the top of the glass. Dr. Pepper Ten instead continued the action movie parody and depicted its star pouring a glass of Dr. Pepper Ten while seated in a safari vehicle, bouncing along a rough road and spilling the drink every which way. The commercial also qualified the calories in Dr. Pepper Ten as manly and something that guys desire, attempting to thwart calories and concern for them as feminine and feminizing. The commercial's star assures viewers, "It's only ten manly calories but with all twenty-three flavors of Dr. Pepper. It's what guys want." At the end of the commercial, the action star signed off, telling women they can "keep the romantic comedies and lady drinks. We're good." In order to render Dr. Pepper Ten a diet soda suitable for men, the ad portrayed the beverage as wholly separate from "lady drinks," that is, other diet sodas. The ad further reinforced the binary divide between masculinity and femininity, men's diet soda and women's diet soda, through the parallel comparison between action movies and romantic comedies.

Dr. Pepper strategically placed the commercial in order to reach a male audience. The ad launched on all major networks, FX Network's Macho Movie Night, and on ESPN during college football games. Dr. Pepper Ten also partnered with *The Voice* competition singing program, country star Blake Shelton, and the Academy of Country Music awards to make it "into the most manly award show on television."[68] Not coincidentally, these cross-promotions transpired at the moment when "the tatted, gym-toned, party-hearty young American white dude" sounds of "bro-country" began to dominate the country charts.[69]

Dr. Pepper Ten's inaugural commercial garnered mixed results for its gender targeted approach. According to Ace Metrix, the ad scored higher than the industry norm for non-alcoholic beverage TV commercials and more favorably with men than women (though women's scores were still above the industry norm) and highest among men aged 36 to 49.[70] Dave Fleming, director of marketing at Dr. Pepper, said, "Did we have a conversation about how far we wanted to go with this message? Absolutely. But we did the research, and it scored well with men and women."[71] Even if that was the case, Dr. Pepper Ten drew feminist critique after it launched nationwide. For example, *Salon* staff writer Mary Elizabeth Williams described the campaign as tone deaf, lame, obvious, full of "good old-fashioned misplaced machismo," and "designed to reassure men that they can drink diet soda without growing a vagina"—all comments that address gender contamination and the limits of gendered marketing.[72]

Women consumers were not the only ones to question Dr. Pepper Ten's anti-woman marketing. The (now defunct) Fast Food Geek website reviewed Dr. Pepper Ten favorably, but questioned its marketing, as writer Andrew (no last name) quipped, "Why would you ever want to alienate half of the earth?" Nevertheless, he copied the ad's gendered tone as he wrote, "I'm giving Dr. Pepper Ten and all of its bad ass, smack you in the mouth, eat you for lunch, crush your chest, donkey flip your dungarees calories a 4 [out of] 5 stars."[73] The misogyny of Dr. Pepper Ten's messaging became an ambivalent part of how consumers perceived the beverage and its meaning, even when they were inclined to resist it.

Deutsch L.A.'s "Like Report" for Dr. Pepper Ten was an official honoree at the seventeenth Webby Awards in 2013 in the Food and Beverage category, but it further demonstrated how the dude's humor and ironic potentials still endorse misogynistic messaging. For the interactive report, the firm claimed to have analyzed 536 million pieces of Facebook data to develop a database of what men like.[74] The concept overview stated, "At Dr. Pepper Ten, we make the only 10-calorie soft drink for men. So we set out to find the true definition of manliness, we invented the only ranking system based on social science. . . . The Like Report."[75] Animated by the dude's playful absurdity, the Like Report's data was available for users to click through as they considered questions like, "In a cage fight of manliness, who would win?" and choices like: socks or watches, grilling out or Friday nights, bonfires or hot showers, vegetarianism or eagles. Users could also rank their own manliness using the "Man Meter" and challenge others to compare scores, earning final judgments like, "You are 17.58 percent manlier than X." In addition, Dr. Pepper Ten's Facebook page was called "The Man'ments." It used an application that excluded women from joining, ensuring a men-only space for games and videos. In a shooting gallery game, male users could take aim at symbols of femininity like high heels, lipstick, and potholders. "Man'ments" included a list of "thou shalt not" statements, such as: "OMG," "pucker up," "post pics of your outfit," "post furry animal videos," "untag unflattering pics," "end a comment with =)," or "make a Facebook profile for your pet"—all actions deemed derisively feminine.[76]

Dr. Pepper Snapple Group described these social media campaigns as tongue-in-cheek humor. Even if funny to some, this humor sustains unequal power relations that bolster masculinity, denigrate femininity, and simulate violence. Even if intended as a joke, the concept "Bro's Law" suggests that such statements negatively affect women, regardless of the intended sincerity of the commenter.[77] In our current cultural moment stained by popular misogyny, it can be difficult to distinguish overt misogyny from parody in food advertising and throughout popular culture.[78]

The dude also shaped the advertising that launched yogurt brands for men. With a heavy hand, Powerful Yogurt's initial campaign, developed by Vidal Partnership in 2013, mirrored the misogynistic threads of Dr. Pepper

Ten, mixing quirky dude humor with outright sexism. In two of Powerful Yogurt's first TV spots, an attractive and fit white man with six-pack abs used his muscles to assist a beautiful, thin, scantily clad white damsel in distress. In a third commercial, "Ping Pong Man," a white man with long curly hair, his body obscured by a velour jumpsuit, played ping-pong not against an opponent's paddle, but against a fit Asian man's bare abs. Rather than a close up of a woman's buttocks or breasts as present in the other TV spots, this commercial zoomed in on the Asian man's buttock from behind—dressed in very short, tight, white shorts—as it flexed and thrust forward repeatedly to return the ping-pong ball across the net. At the end of the commercial, the Asian man eats a Powerful Yogurt and dances with an Asian woman, visually demonstrating that abs, fitness, and Powerful Yogurt defeat unfit whiteness. At the same time, this third spot followed the format of the previous two. It thus placed the Asian man and his objectified body in the marginalized position of the white damsel in distress from the previous ads, reinforcing the stereotype of Asian men as effeminate.[79] Overall, the ad's playful weirdness reinforced dudeness in an effort to reach male consumers. Beyond these three commercials, a subsequent print campaign extended the power of abs, arguing, "In the battle for women, abs always win," depicting images of six-pack abs defeating puppies and babies in a competition for women's attention.[80] As they attempted to sell yogurt to men, these advertisements positioned abs as a tool for seducing, securing, and controlling women.

Beyond commercials, the abs theme infiltrated the brand's entire promotional strategy, from the shape of the plastic container to the tagline on the label, but in every instance with a heterosexual presumption. For example, dude-infused product promotions emphasized abdomens through games, such as a microsite called "Scroll with Abs," which could be navigated only by doing crunches. The site rewarded men's abdominal persistence with eroticized photographs of women, referred to as "eye candy" in the brand's launch summary. Men earned the opportunity to download the browser plug-in so that all of their web surfing could be part of a semi-pornographic ab workout. While heteronormative and misogynistic, the playful absurdity of "Scroll with Abs" speaks of the dude. Similarly, Powerful Yogurt used an ultrasound machine that revealed men's "inner abs" as a booth activity at the 2013 Food Expo of Natural Products. At the expo, 5,000 men tried it out with the assistance of a female technician dressed in a tight-fitting, low-cut nurse's costume more typical of a Halloween party than a health-care setting.[81] Such promotions demonstrate how this men's yogurt initially incorporated

Powerful Yogurt used an ab ultrasound promotion staffed by sexy nurses to launch their product at the 2013 Food Expo of Natural Products in a misogynistic way.

women and femininity into their product only in highly objectified ways, while emphasizing the playful and somewhat immature qualities of the dude.

Compared to Powerful Yogurt, Dannon took a more measured approach with Oikos Triple Zero. Campaigns for the regular Oikos brand (including Super Bowl ads in 2012 and 2014) featured aging hunk and former *Full House* star John Stamos with playful gestures that aligned his Greek heritage with Greek yogurt. Dropping Stamos, Dannon kicked off Oikos Triple Zero with a new aspirational star to attract young male consumers: Carolina Panthers' quarterback Cam Newton. TV commercials designed by ad agency Y&R started early in January 2015. They featured Newton in his game day uniform directing grocery store customers dressed in gym attire away from the protein snacks aisle and toward the dairy case. Debuting on the NFL Network in January and running during the NFC and AFC championship games, the ad featured both male and female customers and sought to rebrand yogurt as a high-protein snack with a casual and sports-based message.

After ultimately concluding that alienating women was not smart business, Dannon marketed Oikos Triple Zero to both men and women. A Dannon executive described Powerful Yogurt's male-targeted approach as "very narrowly targeted at a small sub-segment of men. We wanted to take a less polarizing approach with a more mainstream offering."[82] Oikos' Greek-style yogurt had previously tried a male-specific approach that emphasized the yogurt's high-protein content. Dannon executives conceded, "Women are still bringing most of the food choices into the home," echoing admen's early-twentieth-century frustrations with Mrs. Consumer, who controlled as much as 80 percent of household purchases.[83] Despite not wanting to alienate today's female consumers, Oikos pointedly targeted men with a multi-million-dollar product launch that targeted media properties with significant male reach, such as cable networks Spike and ESPN, *Men's Health* magazine, and digital takeovers on NFL.com.[84] Even with its more moderate approach, Oikos Triple Zero's launch demonstrates, yet again, how food advertising deployed the dude in ways that ultimately upheld conventional notions of gender and authority.

IN DIFFERENT WAYS and to varying degrees, the advertising campaigns that launched these four products incorporated the dude into their pitches. The dude endeavored to masculinize diet sodas and yogurts, and in some ways succeeded to do so, at least in sales numbers. The question remains, however, do men regularly drink diet soda and eat yogurt, or do they perceive them as feminine and avoid such products? While a 2013 Gallup poll found that more women drank diet soda than men—46 percent of women versus 39 percent of men—results from the 2009–2010 National Health and Nutrition Examination Survey found that diet soda consumption was similar among men and women, except between the ages of twelve and nineteen, when more women consumed diet soda.[85] According to Coca-Cola, in 2007, men made up 45 percent of all Diet Coke drinkers and 55 percent of all Coke Zero drinkers.[86] Coca-Cola reported in 2010 that in the sixteen-to-twenty-four age group, about 60 percent of Coke Zero's drinkers were male.[87]

Despite these figures, as I have shared this research in conference presentations and casual conversations, I have heard plenty of push back. Colleagues and friends have shared examples of husbands, boyfriends, sons, and male colleagues who consume diet sodas without giving it another thought. My own body-building, power-lifting, protein-consuming husband drinks diet soda just about every day. He also eats yogurt regularly, and he isn't the only one. The Straight Dope website, inspired by the *Chicago Reader* column by the same name, posted a poll in April 2009 asking, "Do guys eat yogurt?"[88] The seventy-eight responses reveal numerous instances of men who did, leading the initial poster to conclude, "Well, I'll be! All those yogurt ad campaign people really need to re-think their target audience, apparently." In addition, on the product review site Influenster, the hundreds of reviews for Oikos Triple Zero are authored primarily by women, revealing more evidence that the market success of these products was not due to men alone.[89]

The conflicting nature of this consumption data demonstrates how food advertising purposefully participates in a dynamic process of food gender recoding that may, or may not, reflect actual consumer experiences, beliefs, or preferences. Food brands and their marketers employ cultural definitions of masculinity and femininity in efforts to influence sales. Advertisers also work to combat gender contamination and rewrite cultural scripts in an effort to expand market share. While advertising forms the language of consumer culture, and food marketers routinely exploit identities to create and sell brands, it is ultimately true that advertisers' target audience is simply one that consumes their product repeatedly. The examples of diet soda and yogurt demonstrate how the concept of gender contamination serves to benefit the marketplace, not consumers and their notions of identity.

Lastly, the sales success of "men's" diet soda and yogurt was not without consequences. In the end, these advertising campaigns reinforced and extended cultural definitions that limit and constrain the expression of gender and maintain existing hierarchies of power and inequality. In such ways, foods like diet sodas and yogurts reveal the circuits that exist between notions of taste, product development, packaging design, advertising campaigns, ideal body types, nutrition trends, and global food systems. They also show how these elements intersect with notions of gender contamination and the dude as a strategy to combat it. These dynamics grow further complicated when considering not just food and eating but dieting for weight loss, the topic of the next chapter.

CHAPTER FOUR

Marketing Diets to Dudes

Health, Bodies, and Selves on Weight Watchers

"Real men don't diet. They eat real food, and can achieve real weight loss with a customized online system built just for them." So decreed Weight Watchers when they launched their online program for men in 2007. At the time, the diet industry exerted a strong hold in the United States. More than 100 million dieters spent $20 billion annually on weight loss, a number that has only ballooned since.[1] I've been studying dieting from a cultural perspective since I was twenty years old because dieting encapsulates the paradoxes and conflicts at the core of American identity: abundance and restriction, freedom and containment, dreams and expectations. Diets extend and exaggerate advertising's central promise of aspirational transformation. The public faces of commercial diet programs illuminate American identities, not through what we eat, but through what we aspire so vehemently to limit and avoid.

Dieting in America also documents how gender is constructed at the intersection of food, eating, the body, and ideas that link health with productive citizenship. Although dieting was once a supremely masculine concern, dieting has since been culturally coded as a feminine practice, even one of the most feminine preoccupations of womanhood.[2] As a result, conventional masculine norms deem male dieting taboo and transgressive.[3] While exercise and working out do not encroach upon masculinity's prowess, the dietary changes required to lose weight are considered unduly feminine. According to the impossible rules of ambivalent masculine body discipline, nutrition and health knowledge, "healthy" eating, concern for one's weight, and earnestly pursuing weight loss are each rendered feminizing and in conflict with normative masculinity.[4] The dude-inspired dad bod resists the strictures of hegemonic masculinity that endorse a fit, lean, muscular body, but this ideal continues to shape dudes' experiences with their bodies.

Despite the feminine coding of dieting, weight loss companies Weight Watchers, Nutrisystem, and Jenny Craig each began targeting male clients between 2005 and 2010, seeking to increase their consumer base and market potential.[5] Men have typically made up approximately 10 percent (or less) of commercial weight loss clients, so these programs had to manipulate gender

Weight Watchers' multi-million-dollar "Lose Like a Man" campaign sought to masculinize weight loss with celebrity spokesman Charles Barkley and by including dude food as part of the diet.

in order to convince male consumers that real men can and do diet. The Nutrisystem for Men program began in 2005, reportedly increasing Nutrisystem's male customer share from 13 percent in 2002 to 30 percent in 2007. That year, Weight Watchers launched Weight Watchers Online for Men as a program "customized just for guys" with men-only discussion boards, workout videos, and tips for eating out at sporting events. Weight Watchers reported a more than 28 percent increase in male subscribers between 2006 and 2007 and sought further gains.[6] In 2011, the company heavily promoted Weight Watchers Online for Men with a $10 million campaign, including commercials starring spokesman Charles Barkley, aired during the NBA and NHL playoffs. The "Lose Like a Man" campaign represented a significant investment, as much as 10 percent of Weight Watchers' total ad budget.[7] Similarly seeking male clients, Jenny Craig launched "Jen Works for Men" in February 2010.

As the weight loss industry endeavored to attract male clients, these market changes incited complicated questions, particularly within the gender destabilizing context of the Great Recession. What is suitably masculine when it comes to food, eating, and cooking for weight loss? What is a masculine body? What are masculine ways of shaping and caring for the body? Or for mastering and knowing it? Engaging both food and the body, weight loss shapes gender in myriad ways.

Dieting's dedication to idealized whiteness, middle-class authority, personal responsibility, and social respectability also influence arrangements of power within the shifting landscape of American life. Often expensive and exclusive, commercial diet programs are part of a complex system comprised of economic forces and capitalist aims, definitions of health, the foodscape, and cultural understandings of identities and "good" bodies. In post-9/11 America, public health anti-obesity campaigns framed good health, weight loss, and bodily surveillance as increasingly mandatory conditions of patriotic American citizenship.[8] Indeed, Weight Watchers success stories most often depict white, middle-class, heterosexual, youthful, able-bodied, and attractive people. These "successful losers" enact normative standards of gender and bodily control, which are ever-increasing requirements within neoliberal contexts where bodies are read as evidence, or not, of self-sufficiency and productivity. Constructing male weight loss clients not as men but as dudes proved a simple strategy to answer these complicated questions and context. The dude could transform the feminized character of dieting. Dudes on a diet could still eat, do, and be whatever and whoever they wanted.

A History of Weight Watchers and Men, 1960s–1990s

Founded in 1963, Weight Watchers' history reveals how dominant weight loss models incorporated men and masculinity before the company created a distinct men's program. Although diet programs have struggled in recent years given cultural shifts away from overt dieting and toward wellness, Weight Watchers has been one of the most popular, financially successful, and long-standing commercial weight loss programs in the United States, even referred to by some as "the Coke of the weight loss industry."[9] Some scholars have presumed that Weight Watchers has always been a program by and for women, but I approach the history of Weight Watchers to ask, "Where were the men?" This question does not intend to center men or masculinity in the history of the commercial weight loss industry. Nor does it aim to diminish the way the industry has contributed to the surveillance of women's bodies and profited from women's oppression. Rather, I demonstrate how the weight loss industry—as an institution and cultural force—has constructed notions of gender, both masculinities and femininities. This question digs down to the roots of Weight Watchers' twenty-first-century men's campaign—"Lose Like a Man"—to reveal how the company's gendered interventions have indexed social power and consumer agency for more than fifty years.

Men have had a presence in the Weight Watchers program since its inception, including within its leadership. Jean Nidetch incorporated Weight Watchers in 1963 with herself, her husband (Marty Nidetch), and Felice and Albert Lippert as the four founding members, who each lost significant weight on the program.[10] In fact, Weight Watchers became as central to Albert Lippert's life story as it was for Jean Nidetch, though she is more routinely profiled as Weight Watchers' founder. Before Albert met Jean, he was an army veteran and married father of two sons, who worked as a buyer of women's coats and suits. Having heard about Jean's first successful weight loss meetings in her own living room, Albert and Felice invited Jean to their home with more meetings to follow. As both Albert and Felice lost weight, the group coined the name Weight Watchers and, so the story goes, Albert suggested incorporating the business. In Albert's words, he "really administered and ran the business. Jean was the evangelist and did all the up-front work."[11] In a *New York Times* interview, Albert said, "I still get goosebumps when I feel that I, as an individual, was instrumental in developing what today is the world's foremost weight-reduction organization."[12] Weight Watchers became Albert Lippert's legacy, even in his 1998 *New York Times* obituary, as he remained a Weight Watchers business consultant until his death at the age of seventy-two.[13] His headstone even acknowledges his work with Weight Watchers, as it bears the inscription, "He changed the shape of the world."[14]

Beyond covering news of Weight Watchers' founders, the press throughout the 1960s, 1970s, and 1980s consistently cited and quoted male dieters on the program, despite the fact that most members were women.[15] In one of the first *New York Times* articles covering Weight Watchers, written in 1967, Nan Ickeringill quoted eight members, two of whom were men.[16] One man was a Weight Watchers group leader at a meeting of forty-seven members where four were men. The same year, the *Chicago Tribune* profiled Richard Cooper, the president of the Chicago Weight Watchers Inc. franchise, who himself lost forty pounds on the program and led meetings at ten Chicago locations attended by both men and women, making Cooper quite wealthy.[17]

In 1976, the *Chicago Tribune* sympathetically featured the Lavender Elephants, a group of approximately fifty gay men, many of whom had previously participated in Weight Watchers, but sought a meeting space less feminine and less heteronormative. In the story, participants freely used profanity, which they implied would not have been considered appropriate at a Weight Watchers meeting. Furthermore, one participant shared, "If I were at a Weight Watchers meeting tonight, I couldn't get up before the group and say I went home and ate and ate because I was rejected at a [gay] bar. They'd be shocked."[18] Such comments suggest that Weight Watchers provided a needed forum, but one with limitations for both gay and straight men. Such limitations did not affect Jean Nidetch's image as a sought-after "apostle of thin," however. According to the *LA Times*, a Jean Nidetch talk in Los Angeles in 1982 drew a crowd of "some 420 women and at least 20 men," all equally eager to witness Nidetch as a Weight Watchers founder.[19] During one of Weight Watchers' peaks in popularity in 1993, the *New York Times* summarized the happenings at a meeting in Scarsdale attended by "fifty or so women and a handful of men."[20]

These off-hand summaries of gendered demographics and quotes from male dieters provide evidence of men's small, but consistent membership in the Weight Watchers program across decades and geographies, as well as the press's fascination with them. Despite this, pre-2000 Weight Watchers often employed gender-neutral language, thus subtly including men among Weight Watchers participants and potential clients. When quoted in the press and writing in her cookbooks and other publications, Nidetch most often spoke of "people," "members," and "the overweight," rather than addressing only the women who consistently made up 90 percent or more of the program's membership.

Male Weight Watchers members were specifically considered in the development of Weight Watchers cookbooks and *Weight Watchers Magazine*. For example, the *Weight Watchers Program Cookbook*, first published in 1972, listed menu plans for both women and men, including male customizations such as an extra slice of bread at breakfast and lunch, two extra daily servings of fruit, and an additional two ounces of fish, meat, or poultry at dinner.[21] Furthermore, *Weight Watchers Magazine* included men as part of its intended audience, a venture lead by male executives. Albert Lippert worked with editor Matty Simmons and publisher Leonard A. Mogel to launch *Weight Watchers Magazine* in February 1968.[22] The magazine endeavored to be "the first and only monthly magazine that reports realistically, completely and interestingly on one of the most serious problems of our day . . . the simple problem of weighing too much."[23] Simmons noted broad interest in such a periodical, citing that "a high proportion of our population, at every age and in both sexes" were overweight.[24] Targeting male interests, the magazine's first issue included a special column "For Men Only" and a feature about men and golf. While the magazine was initially conceived of as a women's periodical, Simmons shared in an interview that "there were men who would read it," and the publishers wanted to reach out to them. Some men did read *Weight Watchers Magazine*. In 1993, 700,000 of the magazine's 4.7 million subscribers purportedly were men, a small but present readership. For reasons not immediately clear, the magazine's editorial approach shifted in the 1990s, however, dropping its inclusion of male Weight Watchers to focus solely on female readers.[25]

Although mostly women have served as Weight Watchers spokespeople, men have also broken the cultural silence around male dieting.[26] A 1967 *New York Times* article included the subheading "Men Are Vain, Too," and covered the weight loss stories of several male Weight Watchers, including the meeting leader Chuck Ashkenas. He had lost 65 ½ pounds and quipped, "It gives me a kick to be able to wear clothes with horizontal stripes. You think only women are vain about clothes?"[27] In 1973, Weight Watchers celebrated its tenth anniversary with an event that drew 15,000 program devotees to Madison Square Garden. The evening's entertainment included Bob Hope, who told the audience he was on a diet most of the time, offering a somewhat rare glimpse into a male celebrity's experience with weight and dieting.[28] A 1986 expose, "The Ever-Fatter Business of Selling Thinness," quoted then president of Weight Watchers International, Charles Berger, who admitted that 92 percent of program members were women, but saw opportunities for male growth. He said, "You have things like ads of men dressed in tight jeans. Well, guess what, a lot of men can't get into those tight jeans. They can if they come to us."[29] From Weight Watchers leadership and male dieters alike, these admissions of male vanity and body self-consciousness reveal the ways in which men and women were similarly drawn to Weight Watchers in an effort to lose weight.

Since Weight Watchers' origins, men have also been among the program's most "successful" clients, revealing the universalizing, though not equal, impacts of fat stigma. For example, in 1972 the *New York Times* covered the "Big Losers" present at a Weight Watchers press conference announcing an update to the meal plan. These "losers" included junior high school principal James Bennett, who had lost 208 pounds, and Ronald Pomerleau, who lost 250 pounds after his doctor "told him he would never live to be 35."[30] The article pictured a svelte Pomerleau wearing a light-colored dress shirt, diagonally striped tie, and dark jacket with a carnation jauntily adorning the lapel. He sat with his hands comfortably folded in his lap, his left ankle crossed easily over his right knee. The article featured a similar image of another Weight Watcher, Grace King, who had lost 205 pounds. They both sat before easels that held up poster-sized photographs of their formerly fat selves. The photos depict their "before" bodies dressed in white, as if made to appear as large as possible. Shot in profile, their fleshy faces look away from the audience. Without two eyes in view, without a gaze to speak of, these former fat selves were visually depicted as objects, compared to the full subjectivity of the dieters' thin "after" bodies, which were dressed in dark colors and looked directly at the audience and the camera.

These stories and images reinforce not only that men have been present in the Weight Watchers story from its beginning but also that they have been subjected to fat stigma and social assumptions about personal, physiological, and moral fitness. Sports journalist and fiction author Robert Lipsyte emphasized these points in a 1996 piece in the New York Times, "Confronting the Fat in Me: A Journey Begins," in which he discussed his lifelong weight struggles as he returned to his neighborhood Weight Watchers. He wrote, "I relaxed, safe among my people. We could let down, tell off-calorie jokes, use the F-word that hurt us most. . . . Forget race, ethnicity, gender, class, and the false divisions of the city; the struggle is between the Fatsos and the Civilians."[31] As Lipsyte poignantly emphasizes, fat stigma affects both men and women—further compounded by race, class, and sexuality—and has contributed to the gendered history of dieting in the United States. Lipsyte's life as a man dealing with fatness and dieting introduces a fat/thin binary into discussions of intersectionality that modifies the experience of other identity categories.[32] Social perceptions of fatness produce inequality, exclusion, and marginalization.[33]

As a result, men *do* diet. Commercial weight loss programs have sought to profit from shifting male body ideals, men's increasing discontent with their bodies, and heightened social concerns for health and fitness. This desire for social legibility affects men deeply enough that they have, throughout the histories of commercial weight loss programs, waded into the waters of supposed emasculation to join Weight Watchers or Nutrisystem or Jenny Craig, even if they are one of very few men in attendance.

Diet Culture in Men's Magazines and Diet Books, 1990s–2000s

Beyond men's small but consistent participation in Weight Watchers, men's diet culture further blossomed in the 1990s and early 2000s with men's health and fitness magazines, such as *Men's Health*, and diet books that drew a larger male audience, such as *Dr. Atkins New Diet Revolution*, *The Paleo Diet*, and *The Abs Diet*. These sources of health, fitness, and weight loss advice voiced anxieties about modern life and identity, as they served as precursors to the weight loss industry's programs for men, and their advertising campaigns that emphasized the dude. *Men's Health* in particular paved the way for men's diet programs. Rodale Press piloted *Men's Health* magazine in 1986, but by 1994 its circulation numbers were double that of industry-leading men's magazines such as *Esquire* and *GQ*, proving the significant potential for men's periodicals dedicated to active living, health, and fitness.[34] Culturally, however, such magazines produced contradictory models of masculinity that fervently endorsed self-regulation, personal responsibility for health, whiteness, and heteronormativity.

Rodale Press and *Men's Health* editors further extended their emphasis on personal responsibility when they published *The Abs Diet: The Six-Week Plan to Flatten Your Stomach and Keep You Lean for Life* in 2004. Alongside recipes for "Macho Meatballs" and exercises for sculpting a six pack, *The Abs Diet* authors endorsed a slim and muscular body as part of ideal and erotic citizenship. In the book's opening pages, the authors declared, "When you have abs, you're telling the world that you're a disciplined, motivated, confident, and healthy person—and hence a desirable partner."[35] Abs form a physical and cultural shorthand for adjudicating "good" health and conventional attractiveness, imbuing their pursuit with importance and anxiety.[36] Unsurprisingly, searching online for "how to get six pack abs" returns more than 80 million results. These include not just ab-centric workout routines, but the nutritional admonition that "abs are made in the kitchen," which the Powerful Yogurt brand built upon, as shown in chapter 3. Achieving and maintaining abs represents a key attribute of productive male citizenship, defined by whiteness, normative masculinity, and proper middle-class consumption.

As discussed in chapter 1, *Men's Health* also broached dieting for men within the pages of their cookbooks, such as *Guy Gourmet*, which promoted brawny dude food alongside a fit muscular body, foodie sensibilities, and masculine prowess in both the kitchen and the gym. This juxtaposition echoes the "bulimic double bind" depicted on the covers of women's magazines that promise, for example, the secret to losing 10 pounds alongside a recipe for the best chocolate cake.[37] Despite this similarity between men's and women's magazines, *Guy Gourmet* upheld conventional notions of male appetite and satisfaction, typically withheld from women. *Guy Gourmet* framed maintaining one's weight in the masculine, athletic terms of "stay lean." It placed weight loss within an individual man's controlled desires, assertive goals, and wholly subjective intensions to lose the weight *he wants*.

Other diet books published in the 1990s and early 2000s appealed to men with masculine diet fare. They similarly hailed and applauded the productive, healthy, male citizen. Published in 1992, *Dr. Atkins New Diet Revolution* stands as one of the best-selling diet books of all time and one that significantly masculinized dieting, as men and women followed the program in equal numbers.[38] Men have been historically less inclined to follow low-fat diets, which feature femininized and overtly health conscious foods like yogurt and salads. Men following the Atkins diet ate high-protein foods considered masculine in American culture, food that approached dude food status, such as steak, burgers without buns, chicken, bacon, and eggs. Men could diet without adopting any of dieting's conventional (and derisively feminine) rituals, such as counting calories, avoiding desirable foods, or engaging in constant dietary surveillance. In this way, low-carbohydrate diets—such as Atkins, South Beach Diet, and Zone Diet—set masculine dietary and behavioral precedents that Weight Watchers, Nutrisystem, and Jenny Craig would adopt and augment.

These diets also paved the way for Loren Cordain's *Paleo Diet*, first published in 2002 but reached popularity in the years afterward. The book sought to imbue the low-carb trend with a distinctly masculine historical and evolutionary legitimacy. The Paleo Diet evangelized Darwinian medicine and promoted the eating habits of Stone Age hunter-gatherers, encouraging dieters to "eat like a caveman," evoking the purposefully masculine imagery long referenced in men's cookbooks.[39] The diet endorsed considerable meat consumption while restricting foods generally considered healthful, such as grains, legumes, and dairy products.

Today's Paleo Diet movement represents a culmination of various twentieth-century researchers' aims to establish connections between not just diet and health but between modern civilization and the supposed degeneration of vigor and strength, tensions that have long motivated masculinity crisis, as discussed in the introduction.[40] Today's Paleo Diet echoes the practices and motivations of the nineteenth-century physical culture movement that expressed anxieties about the effects of modern life. Paleo

Diet followers convey legitimate concerns over the caloric effect of sedentary jobs and leisure activities, the overstimulation of digital technologies, and the effect of industrial agriculture upon the quality of the food supply. The gendered effects of modernity may be perceived as even more dire now than at the turn of the century, as significant numbers of women also follow the Paleo Diet, evangelizing their experiences on blogs and social media.[41] Like their nineteenth-century forbearers, followers of the Paleo Diet movement resist the supposedly deleterious effects of modern life through the controlled cultivation of their bodies, following specific dietary practices and fitness regimens, most notably CrossFit. Taken together, diet books from Atkins to Paleo and magazines like *Men's Health* engaged masculinities through specific foods and ways of eating. They emphasized the body's relationship to everyday American life, echoing long-standing anxieties regarding modernity's potentially negative effects on masculinity, which the dude communicated as well.

These earlier diet trends shaped the context in which commercial diet programs would seek out more male dieters and hail them as dudes. Weight loss programs for men defeminized and masculinized dieting using three main strategies. First, each program presented men's weight loss as fundamentally different from women's weight loss, a tactic long popular within the pages of men's cookbooks like those analyzed in chapter 1. Gender difference resonated strongly as a strategy to combat gender contamination, especially given the context of the Great Recession era and its blurring of traditional gender lines. Second, each program appealed to men through dude tropes, such as boyish humor and sports. Third, programs made weight loss "safe" for men by keeping the work of weight loss a secret.

Real Men Don't Diet: The Construction of Gendered Difference

To combat the cultural refrain that real men don't diet, diet programs capitalized upon the ways men themselves have described their weight loss as different from women's in order to protect their masculinity.[42] For example, in the press release launching Weight Watchers Online for Men, the company emphasized "guys' unique approach to weight loss" in a Weight-Loss Gender Differences Chart.[43] The chart compared characteristics such as the "weight loss vernacular" of women (diet) versus men (get in shape) and women's and men's overall approach to weight loss. Weight Watchers claimed that women are "quick to initiate, but prone to start and stop," while men are "serious, disciplined, structured."[44]

Despite offering men and women basically the same weight loss approach, tools, and food options (though in different serving sizes), program advertising routinely employed the dude to construct the experience of weight loss along gendered lines. For example, the 2013 Nutrisystem homepage had separate tabs for Women's Plans and Men's Plans. The women's page read, "Easy weight loss that works," with a series of bullet points that explained the program in detail.[45] Conversely, the men's page described the program with simplified and abridged language: "Eat. Move. Lose. . . . With foods you actually enjoy, simple plans that spell everything out, and 40 years of balanced science to bet on, you're just one choice short of the body you want."[46] Such program descriptions differentiated masculine versus feminine weight loss through variation in language, tone, and style, as well as through subtly gendered references to satisfying food and scientific legitimacy.

These programs also differentiated men's and women's weight loss through dichotomous depictions of foods and appetites matching masculine/feminine with satisfaction/restraint. Men's diet programs did not endorse regendered foods, like the diet sodas and yogurts discussed in chapter 3. They also did not endorse foods typically framed as healthy. Instead, men's diet programs promoted dude food: foods considered irrefutably masculine and decidedly anti-diet. Men's diet programs emphasized the flavor, satisfaction, and quantity that dieting tends to curtail. In their program launch, Nutrisystem for Men assured male dieters that they would eat hearty amounts of "man food—burgers, pizza, pasta, and chips."[47] In a section titled, "What can I eat?" the 2013 Weight Watchers website assured men that they can eat, "Anything. (Seriously, have that burger.)"[48] Alongside images of hot dogs, chicken wings, mac and cheese, ice cream sandwiches, and steak kabobs, Weight Watchers assured male dieters, "Seriously—*no* food is off-limits. You can eat anything you want. You'll just learn to do it a whole lot smarter." Diet programs assured men that their appetites need not be restrained in order to lose weight. They promoted and protected dude food—and by extension masculinity itself—from the feminine encroachment of dieting. With Weight Watchers, Nutrisystem, or Jenny Craig, men did not need to fear the assumed gustatory dissatisfaction of "healthy" foods, framed as the opposite of tasty and hearty dude food.

In recent years, digital programs, devices, and apps have changed the weight loss landscape, but Weight Watchers framed these tools in distinctly gendered ways. For women, weight loss technologies—such as Weight Watchers points tracking app—furthered the emotional, psychological,

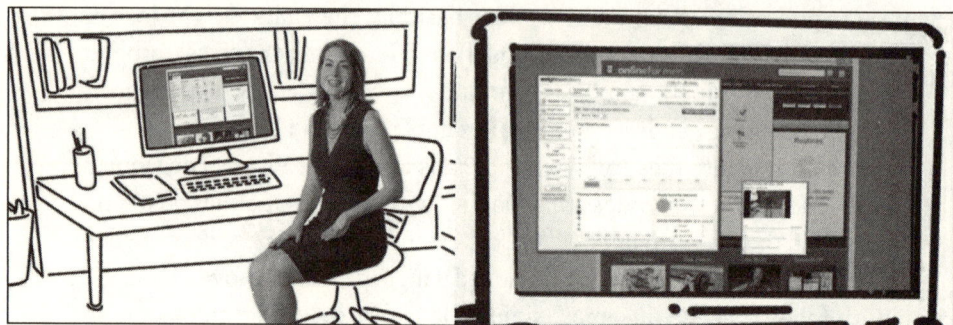

Weight Watchers Online presented the effort of weight loss as satisfying work for women but as play for men, depicted in these opposing screen grabs from an informational video.

and highly internalized project of self-discipline and chronic, unwavering restraint. Weight Watchers portrayed female dieters on a difficult but actualizing and empowering journey toward not just idealized thinness but a new and better self. For men, Weight Watchers portrayed the same dieting technology as keeping the work of weight loss at arm's length. Weight Watchers depicted male clients losing weight as dudes. They lost weight easily, even effortlessly, while remaining stably and immutably masculine throughout the process. Weight Watchers depicted dieters' gendered relationship to technology spatially as well. A program video depicted a female dieter, Bonnie, seated at a desk with a computer as if at work. She actively interacts with her weight loss effort of restraint, which the program measures, tracks, and visualizes on the screen. Conversely, a male dieter exclaimed, "The tools are kind of like a video game," emphasizing the supposedly easy satisfaction of male weight loss and the playful register of the dude.[49] For women, dieting is hard work. For men, it's a game, made to appeal to dudes who play rather than labor.

Just as diet soda brands emphasized real taste for men, so too did weight loss programs. Weight Watchers assured men they would eat only real food, and the Jenny Craig for Men homepage told men: "Eat real food with real taste. You want to lose weight, not taste."[50] With such comments, commercial weight loss programs reinforced the perception among men that "healthy" foods are unsatiating and unmanly. This supposedly masculine appetite and sense of taste contrast strongly with the flavor profile of diet food, which women have traditionally consumed when attempting to lose weight. These diet foods for women are distinctly *unreal*, as they create substitutes for the appearance and palatability of pleasurable flavors. Since male

These screen grabs from an informational video depict how Weight Watchers Online presented the program differently for male versus female clients through gendered representations of food, eating spaces, and cooking.

appetites and bodies have typically not been restrained to the same extent as women's, masculine diet food is relatively free from this unrealness in flavor, texture, quantity, and expression. Even when dieting, the food men consume is liberating. Men's diet food is real food, eaten in masculine ways.

Weight loss programs also depict food practices, such as shopping and cooking, within a strict gendered divide between public and private. In a program video, "successful" Weight Watcher Bonnie used a barcode scanner on her smart phone to learn the point value of a box of whole-wheat pasta at the supermarket, a site that since its inception has been framed as a feminized space, even "a housewife's paradise."[51] In contrast, male Weight Watchers success story Dan used the same tool at a convenience store to purchase a bag of chips, so that he "can stay on plan" while "on the go," separating his food shopping from feminized domestic work. Such contrasting depictions repeat the gendered division between "healthy" (feminine) and "unhealthy" (masculine) food choices that promote restraint and satisfaction respectively.

Bonnie's and Dan's stories also reinforced the gendered divide between the public and private spheres. Unlike Dan, who used the tool while out and about, Bonnie's video seamlessly transported her from the supermarket aisle to a kitchen, spatially reinforcing the enduring, feminized character of food shopping and preparation.[52] While Bonnie discussed cooking and recipe tools in the kitchen, Dan never mentioned these tools or appeared in such a space. Instead, he used a cheat sheet tool to prepare one of his favorite foods (porterhouse steak) outdoors on the grill. Weight Watchers reinforced the perception of cooking as wholly feminine, but they were not alone in these gendered depictions of food preparation.[53] The Jenny Craig for Men website proclaimed, "With Jenny's highly satisfying meals, all you have to do is pop them in the microwave or oven and they're ready to eat."[54] These simplified instructions distance men from the intention, skill, and act of cooking and the private sphere, even when following a diet.

In addition to food and food practices, weight loss programs positioned views of the body along these gender lines and reinforced divisions between public and private spheres. For example, although both Bonnie and Dan lost significant weight on Weight Watchers (forty-seven and sixty-seven pounds respectively), their success story videos depicted the meaning of their weight loss differently. On the one hand, Weight Watchers framed Dan's weight within a professional capacity, orienting his body (and its purported fat disability and thin ability) toward the masculinized, public sphere. On the other hand, Bonnie's weight loss was oriented toward the private sphere and about how she felt about herself.

At the beginning of her video, Bonnie shared the screen with her "before" photo and attributed her weight gain to family gatherings marked by lots of fattening food. Prompted by personal concerns for her health and weight, Bonnie joined Weight Watchers Online. Bonnie engaged in the self-reflective work endorsed by the Weight Watchers approach. Dan did not. Instead, he stated that he was a sergeant in the military who "could have been honorably discharged" for "barely meeting the fitness requirements." The video portrayed Dan as joining Weight Watchers not to transform himself both inside and out, as Bonnie did, but to salvage his career by changing his body. As such, Dan's motivation to lose weight was made to appear more legitimate to potential male Weight Watchers clients than Bonnie's. While Bonnie's weight loss was rooted in family and emotions, the video depicted Dan's weight loss as central to his public life and career success, and, as a military sergeant, to the health of the nation as well.

Weight Watchers Online presented weight loss as emotionally driven for women, but as career-driven for men. These opposing screen grabs from an informational video also reveal different uses of before and after photos in ads targeting women versus men.

The video's conclusion reinforced this perspective as Dan claimed, "I've become an officer and a role model for my men," after he lost weight and started training to run a marathon. His weight loss communicated achievement, complete with a professional promotion, accolades, self-confidence, and leadership status. Conversely, after losing weight, Bonnie said, "Now I'm hiking, I'm biking, I'm dancing. But mostly, I'm more comfortable with myself than I've ever been," emphasizing the emotional, personal, and private nature of her weight loss, a perspective emblematic of therapeutic culture, which forms both a healing process and a worldview.[55]

The therapeutic ethos naturalizes the pursuit of an ideal self, framing its cultivation "not merely as a personal good, but a social obligation, the central purpose of human existence."[56] Programs like Weight Watchers fuse the ideal self to the cultivation of the ideal body, which closely follows gender ideals as well. Bonnie repeatedly demonstrated this relationship. At the end of the video, she appeared beside another before photo to which she said, "This used to be me. I transformed my life with Weight Watchers Online and I've never looked back and I know that you can too." Alternatively, Dan never appeared in the same frame as his fat body. While Dan did say, "Weight Watchers changed my life," his video concluded by focusing on his continual progress, embodied in his ongoing fitness journey. The final frames of his video show Dan in exercise clothes crossing a finish line, again reinforcing his body's public capacity rather than its private, interior achievements.

Commercial diet companies also constructed men's dieting as different from women's through expressions of rational versus irrational emotion. Men's weight loss programs adhered to hegemonic masculinity's expectation for rational thought, strength, and self-control when they described male weight loss success stories. Charles Barkley said he started Weight Watchers because "I was just getting too fat . . . the last thing I wanted to do was be an old fat guy taking a lot of medications."[57] Terry Bradshaw told a similar story: "I was so tired of looking old and fat and ugly that I couldn't take it one more minute. So you know what I did? I ordered . . . Nutrisystem."[58] Noncelebrity spokesmen also described weight loss in such unemotional terms. Weight Watchers success story Pete articulated the meaning of weight loss materially, as he reflected on his newly thin body, saying, "Oh my God. That's what an ab looks like," a comment that also reinforces the symbolic power of abs to communicate weight loss success and masculine healthfulness.[59] Daniel, another successful Weight Watcher, concluded his story by gesturing to his trim physique and saying, "I always say to my wife, 'How do you keep your hands off this?'"[60] Men's weight loss success stories highlight simple, unemotional physical change or the triumphant achievement of physical prowess, including heteronormative attractiveness.

In contrast, a Weight Watchers commercial featuring Kendra, a successful female client, reflected the tone and content of typical women's success stories. She described her eighty-seven-pound weight loss as a story of fear and courage, renewal and rebirth. She said, "This is a body that I have never lived in before," raising her arms to the sky, not only showing off her slim physique, but as if in religious thanks for her transformation.[61] She confessed that she had never been to a swimming pool for fear of showing her body in public. She continued saying, "I got the courage to learn how to swim. It's never too late to start anew."

Commercial weight loss programs require women to constantly surveil and discipline their bodies in the pursuit of the transformed self that Kendra described, which has destructive consequences.[62] Furthermore, weight loss promises of thin transformation reinforce negative portrayals and assumptions regarding fat bodies, particularly for women but also for men.[63] And even if weight loss yields a transformed self, it is conscribed to a particular type of potential womanhood that is subordinate; one with a curtailed autonomy and agency that is only powerful when thin.

It is also true, however, that dieting may afford a sense of agency.[64] Dieting can cultivate disciplined "technologies of the self" that are enabling and positively productive.[65] Dieting engenders new skills and ways for mastering, knowing, and caring for the self. Weight loss program advertising withholds this promise of transformation from men, however ambivalent it may be. This is why Kendra's success story followed the emotional template typical of women's weight loss stories, which are rooted in therapeutic culture. Conversely, male dieters shared unemotional narratives, which adhered to hegemonic masculinity and communicated the nonchalance of the dude.

Word choice further reinforces the orientation of male weight loss outside of the self. Dan talked of "losing *the* weight" (italics added), while Bonnie spoke of "*my* health," "*my* weight," and "*my* weight loss" (italics added). Dan did not address his role in gaining weight; he did not adopt the therapeutic ethos or the mantle of personal responsibility that Weight Watchers requires. He did not mention, for example, wanting to be there for his children, feeling guilty, or suffering low self-esteem. Engaging the distance that "the" produces, he did not speak of fatness, weight, or weight loss in terms that relate to his identity and sense of self. For dieters, weight loss is constructed as a disciplined act that "will eventually demarcate them as intelligible men and women."[66] Dan thus distanced himself from his previously fat body in order to adhere to masculine norms.

Analyzing the ways that Weight Watchers constructs male versus female weight loss reveals how the program manipulates the dude to its benefit, negatively affecting both women and men. Patriarchy oppresses women's bodies by idealizing thinness and scorning fatness. It also constrains the ways men can be men. It does so in part through socially constructed expectations for male character that devalue and discourage food and health-related knowledge and practices, the central tension in ambivalent masculine body discipline.

What's more, framing male weight loss as distinctly different from female weight loss has real consequences. For example, in a randomized trial of a weight loss program designed for men, published in *Obesity* in 2015, the authors based their intervention design on the understanding that men want different things from weight loss than women do. The authors wrote, "Men report wanting individually focused programs that do not include strict meal plans and provide the ability to tailor the diet to their preferences. Additionally, they prefer programs that do not disrupt their daily routine and provide information in a clear and direct manner."[67]

Such statements further naturalize aspects of normative discontent, a concept that describes the widespread nature of women's dissatisfaction with their bodies.[68] This weight loss study privileged men as it assumed that women *do* want things like strict meal plans, not tailored to their tastes and that disrupt their daily life. In such cases, women's more willing compliance with weight loss protocols can be misread as inherent characteristics of female study subjects. In reality, such a readiness to diet represents deeply ingrained and damaging behaviors into which women are more commonly socialized than men; an adherence practiced over years of dieting and often motivated by unyielding social demands for thinness. The oppositional framing of male versus female weight loss is built upon binaries of satisfaction/restraint, real/unreal, public/private, and rational/irrational. These binaries reinforce and further disparities and inequalities along axes of identity. They form the foundational assumptions upon which diet programs employed the dude in their sales pitch to men.

Appealing to Men, Endorsing Dude Masculinity

Diet program materials and advertising appealed to men through the dude's detached coolness with tropes such as casual language, misogynistic humor, and connections to professional sports. While all the programs included the word "men" in the diet name, advertising more often employed the laidback togetherness of the dude, speaking to the male audience as guys. The Nutrisystem website called out, "Hey guys—this isn't your wife's diet," establishing a homosocial and heteronormative connection, while also differentiating the program from women and women's dieting. In a Weight Watchers Online for Men commercial, two clients said, "We lost a ton of weight on Weight Watchers and we did it all online. There's a plan. It's just for guys."[69] Using plainspoken and direct language, commercial weight loss programs each embodied the ethos of the dude, as they forged a casual and yet heterosexually intimate connection with male consumers, and by extension with the act of dieting.

These advertisements also employed dude humor. In the Weight Watchers advertisement, "Roll Call," spokesman Charles Barkley stood at a podium,

Charles Barkley appeared in drag in the "Sir Charles for Weight Loss" Weight Watchers commercial (2012), assertively directing the male gaze to his newly reduced body.

reading in a melodramatic tone a long list of euphemistic and colloquial terms for penis.[70] After thirty seconds of penile oratory, a male narrator announced, "For every thirty-five pounds you lose, you may gain an extra inch of . . ."—at which point the audio cut to Barkley saying "wang." The announcer continued, "Well, now there's a Weight Watchers just for guys. Just think of all you'll gain." By relating weight loss to penis length, a pseudo-measure for manliness that abounds in popular culture, Weight Watchers aligned itself with a potent symbol of masculinity in a light-hearted, but visceral (and potentially anxiety-inducing) way.[71] The commercial also endorsed the anti-diet zero concept discussed in the previous chapter, as it emphasized what men gain from the program, rather than simply the weight they could lose.

Weight Watchers again employed sexually infused humor in the advertisement, "Sir Charles for Weight Loss," which framed weight loss and Weight Watchers as appropriately masculine through drag and the direction of the male gaze.[72] In this ad, Barkley dressed in a body hugging, low-cut, black dress, padded at the chest to create the appearance of breasts. He wore make up, silver jewelry, and a wig of long curly brown hair. He awkwardly strutted toward the camera in strappy open-toed heels and struck a pose with hands on his hips. "I hear some of you guys still think that Weight Watchers is just for women," Barkely said, "Even though I, Sir Charles, have been telling you that Weight Watchers has helped me lose 42 pounds and counting. And I can still eat man food like steak and pizza. So if this is what I gotta do to get you to listen, take a good look. But my eyes are up here guys."[73]

Some scholars read transphobia in this ad, but the commercial's use of drag and humor were also an overt expression of masculinity.[74] Barkley's mimicry and exaggeration of feminine dress, comportment, and gestures did not diminish his masculinity, but rather highlighted it, as he self-directed the male gaze toward his own body. Through his performance of femininity, Barkley emphasized his masculine mastery of the weight loss process. He directed the spotlight to his now lean and muscular body. His body was more visible and objectified in a sleeveless formfitting dress than it would have been in the dress shirt and pants that he wore in other commercials. At the same time, the drag performance taps into the playful, yet privileged, status of the dude. Barkley could dress up, joke, and play around because his weight loss achievement and established celebrity status reinforced his masculinity.

In their effort to combat gender contamination, diet sodas and yogurt ads depicted men watching sports, but men's weight loss programs often invoked athletes directly. Even as female participation in sports has increased and the once gendered divisions of athletics are increasingly blurred, weight loss programs for men promoted sports as supremely masculine, and athletes as aspirational models of fitness and health.[75] In the early 1990s, former professional athletes Tommy Lasorda and Dan Dierdorf served as spokesmen for Slim-Fast, a meal replacement shake, which reported in 2008 that 35 percent of their customers were men.[76] Weight Watchers employed Barkley as spokesman and sought to both reach male audiences and masculinize dieting through media context, launching new TV ads during the NBA and NHL playoffs. Nutrisystem endeavored to do the same. They expanded ad placement into masculine media terrain such as ESPN, *Sports Illustrated*, and *Men's Health* and invested 29 percent of their overall TV advertising budget on male-oriented networks.[77]

Both Nutrisystem and Weight Watchers have employed retired male sports stars as spokesmen, attempting to capture and channel the perceived masculinity of their athletic careers and bodies. Former NFL players Jim Stuckey, Dan Marino, Don Shula, and Terry Bradshaw have each endorsed Nutrisystem. Praising Marino, Nutrisystem nutritionist Delphine Carroll said, "You see an athlete like Dan Marino and he's a real man's man. . . . Having Dan Marino lose with Nutrisystem kind of gave men permission to diet."[78] Conversely, Jen Works for Men selected actor Jason Alexander, best known for playing George Costanza on *Seinfeld*, who the company considered relatable for everyday men. Alexander's less hegemonic performance of masculinity might have played a role in Jenny Craig's more modest success gaining male clients.[79] While Weight Watchers and Nutrisystem emphasized the dude in their advertising messages, they also specifically selected retired athletes as spokesmen to reinforce conventional connections between masculinity, sports, and a fit and controlled male body.

These choices of spokesman also reveal the interrelationship between gender and race in representations of dieting. Nutrisystem has hired white spokesmen for their men's program, while Weight Watchers hired Barkley. He was a reasonable candidate for a weight loss spokesman because of his accomplished career in the NBA and as a sports analyst and because of his 100-pound post-career weight gain. While not a dude himself, Barkley was a successful athlete and masculine role model carefully selected for his ability to resonate with male consumers. Weight Watchers' choice of Barkley cannot be critically read, however, outside of the cultural context of centuries-old racial stereotypes that read the Black male body as hypermasculine, hypersexual, and dangerous.[80] Whether invoking sports or not, such representations of Black bodies demonstrate how commercial weight loss normalizes whiteness, as it upholds a "racial and cultural ideology that sees white bodies as controllable, desirable, and beautiful and Black bodies as uncontrollable and deviant."[81] Within such a context, Weight Watchers' choice of Barkley as the Weight Watchers Online for Men program spokesman sought to masculinize the program and confirm its effectiveness via its ability to control "deviant" bodies marked by gender, race, fatness, and bodily ability. This manipulation of Barkley as spokesman grows more apparent when considered against the racial makeup of weight loss advertisements more broadly. A study of advertisements in a decade's worth of ten high-circulation magazines found that 80.2 percent of weight-loss ads featuring people depicted white people, an overwhelming majority.[82]

Against a subtext of both gender and race, ads also included sports metaphors in their program pitches. Jenny Craig incorporated sports (and a Weight Watchers dig) into one of their advertisements, saying, "Jenny Craig knows that the only time you want to count points is at a basketball game."[83] Nutrisystem incorporated sports imagery and context, filming one commercial against a digital football field background. In the ad spokesman Dan Marino declared that he had lost twenty-two pounds on the programs and is "back down to his playing weight."[84] In 2013, the Nutrisystem website also employed sports-related language, as it read, "Sometimes the thought of 'diet food' can sideline you before you even start a weight loss program. . . . [Nutrisystem has] the variety you want and the flexibility you need to fit your lifestyle and get your body back in the game." Terry Bradshaw, who claimed to have lost thirty-two pounds using Nutrisystem, discussed in a commercial weight lifting, sprints, long distance running, and passing practice in parallel with his experience following the Nutrisystem diet with its set meal options for breakfast, lunch, and dinner.[85] In this way, he masculinized diet food as part of an intense, athletic training routine.

Sports and an athletic desire to win may also lead men to start a diet. Nutrisystem reported that the Monday following the Super Bowl was one of the top days of the year that men start a diet, with one man calling or visiting the Nutrisystem website every 1.5 seconds.[86] Terry Bradshaw explained the phenomenon using sports imagery, saying, "It makes perfect sense. You go for the chips, you go long for the guacamole and you just keep going. Then, you wake up the next day and think, 'Man, I gotta do something I know will work. I need a winning game plan.'"[87] While Nutrisystem's Super Bowl sales claims are likely difficult to prove definitively, all of the celebrity athlete spokesmen asserted that losing weight makes men winners. Winning endorses an anti-diet zero approach, as it breathes an athletic fervor into the concept of lose like a man. These sports metaphors also made visceral the stakes of winning and losing, as they refer to the supposedly proper control of the male body and performance of masculinity. Emphasizing themes like sports and boyish humor, weight loss advertising spoke to men as consumers who could engage with dieting at a distance, through play rather than laborious restraint, as dudes rather than men.

Making Dieting Safe for Men: Anonymity, Secrets, and Silence

Commercial weight loss programs also sought to address the social stigma attached to male dieting by keeping secret its supposedly objectionable aspects. It turned out, dudes can do whatever they want, but there are still some things they do not, or cannot, talk about. Even as they attempted to sell weight loss programs to men, diet companies reinforced aspects of hegemonic masculinity that characterize weight loss as feminine, a belief that even some men on diets continue to hold. As Weight Watchers Online for Men spokesman Charles Barkley said at the program launch, "Men talk about a lot of things. Being fat ain't one of them." A 2007 *New York Times* article also reinforced this sentiment as it reported on a group of men using Weight Watchers and Nutrisystem with the title, "It Takes a Big Man to

Seek Help on Weight Loss."[88] Even David Kirchhoff, who worked for Weight Watchers for more than a decade and was company president and CEO from 2007–2013, described his weight problem as "hidden." He said his opportunity to lose weight on Weight Watchers while working for the company was a "secret" endeavor.[89] He also invoked the taboo nature of male dieting in his endorsement of Barkley. "When you have a role model like Charles Barkley," he said, "who's about as manly as anybody can possibly get, who's actually eating fruits and vegetables for the first time in his life — it signals to men everywhere that this is OK to do."[90]

To combat the cultural taboo of male dieting and to make dieting permissible for men, commercial weight loss programs constructed what I call — building from queer theorist Eve Sedgwick's work — a weight loss closet, as they endeavored to leave certain aspects of male weight loss unspoken.[91] Through purposefully produced silences about the work and meaning of weight loss, these programs hid aspects of dieting that fell outside of hegemonic masculinity and heteronormativity. These silent aspects included consuming diet foods, restraining one's appetite, or openly discussing how difficult weight loss is. These silences about male dieting ensured the subordination of marginalized masculinities and femininities, as commercial weight loss programs maintained the boundaries of hegemonic masculinity even as they promoted a supposedly feminine activity to men.

Commercial weight loss programs constructed the weight loss closet for male customers in multiple ways. Nutrisystem inconspicuously delivered packaged meals right to one's door, a program feature credited for attracting male clients.[92] Nutrisystem also reported that switching from meeting-based programming to online and telephonic options made men "feel more comfortable with the program."[93] If in-person meetings were held, they were made men-only and depicted as different than a women's or coed weight loss group. For example, Hal Majar Jr. lost eighty-one pounds on Weight Watchers and joined the company as a full-time group leader for a men's only group in Nashua, New Hampshire. He argued there are stark differences between men-only and coed meetings. "I don't think I've ever had a response in a men's group to a general question like 'Did you struggle this week,'" he said. "But if you talk about what you did for snacks during the six-hour Red Sox game, the frame of reference changes. The biggest difference I really see is that women talk about weight in very emotional terms. Women cry about weight. Men don't."[94] Such a statement sought to depict masculine weight loss as different from female weight loss, rendering emotions or challenges unspoken for men, even if they exist. As I've read men-only message boards, followed male Weight Watcher Instagram accounts, and listened to weight loss podcasts, men *do* cry about weight and have every reason to. Most diets fail and maintaining lost weight is outrageously difficult, if not impossible, for many people.[95]

Despite the real challenges of weight loss, these programs manipulated the perceived anonymity of online spaces to fashion the weight loss closet. For Weight Watchers, the shift to online programs also sought to keep pace with the ways in which digital technology increasingly shapes elements of everyday life. The digital health and wellness landscape has changed significantly in recent years with biometric self-tracking devices like the FitBit, released in 2008, and an ever-growing corpus of apps. While dieting has always endorsed and enhanced bodily surveillance, self-tracking devices "direct the gaze directly at the body. They privilege an intense focus on and highly detailed knowledge of the body."[96] Conceptually straddling the analogue and the digital, Weight Watchers Online reproduced constructions of gender and negotiations of power in this pursuit of body data, particularly in creating seemingly anonymous weight loss experiences.

For Weight Watchers, going digital also required a dramatic shift in the program's hallmark approach. Featuring online tools and downloadable apps, the online program was divorced from the in-person weigh-ins, group meetings, and tangible resources that characterized the traditional Weight Watchers program—and the face-to-face social support credited for the program's success.[97] Eschewing social support as feminine, Weight Watchers Online for Men assured members that the online message boards were men only, seeking to masculinize the Weight Watchers experience through excluding women spatially and conceptually. As part of the weight loss closet, Weight Watchers Online also largely framed weight loss as an individualized experience mediated by digital tools. For example, the Weight Watchers Online homepage invited dieters to "Lose weight completely online," as if the work and results of weight loss occurred within a suspended, cyber reality: a secret space. In a program video, a male Weight Watcher confessed that he thought "Weight Watchers was just for the ladies," but then he "got the trusted plan, completely online, customized just for guys." This pivot from Weight Watchers as derisively feminine to acceptably masculine depended upon the anonymity and strict gender binary that the online program and app endorsed.

Through the assurance of anonymity, diet programs constructed a weight loss closet that kept aspects of weight loss deemed feminine outside of male customers' experience. These programs presented gender typed depictions of real foods and ways of losing weight, as they incorporated dude language and humor, anti-intellectualism, and connections to sports. Commercial diet programs created and sustained the weight loss closet through men-only spaces, online programs, apps, and home delivery services. These combined efforts sought to engage men as dudes who *do* diet, but in passive, casual, and secret ways that did not threaten conventional masculinity.

Dudes Stepping Out of the Weight Loss Closet

Compared to men's cookbooks, food TV, diet sodas, and yogurts, men's weight loss programs posed a greater perceived threat of gender contamination for marketers to address. Campaigns such as "Lose Like a Man" poignantly reveal the significant ambivalence of the dude as a marketing strategy to combat gender contamination fears. Furthermore, these representations of the dude in weight loss campaigns likely diverge from men's actual lives. Glimpses into the experiences of men participating in weight loss programs reveal more fluid definitions and processes of gender, as well as ongoing tensions and contradictions.

Even men who diet must navigate the social view that dieting and losing weight are not suitably masculine endeavors. When he was twenty-nine years old, Jon Grigio lost 100 pounds following a hybrid of the Atkins and Glycemic Index diets. "Men are supposed to be tough and rugged and not need the help of a diet," he still said.[98] Jonathan Giordano, a weight loss influencer known for his recipes, seemed to concur in a 2017 Weight Watchers "Bropocalypse" event streamed on Facebook Live. "As a man and a Weight Watcher, it's a woman's world here," he said. "It's different. It's not easy for us to share and be vulnerable and be open about these things because, like . . . be a man, it's not a manly thing. This is new ground for us."[99] Weight Watchers participant M. Kevin Howland revealed another dimension of gender negotiation when weight loss is positioned in a men's-only space. "Without the women here, you don't have to be as masculine because we're all in the same boat," he said. "We don't have to show off for anyone. We can all be ourselves."[100]

The notion of self—of who we are and want to be—is central to the promises commercial weight loss programs make, but Weight Watchers has typically endorsed different types of self for men and women. These differences reveal the contradictions and constraints of the dude. For women, programs like Weight Watchers promise a transformed self and the opportunity to start life afresh in a thin body that purportedly reflects a woman's inner hopes and desires. Weight Watchers excluded this process of trans-formation and this yet-to-be-imagined self from the male weight loss prom-ise. While men keeping the therapeutic work of dieting at arm's length likely proves psychologically protective, it also reveals how patriarchy traps and limits who (and how) men can be, not to mention how it erases differ-ently gendered bodies and selves. These gender rules allow little space for the potentially empowering and actualizing effects of personal change. In-deed, the dude resists deep thinking or earnest effort in order to maintain an easy, unconflicted coolness. "Real men" must refrain from too much self-reflection in order to maintain their status. Because of this, Weight Watchers success stories, such as Bonnie and Dan, depict women glowing with the exhilaration of successful weight loss and newfound sense of self, while men must demonstrate how a changed body yields productive accom-plishments, such as a career promotion and new athletic abilities.

The Weight Watchers videos featuring Bonnie and Dan appeared on the Weight Watchers website in the early 2010s and depicted a constrained promise of transformation to men that eschewed social support and the emotional side of weight loss. More recent iterations of Weight Watchers Online have tried to create new digital spaces for men to seek social support with the hashtag #WWBros, which originated among male Weight Watcher members themselves. While in the language of bro instead of dude, this choice of hashtag still demarcates an identity more akin to the dude than #WWMen, for example, might have. Furthermore, the program website promises men, "#WWBros are behind you" and explains the community as, "Get props on our social network, Connect, where you can share updates with thousands of other members as you're all losing weight. Follow the #WWBros, our tight-knit community of men, and see how other members are getting #backontrack."

While Connect is part of the private Weight Watchers app for members, a number of Weight Watchers members use the hashtag on Instagram, making it part of their personal and public "weight loss journeys." In spring 2020, there were more than 31,000 posts on Instagram using the hashtag #WWBros to accompany photos of Weight Watchers point conscious meals and recipes, workouts, weigh-in results, and before and after photos. A number of men use the hashtag, but women do as well, along with hashtags related to Weight Watchers, such as #weightwatchersfam, #WeAreWW, #IAmAWeightWatcher, #beyondthescale (a program introduced in Decem-ber 2015), and #wwfreestyle (a program launched in December 2017), along with more general markers, such as #healthychoices, #healthylifestyle, and #weightlossjourney.

An "off and on" Weight Watcher over the course of a decade, Jonathan Giordano, previously mentioned, runs the Mudhustler website and related social media accounts as "the original #wwbro."[101] He develops and publishes recipes with low Weight Watchers point counts with the mantra "we don't eat no stinkin' diet food" and promising one can "eat like a fat kid and still lose weight." He became relatively well known within the weight loss community for creating Weight Watchers compliant recipes for dude food, such as Bigasswaffles (waffles made with protein powder and high-protein pancake mix) and Birdballs (turkey and chicken meatballs). Giordano created diet food infused with realness, which appealed to both women and men on diets. At the same time, his recipes endorsed conventionally masculine characteristics, including exaggerated recipe names that echo those found in *The Abs Diet* or men's cookbooks. When I asked him about how he named these recipes, he said, "I knew that from past experience that I could live on salad and skinless chicken breast for a little while but that doesn't last long. I wanted to be able to eat a big ass waffle." Giordano also cites his love of food TV, especially Guy Fieri's *Diners, Drive-Ins and Dives*, as part of his inspiration to develop recipes despite lacking a culinary background, revealing how Fieri's enthusiastic populism circulates among his viewers.

Giordano has achieved some public success as a weight loss influencer. His Instagram account boasts more than 66,000 followers, his posts routinely feature product sponsors and deals, and he has participated and hosted large events, some affiliated with Weight Watchers. Giordano speaks candidly about his challenges with food, weight, and body image. He insists that openly sharing about his weight loss experience not only helps other men, but defines what it means to be a man. Giordano uses social media to dismantle the weight loss closet that Weight Watchers maintained, revealing how the dude operates outside of commercial spaces. Indeed, other men, such as comedian Anthony DiDomenico of the WW Bro Podcast and Jay Casale of The Lighter Side Podcast (which features interviews about weight loss and transformation) also share personal stories of weight loss struggles and their Weight Watchers membership. For all three of these men, publicly sharing weight loss experiences serves as a form of advocacy. They are actively reimagining weight loss for men beyond what commercial programs like Weight Watchers have traditionally offered to male members.

These few examples present different ways of negotiating masculinity in and through commercial diet programs, weight loss, food, and digital media. In the case of #WWBros, users co-opted a company's social media campaign and made it newly meaningful. The story of #WWBros also reveals the ongoing effects of not only fat stigma, but also weight loss stigma for men. Compared to #WWBros' 31,000 posts on Instagram, #wwsisterhood marked more than two million. Giordano told me that even though he shares his experiences "as a man and for men" his audience is 96 percent women. "From what I can tell (through email and conversation)," he said, "that is because they are concerned with the men (sons and husbands) in their life that need help."

While commercial diet programs produce and reinforce many of the most damaging elements of diet culture for women, the social strictures of masculinity and notions of gender contamination further complicate men's experiences with their bodies. The increasingly public and confessional expectations of our digital media lives bring risks but also afford opportunities. Some men, including those briefly profiled here, may feel more comfortable speaking out about weight loss on social media and actively seeking virtual social support. Others will not. Instead, they'll remain in the weight loss closet. The dude and dude food provided the commercial diet industry avenues on which to meet men at the crossroads of gender negotiation, the body, appetite, and health. The dude has also afforded some opportunities for men themselves. Men, like Giordano, have openly participated in weight loss programs, created their own recipes, and shared their stories on social media and on podcasts. These men's weight loss experiences are more agentive than those created by commercial success stories or advertising campaigns. These men are working to redefine what it means to be "a real man." In the conclusion, I consider more of the dude's opportunities, and limits.

Conclusion
Dude, What Happened?

For all his privileged slacking, the dude proved valuable to industry, who quickly put him to work selling cookbooks, food television, diet sodas, yogurts, and weight loss programs to men with cool insincerity. Far more than a marketing strategy alone, the dude emerged from the specific social, cultural, economic, and political tensions that collided in the first decades of the new millennium. The dude spoke of the period's crisis of white masculinity under Barack Obama and before him, George W. Bush, who was arguably a dude president who resisted the full demands of the office.[1] This crisis began a new chapter with the presidential election of Donald Trump in 2016. The dude responded to a cultural context in which concerns for identity and status reached a fever pitch, which have only escalated since then. These years of Trump have been marked by increases in hate crimes, white supremacist movements, overt racism, and new racism.[2] There have been responses, too, such as the sustained efforts of Black Lives Matter. When it comes to gender, the dude's transformation similarly speaks to a frenzied and highly reactionary cultural moment.

Post-2016 America wrestled with bursts of popular misogyny, even stronger anti-feminist backlash, and a resurgence of toxic masculinity, including by Donald Trump himself. At the same time, commodified feminism came into mainstream fashion and the #MeToo movement expanded in 2017.[3] The "transgender tipping point" Katy Steinmetz proclaimed in *Time* in 2014 resulted in years of increasing media visibility but has yet to cultivate equal civil rights, and the transgender community still faces significant legislative inequality.[4] At the same time, the American cultural landscape shows some signs of change, starting with our language. By 2019, three of the most-referenced online dictionaries—Merriam-Webster, Oxford, and Dictionary.com—each included *they* as a singular personal pronoun. Merriam-Webster named *they* as 2019's word of the year, as their data revealed a 313 percent increase in lookups compared to 2018.[5] What's more, members of Generation Z, those born since the mid- and late-1990s, purportedly express more flexible views on gender identity and fluidity, which differentiates them from my Millennial generation.[6] Bathroom signs decreeing "We don't care" loudly speak the opposite, of caring deeply, constituting a politicization of the dude's "whatever" attitude.

With regard to the recession and its gendered effects, we were told the American economy had recovered. And yet precarity lurked in every corner of the American labor system. Workers in nearly all industries and fields battle an uncertain future characterized by stagnating wages, increasing health-care costs, inadequate parental leave policies, and the day-to-day realities of a changed climate in crisis. (The COVID-19 global pandemic laid bare the severity of these problems for all to see.) Amid such a context, the dude lost his footing. Strongly gendered and exclusionary advertising tactics, always limited in their potential, grew increasingly insensitive and culturally out-of-step within these political shifts in the late 2010s.

As a result, nearly every example addressed in this book has since shifted course away from the dude and from notions of gender contamination. In some cases, branding instead focused on gender neutrality, dropping the dude along with any emphasis on gender. Other brands adopted a strategy of inclusion, extending the privilege of the dude, for better or worse, to all. Examining these branding changes demonstrates not only how gender discourses like the dude were constructed, deployed, and sustained but also how they have been, and can be, reimagined. In some instances, these gendered branding transformations have had limited effect in the marketplace or on everyday eaters. In others they have proved significant for consumers, but detrimental for a company's bottom line. And in other cases, reimagining the dude has been good for both business and consumers.

As their branding and advertising strategies change, these dude-driven stories reveal how power flows through consumer culture and why food remains such a fraught space for shaping and reflecting identity. They also reveal how something as seemingly trivial as dude food encapsulates the tensions and possibilities of masculinities. The dude navigates the competing desires for satisfaction, freedom, and ease. He balances the demands of personal responsibility, health, and fitness alongside fears of failure, instability, and change. While these processes prove highly ambivalent and perhaps impossible for both men and women, the examples in this book also demonstrate that the dude was not initially deployed in inclusive ways. Instead, the dude circulated in food and throughout media in ways that upheld the power and exclusivity of hegemonic masculinity. In some cases, this process of exclusion has changed, but even these alterations prove as contradictory as the dude himself.

In the case of men's cookbooks, publishers continue to churn out meaty tomes for men, but tracking the evolution of *Men's Health* cookbooks reveals how the dude has transformed. Paul Kita—Food and Nutrition editor at *Men's Health*, who co-authored *Guy Gourmet* in 2013—published *A Man, a Pan, a Plan* in 2017, keeping "man" in the title, but removing most mentions of gendered intent from the recipes themselves. Coming full circle, the title directly plays on the first *Men's Health* cookbook *A Man, a Can, a Plan*, published in 2002. Despite its title and the significant dude precedent set by previous *Men's Health* cookbooks, the introduction to *A Man, a Pan, a Plan* is free of gendered tone. It instead emphasizes cooking as universally central to good health and "a delicious form of self-care."[7] Kita's stated aim is simply to provide "practical advice and straightforward recipes" that use just one pan so to "save stress, prevent mess, and reduce your chances of culinary distress." While previous men's cookbooks incorporated references to cavemen, grilling, and other conventionally masculine symbols, in *A Man, a Pan, a Plan*, Kita likens cooking to "building a birdhouse," a less overtly masculine task. Compared to the genre-busting table of contents in *A Man, a Can, a Plan*, which included sections dedicated to SpaghettiOs and beer, *A Man, a Pan, a Plan* presents recipes for breakfast, not breakfast, appetizers and sides, and desserts. Recipe names also change, as "Crispy Homemade Home Fries" replaces "Homeboy Homefries." The embedded masculine violence of "Border-Patrol Casserole" gives way to dishes like "Porcini Mushroom and Goat Cheese Omelet" and "Huevos Rancheros with Black Bean-Avocado Salsa." Revealing the extent of cultural change after 2016, *A Man, a Pan, a Plan* emphasized self-care and stress prevention instead of gender contamination.

The marketing of Coke Zero and Dr. Pepper Ten also pivoted away from the dude toward a more gender-neutral approach, as the market for soda continued to struggle. Gallup Polls indicated that in 2015, soft drinks (diet and regular) were two of only three foods that Americans were actively trying to avoid in their diets.[8] (The third was sugar.) Key consumer demographics now drink fewer sodas and more carbonated waters, juices, and other beverages viewed as more natural, especially compared to diet soda's artificial sweeteners. More than ever, soft drink companies find themselves desperate to differentiate their products and secure loyal consumers. And so, in 2017, Coca-Cola ended production of Coke Zero in the United States (despite near consistent sales growth since 2006) and launched Coca-Cola Zero Sugar, retaining the promise of zero but extending it to both male and female consumers. With the same design logic as Coke Zero, the Coca-Cola

Zero Sugar cans and bottles retain some black elements, but boast more red ones. These seek to visually signal real Coca-Cola taste, while assuring health-minded consumers that the beverage contains no sugar. Without any gender-targeted messaging, Coca-Cola Zero Sugar's August 2017 launch commercial, "Taste for Yourself," ended not with dudes, but with a white woman's hand with nails painted red holding the bottle. The January 2018 commercial, "Nailed It," featured both men and women sipping the beverage and enjoying its flavor. No longer making ads that decree, "It's Not for Women," Dr. Pepper Ten is still available on grocery store shelves, but at times in limited quantities. This periodically causes panic that it might be discontinued among fans, who take to social media and online forums to voice their concerns. In any event, the dude did not ensure Dr. Pepper Ten's longevity.

While some brands adopted gender neutrality, others adopted a strategy of inclusion, extending the power and privilege of the dude to all. Chefs, writers, and eaters alike have endeavored to rebrand dude food from destructively delicious dishes cooked by and for dudes to something more inclusive, or they openly critiqued dude food for its shortcomings. Tim Carman of the *Washington Post* pondered the potential of the culinary genre as he stated, "Remember that 'dude' has been deemed gender-neutral, and thus [dude food] needs a broader definition. I think of it as a casual gathering of like-minded people over comforting food that would do nothing to divide their tight bond."[9] Such a definition captures the way that Guy Fieri also seeks to extend the dude's easy togetherness and unenthused rule-breaking to all eaters: to eat whatever, however, and as much as you want, while wearing sweats or shorts or sunglasses on the back of one's head without judgment or concern.

Though her food remains entrenched within moralizing food rules, Serena Wolf's *The Dude Diet* (2016) cookbook offered "clean-ish" dude food favorites to all "people who like to eat dirty," not just male dudes. Furthermore, *MEL Magazine*, founded in 2015 by Dollar Shave Club, covers stories about "how to be a guy" without a playbook, conceding they "talk about dicks a lot," but also "aren't entirely sure what 'male' should mean anymore." Within this context, somewhere between dude and more enlightened dude, *MEL* published an article on dude food in 2018—not to celebrate it, but to analyze its "self-destructive psychology" and how it poses yet another way to "eat your feelings."[10] While still not without potential consequences for health and food waste, these less overtly masculine versions of dude food either extend the social privileges of the dude or openly critique them.

Oikos Triple Zero and Powerful Yogurt both moved to an inclusive approach. Still packaged in a black container bearing the NFL logo but with lids rimmed with flavor-themed color, Oikos Triple Zero yogurt endorses a subtly inclusive message. The brand fired Cam Newton as spokesman in October 2017 after he made disparaging comments to a female sports reporter. Dallas Cowboys quarterback Dak Prescott replaced him in January 2018 as the face of the "Fuel Your Hustle" campaign. The brand remains linked to football as a masculine symbol, but a December 2018 ad starred a female boxer, extending the yogurt's sports potential to women. While text at the end of the ad read "Official Yogurt of the NFL," the voiceover said, "Oikos Triple Zero is the official yogurt of never backing down" and "of fueling your hustle," attaching the athletic drive of the NFL to individual consumers, both male and female. Interestingly, although these ads took a more gender inclusive approach, Oikos Triple Zero then double backed in 2019 and 2020 with ads "#YoGlutes" and "Flex Your Cryceps" from agency Lightning Orchard that remixed the dude's ironic humor with hegemonic masculinity's demands for strength and rational emotion.

While Oikos Triple Zero took a more gender balanced approach from the start and later switched course, Powerful Yogurt has significantly shifted their branding away from their initial launch, which employed the dude alongside misogynistic messaging and imagery. On their website's "About" page, the company tells the story of how they "designed the first dairy product for the needs of active men," but then concedes, "The massive positive response from active women and men alike pushed the brand to fully evolve to an active lifestyles brand in late 2013." Although now less emphasized on product packaging, the brand employs the hashtag #FindYourInnerAbs on their website and social media accounts. While they have not acknowledged the misogyny of their initial marketing efforts, Powerful Yogurt frames their earlier tactics as part of an effort to meet an unmet need and to loudly launch their product, ensuring they garnered media attention in a noisy marketplace.

Conversations about the dude's dad bod have also progressed. Writing in *British GQ* in 2019, Justin Myers directly addressed how "women have endured classification and objectification by body type . . . for centuries" to an extent that "men can never fully comprehend the scale of it," discussions not broached during the dad bod moment in 2015.[11] Considering the impossible demands of ambivalent masculine body discipline, Myers describes the dad bod as not just a body type, but a gender ideal, as "a bizarre Zen-like figure, totally at ease with himself but not so at ease that his standards started slipping," revealing the delicate balance required to perform the dude's slacker qualities without pushing them too far. And yet social interest in the dad bod has not waned. A 2019 survey conducted by Kelton Global with Planet Fitness garnered a number of press articles that reported statistics, such as: 65 percent of people surveyed say the dad bod is attractive, 61 percent of women surveyed said men with dad bods are sexy (a 10 percent rise from 2018), and 23 million men in the United States claim to have a dad bod, a physique that they accept and assert makes them happy.[12] While such developments in body positivity and self-acceptance may prove beneficial for men, they engage the same contradictions as body positivity efforts for women, which emphasize individual empowerment rather than collective change. Dad bod reporting also continues to frame the dad bod in heteronormative ways. It also poses a challenge for weight loss programs like Weight Watchers, which now engage differently with the dude.

Weight Watchers extended the notion of anti-diet zero, previously reserved for men, to all dieters. Released in 2015, the Freestyle plan with more zero-point foods promised dieters what they once only endorsed for men: to "eat what you love and still lose weight" and that "everything is on the menu." This programmatic pivot reflected a broader cultural shift from blatant dieting to weight loss obscured beneath a veneer of wellness. Despite this change, the U.S. market for weight loss has continued to grow. The industry reached a new peak in 2018, as Americans spent $72 billion on weight loss products and services.[13] Nevertheless, Weight Watchers' expansion of the anti-diet zero approach marks a notable development compared to past versions of the program that endorsed a gender binary that reinforced specific and exclusionary definitions for acceptable genders, bodies, and forms of citizenship.

It remains to be seen if Weight Watchers' shift to wellness, branded freedom, and less restrictive eating will appeal to dieters. After some success when Oprah Winfrey purchased Weight Watchers shares in 2015 and became a brand presence, the company's stock dropped 50.5 percent in the first half of 2019, following their September 2018 rebrand to WW.[14] While these branding changes may affect Weight Watchers' financial future, they did rework the gender binary to which the program previously adhered. Weight Watchers has also amended who it presents as exemplars of masculine weight loss. They brought on new spokesmen who are not professional athletes, as in the past, including film director and actor Kevin Smith (coincidentally the director of the 1994 dude film *Clerks*), chef Eric Greenspan, and music producer DJ Khaled. While their weight loss stories still prove

With sparkly androgyny and ambivalent sex appeal, Diet Dr. Pepper's pint-sized Lil' Sweet applies the dude's playful irreverence to diet soda.

exceptional against most men's experiences, they present more varied ways of being a man and losing weight that include the dude to varying degrees.

Although Dr. Pepper Ten has nearly disappeared along with its anti-woman message, Diet Dr. Pepper began targeting both men and women seeking no-calorie sweetness with the "Lil' Sweet" campaign in 2015. Developed by the ad agency Deutsch, the campaign worked to unravel notions of unreal diet flavor, showing male and female drinkers affirming the sweetness of Diet Dr. Pepper. With unexpected humor, the commercials delighted audiences, as ads found their way into multiple YouTube compilations of funny ads. The commercials star a miniature version of Justin Guarini, known for almost winning the first season of *American Idol* in 2002.

A mash up of glam rock and hair metal, Guarini's character, Lil' Sweet, exudes a masculinity that appeals to both the men and women featured in the commercials. The commercials depict women attracted to Lil' Sweet's sparkly androgyny with allusions to affair-like connections. The ads also show men wanting to work with or be friends with Lil' Sweet, advances that Lil' Sweet rebuffs with a dash of queerness that blurs the traditional boundaries of hegemonic masculinity. For example, when two weather-worn cowboys invite Lil' Sweet to become a hand on their ranch, he instead hops on his tiny horse and sings in falsetto. When a slightly dopey dad invites Lil' Sweet to stay and watch the game, Lil' Sweet instead jumps into a bright pink toy car, driven by the family's cat, leaving the scene in a way inexplicably funny, but not conventionally masculine. Lil' Sweet is able to magically enter everyday spaces such as living rooms, laundry rooms, backyards, and workplace breakrooms where he gently breaks the rules. Made other by his smaller-than-life size and stage-ready hair, costuming, and make-up, Lil' Sweet transgresses traditionally masculine boundaries in ways that extend the more measured resistance of the dude.

While Coke Zero (and Coca-Cola Zero Sugar) dropped the dude and Diet Dr. Pepper reimagined the dude with blurry and almost queer edges, Diet Coke extended the dude to all drinkers, in part because of declining sales. In 2016, six of the top nine diet sodas experienced a sales drop, including best-selling Diet Coke.[15] After two years of research and testing, Coca-Cola rebranded (but did not reformulate) Diet Coke, which they kicked off in 2018 with their first Super Bowl commercial in twenty-one years. Working with the ad agency Anomaly Los Angeles, Coca-Cola company executives described the brand's transition from a woman's diet drink to a "contemporized" millennial beverage for both men and women, one packaged in a thinner and taller 12-ounce can with a vertical stripe.

The "Because I Can" campaign for Diet Coke was directed by Paul Feig, whose work in television and film addressed dudes and gender in novel ways. *Freaks and Geeks* (1999–2000) celebrated geek masculinity as it also launched the dude and dad bod careers of Seth Rogen and Jason Segel. *The Heat* (2013) and the 2016 *Ghostbusters* reboot broke traditional gender norms, casting delightfully foul-mouthed women in roles typically reserved for men. Feig's Diet Coke commercials transformed the "whatever" ethos of the dude into a more agentive sense of purpose and pleasure. A Coca-Cola marketing director described the campaign's message as, "being whatever makes you happy no matter what anyone else thinks."[16] Commercials starred millennial comedians, such as Gillian Jacobs, who spoke directly into the camera, telling viewers to "yurt it up," if they want to live in a yurt. She encourages viewers to run a marathon if they want, even though "that sounds super hard," echoing the dude's slacker views that resist strenuous training and hard work. Lastly Jacobs says, "I mean, just do you, whatever that is. And if you're in the mood for a Diet Coke, have a Diet Coke."

On one level, this commercial's dialogue embodies and endorses the cool nonchalance of the dude. On another, it employs the ironic potential of the millennial dude to riff on soda advertising broadly. Read in another way, the final statement to "have a Diet Coke" serves as a form of cultural permission to do something that may be viewed as transgressive. The ad seeks to give everyone permission to drink Diet Coke, even as many consumers increasingly resist alternative sweeteners and tastes shift toward beverages perceived as more natural and healthier. Subtly, between the lines, the campaign also speaks to men, giving them permission to drink Diet Coke—including in new fruity flavors like Twisted Mango and Feisty Cherry—even if they perceive it as feminine or feminizing.

Tracking these transformations, this book has shown how the food, media, and advertising industries manipulated the dude in the promotion of food, beverages, and food-related products. The idea of gender contamination repeatedly served the purposes of the market, not of consumers and their identities. I offer these critiques of particular campaigns to deconstruct the specific ways that advertising shapes and reflects culture and politics, including ideas about what gender is and can be. Informed media producers and consumers can together consider the implications of these messages. In June 2019, the U.K.'s Advertising Standards Authority took a stronger stand, banning ads that "include gender stereotypes that are likely to cause harm, or serious or widespread offence," guidance that would cover nearly every advertisement analyzed in this book.[17] Interestingly, a number of the agencies that produced the most egregious dude ads—such as Wieden + Kennedy, Droga5, and DAVID Miami—also created some of the industry's most progressive, inspiring, and creative ads in recent years and award seasons. Advertisers *can* do better, so why aren't they?

Advertising, like so many industries in late capitalism, is undergoing a transformation. The days of colorful personalities and creative campaigns have been displaced by branded content, influencers, data analytics, and nanotargeting of increasingly specific demographics and taste profiles. Despite these changes, I still approach advertising as the language of the consumer culture, as a text, however complex and contradictory, that can teach us something poignant about who we are and desire to be. Potentially as powerful as cultural myth, familial heritage, or political message, advertising offers promises of the good life, or life "as it should be." Always entangled with profit seeking and market penetration, advertising can (and does) purposefully incite consumer anxiety and poke at old wounds in order to make a sale and move product. Advertising can also start conversations. Beyond that, with more structural emphasis upon changing the professional make up and social purpose of brands, advertising can offer more than pink-, green-, or rainbow-washed campaigns. Representation matters, deeply, but so does access to producers and production, to seats at the table, to positions of power and decision-making with equal pay.

As I have researched and written this book, I have had opportunities to meet and talk with branding and advertising professionals, as well as with the students I teach. I have shared some of the egregious examples in this book in order to discuss how these products and their advertising play a cultural role in defining gender and, in too many cases, limiting and constraining identity. We discussed why discourses like the dude in food media and advertising matter and have real effects. Brands can reflect, repeat, and reinforce definitions of identity that are conventional or even regressive, which this book documents in spades. But brands can also imagine transformative ways of being. Through repetition and saturation (qualities of ads that consumers usually despise), advertising can play a part in the cultural process of resignification, of opening up possibilities, of refusing the stereotypes that are all too easy and readily observable in ads. A post-gender approach poses one pathway forward and one that has already proved economically viable and culturally meaningful for White Claw, a hard seltzer turned media phenomenon.

Made by Mark Anthony Brands, who also makes Mike's Hard Lemonade, White Claw launched in 2016 and in a short time controlled the category. Today White Claw makes up approximately half of all U.S. spiked seltzer sales. In July 2019, White Claw purportedly outsold every craft beer and longtime juggernaut, Budweiser.[18] In some areas, brand presence is even stronger, as White Claw sales increased 1,000 percent in Southern California in 2019.[19] While White Claw demonstrates the possibility and success of post-gender advertising, it also retains some dude-ish elements.

White Claw picks up where the tale of diet sodas and changing consumer tastes left off. The product pointedly addresses consumer concerns for "healthier" and more "natural" beverage options intertwined with hopes for food that is "clean," safe, and nourishing. White Claw even acquired a registered trademark for their tagline "Made Pure." Nevertheless, just like diet sodas and yogurts, White Claw adopts messaging that emphasizes nutrients, marking on the front of every 12-ounce can its 100 calories, two grams of carbs, and gluten-free status. While White Claw employs the language of calories that the dude eschewed, there is a dude-ish edge of culinary anti-intellectualism in its flavor profile, often described as "watery fruit." Journalists covering young consumers' affinity for the brand report that White Claw's subtle flavor yields simplified consumption.[20] Free from the expectations of informed connoisseurship that have long shaped wine and increasingly guide craft beer as well, White Claw's flavors are accessible and relatively limited in number and complexity. One flavor option is in fact a

The White Claw website and can design emphasize health and purity, dude-ish notions of chilling out, and nutricentric messaging, calling out calories, carbs, and its gluten-free status.

nonflavor that fully merges dude-ish ease with the drive for "healthy" options. White Claw's "Pure Hard Seltzer" is the brand's "purest innovation yet," with an even lighter nutritional impact of "zero carbs, 100 calories, and a clean taste."

White Claw also purposefully adopted post-gender advertising. A number of other hard seltzer brands instead targeted women with more feminine designs, such as Bon & Viv's mermaid imagery, Truly's Instagram-ready fruit arrangements, or Smirnoff's pink cans of rosé spiked sparkling seltzer. Recognizing the shortcomings of past beverage advertising and changing gender norms among young drinkers, White Claw's vice president of marketing, Sanjiv Gajiwala, said, "Whatever we put out creatively and how we positioned the brand really reflects that everyone hangs out together all the time."[21] Like Diet Coke's rebrand, White Claw extends the casual hang once reserved for dudes to all drinkers, but in a way that resonated deeply with quite disparate consumers. As Emily Heil wrote in the *Washington Post*, "Women love it. Even frat boys and the bro-iest of men love it."[22] White Claw has found more than loyal consumers among both men and women. It's created fans. White Claw has inspired memes, YouTube tributes, and unlicensed, unofficial merchandise. It has launched Instagram fan accounts like @itsawhiteclawsummer, @whiteclawbitches, @whiteclawgang, and

@clawdaddycentral, and garnered more than 140,000 posts marked with the hashtag #whiteclaw.

With its fan-fueled emphasis on gender inclusive hanging out, White Claw's branding also harkens back to Coke Zero's original launch campaign, Chilltop. Its messages of opting out of the rat race, of taking time to stop and smile were intended not only to appeal to women but also to men and were specifically inspired by Coca-Cola's study of beer advertising. White Claw similarly invokes the dude's countercultural, surfer, and druggie origins with its logo: a concentric wave, inspired by the "White Claw wave," which the brand website describes as "when three perfect crests come together to create a moment of pure refreshment."

But White Claw isn't just a seltzer water offering refreshment and nutritional promises of purity. It's *hard* seltzer, an alcoholic beverage suited to the toughness of our times. In 2019, the World Health Organization officially classified burnout as a workplace syndrome that negatively affects health, recognizing the toll of job stress. After decades preoccupied by an "obesity epidemic," consumers turned their attention to mental health. In 2019, food marketing research firm The Hartman Group found that anxiety and stress replaced "being overweight" as consumers' top health concern, particularly among women, Gen Z, and Millennials.[23] Zima might have proven the consumer potential for clear, bubbly, water-like alcohol in the 1990s, but White Claw is uniquely situated within burnout culture and consumer products that endeavor to combat it. CBD-infused bath salts, mints, chocolates, coffee, and gummy frogs make a host of alluring promises to relieve anxiety, manage depression, deliver better sleep, and reduce pain. White Claw emerged and exploded alongside the proliferation of such remedies. The 2019 "summer of White Claw" transpired as social acceptance of marijuana use in legal, recreational, and culinary ways increased as part of broader wellness culture.[24] White Claw speaks to the demands of health, labor, consumerism, and identity in late capitalism.

As a result, White Claw retained market prominence in the United States during the COVID-19 pandemic, when many drinkers remained home, under shelter-in-place orders, rather than attending social events or gathering in bars. In March 2020, hard seltzer sales were 327 percent higher than they were in 2019.[25] White Claw sales status continued as millions of Americans practiced social distancing and adapted to working and learning from home, while those deemed essential workers did so under hazardous conditions. During these months, online retailer and delivery apps goPuff and Drizly reported hard seltzer as their top seller nationally, with White

Claw leading the pack.[26] For many drinkers, both male and female, White Claw was the balm of choice during a moment of anxiety and turmoil. Like the privileged dude, White Claw promised an escapist hangout, while BIPOC Americans were disproportionately ravaged by COVID-19.

While White Claw demonstrates how gendered advertising could evolve, dude chef Guy Fieri proves the exception. Fieri's persona retains the slacker qualities of the dude and Velveeta's "that guy you know," even as he has become a successful and affluent celebrity chef and food businessman. As he gathers friends around the grill, he provides a model for domestically masculine fathers who cook to feed their families, while his cool nonchalance echoes the beer-ad tone Coke Zero aspired to when assuring men, "It's not your fault." Like Emeril Lagasse before him and like Dr. Pepper Ten's ostentatious marketing campaign, Guy Fieri kicked it up a notch, purposefully bursting out of bounds with his persona and his food, which has annoyed critics and won loyal fans. When vying to become Food Network's next star, Guy Fieri told the show's judges that the network was missing out on a masculine younger audience, and he was right. Just as Greek yogurt producers and commercial weight loss programs did as they sought to capture a male market, Fieri manipulated notions of white, middle-class, heterosexual, cisgender masculinity and authority—including how these identities are mapped upon the male body and cultural ideas about health. In these various ways, Guy Fieri articulates the ongoing anxiety regarding how to be a "real man" in the twenty-first century, whether one eats steak or quiche or trash can nachos.

First forged on *Next Food Network Star*, Fieri's enduring out-of-bounds culinary persona and dude masculinity also tell a larger story about America today. For his fans, Fieri represents a people's celebrity chef, one who pushes the limits of middle-class respectability in his persona and food, as he acknowledges the tastes of everyday people. As he transgresses such boundaries, he has earned a slew of critics. And yet, the critiques—that he eats more than he cooks, that he's more personality than skill, that he has so many currently airing shows he is inescapable, that he's commercial and grating—each represent broader dissatisfactions with the state of food media and with our current historical moment. Fieri's populist persona speaks directly to eaters who oppose culinary elites and who experience a sense of disenfranchisement regarding their own sociocultural status. Through the language of food, Guy Fieri's expansive food media empire illuminates the most recent rise of populist sentiment in the United States, what motivates it, and what feeds it. At the same time, alongside food activists and humanitarians like José Andrés, Fieri seems to emerge as a good dude savior, cooking to feed people during the California wildfires of 2017 and 2018 and partnering with the National Restaurant Association to support food workers whose employment prospects collapsed in the global health and economic crises that seized the world in the spring of 2020.[27]

Guy Fieri is but a paragon for broader concerns about the twenty-first-century American experience. Guy Fieri's media persona (as opposed to the man himself) forces us to ask difficult questions with complex answers: What does it mean to be "a real man" and a good father when our social world continues to shift beneath our feet? What should we eat? Does it matter if we cook? How should we care for our bodies, the earth, and those around us? What will our future of food be? And why have we always been so worried about it?

As I ponder these questions myself, I'm brought back to the imperfect reason I went to public health school: a belief that food could change the world, or at least the individual lives we live within it. I'm now less interested in how food might change the world and more invested in why we think that might be the case, to understand why we continue to find in food such profound power. Throughout history, we have repeatedly turned to food as a potential solution for the overwhelming social problems facing us, including gender crisis. The same holds true for our current moment. So much around us feels fake, from highly curated Instagram feeds to influencers' supposedly authentic marketing to a post-truth media era peppered with claims of fake news. Surrounded by this fakery, food—especially food marketed as natural and whole, pure and safe—feels all the more real. It is this sense of timeless realness that makes us love and obsess about food, to find in it comfort and pain. It is why food remains a uniquely meaningful and anxious arena within our consumer culture. It is why food incited such grave concerns for gender contamination. It's part of what brought us the dude. Despite decades of resistance and progress toward greater gender equality, the dude revealed the reactionary shoring up of gendered categories that began in the early years of the twenty-first century and only grew stronger after the 2016 election. This book has shown how the Great Recession era shaped food and gender norms, and not for the better. I hope it might provide clues to how we can move forward and reimagine ourselves and our world following the economic fallout of the COVID-19 pandemic. These complex and contradictory sociocultural processes are made all the more visible when mapped onto the terrain of food, the body, and media. They chart a way forward. It is our duty and our joy to find it.

Acknowledgments

I could not have written this book without the support of a great many people. I thank Warren Belasco, Carole Counihan, and Rachel Black for their mentorship while I was at Boston University and their support in all the years since. I am grateful to Brown University's Graduate School for the University Fellowship that made it possible for me to research and write full time while pursuing my PhD. I warmly thank Susan Smulyan, Richard Meckel, and Debbie Weinstein, a trio of historians, who richly transformed my methods for studying the present as they provided critical feedback and unending support. Susan knows how much she means to me, so I will not embarrass her further here. I thank the five women in my PhD cohort—Alyssa Anderson, Felicia Bevel, Kate Duffy, Suzanne Enzerink, and Diza Rule. They know all the reasons why. I thank Elizabeth Hoover for saying yes when I wanted to launch Food Studies at Brown and for being the perfect pairing to my orderliness. I also thank Ralph Rodriguez for showing me that radical love inspires transformative teaching and learning. That hope is part of this book's aim too.

I thank Matt Guterl for being a text message away for advice (still), and for introducing me to my editor, Mark Simpson-Vos at the University of North Carolina Press. I thank Mark, Kathleen LeBesco, Peter Naccarato, and one anonymous reader who helped me to complete the revisions on this book, my first, a task many presses and readers shy away from. At UNC Press, I also thank Cate Hodorowicz and Dominique Moore in acquisitions, as well as Dino Battista, Ann Bingham, Anna Faison, Gina Mahalek, and Alison Shay in marketing, for all they have done (and will do!) to support this book. I thank Kim Bryant and Matt Avery for my book's cover and interior design. I also thank Diane Cipollone for copy editing and Kate Gibson for production of this book. I am grateful to Jessica Ryan for proof editing and Michelle Martinez for indexing—and to the University of Tulsa's Office of Research and Sponsored Programs, the Kendall College of Arts and Sciences, and the Department of Media Studies for funding them.

At the University of Tulsa, I thank Joli Jensen for the Faculty Writing Program that helped so many of us to write no matter what and all the members of the Department of Media Studies—Zenia Kish, Justin Rawlins, Mark Brewin, Ben Peters, John Coward, Jennifer Jones, Jan Reynolds, and Amy Howe—for their genuine collegiality. I also thank TU for Faculty Development Summer Fellowships in 2019 and 2020. I thank all my students, at TU and at Brown, who've shared in this book's ideas in classes on advertising, popular culture, and food media, especially Val Hinkle who designed preorder promotional materials.

I first presented many of the ideas in this book at the annual meetings of the Association for the Study of Food and Society. At these conferences, I've been fortunate to find critical feedback, helpful comments, mentors, friends, and memorable meals.

It's a community so meaningful I've happily dedicated many hours to serving it. I also thank Zingerman's and all the women connected to Fresh Work and HHH Retreat, especially Ander Wilson.

I thank Diana Garvin, Rachel Laudan, and KC Hysmith for their feedback on chapters and concepts, Julia Ehrhardt, Melissa Hackman, and Warren Belasco for their helpful notes on the entire manuscript, all of them for their friendship. I'm grateful for my rescue pup writing buddy, Raven, who snuggled next to me all the years I worked on this book. I also thank my mother, who has not only read every word of this book (more than once) but quite literally every word I've ever written. Along with my academic peers and students, she is the smart everyday reader for whom I try to write, without too much jargon and with some style and a little humor. (She liked this book, but she is my mom so perhaps she has to say that.) Without the love of my mother, father, sister, and husband this book wouldn't exist. Despite the many hours I spent writing (and revising and revising) this book instead of spending more time with them, I hope they are glad that it does.

Notes

Introduction

1. Anderson, "Will Eating Luna Bars Make a Guy Grow Breasts?"; *Men's Health* Forum, "Luna Bars—Will They Turn Me into a Woman?"; Kryza, "11 Foods That No Man Should Eat . . . Ever."

2. Avery, "Defending the Markers of Masculinity"; Copeland, "Is Diet Soda Girly?"

3. Butler, *Gender Trouble*.

4. In this book, I use the term "soda," specifically "diet soda." The beverage industry more typically uses the term "carbonated soft drinks" (CSDs). I grew up in Montana where these beverages are called pop.

5. Scripts are "models for action" and "mutually shared conventions" that reflect cultural norms regarding categories of identity such as gender, sexuality, and race. For more definitions and examples of application, see Graves and Kwan, "Is There Really 'More to Love'?," 48; Sobal, "Men, Meat, and Marriage,"145.

6. For the history of food gender stereotypes, see Freedman, "How Steak Became Manly and Salads Became Feminine."

7. For "doing gender," see West and Zimmerman, "Doing Gender." For food and gender, see, for example, Counihan, *The Anthropology of Food and Body*; DeVault, *Feeding the Family*; Cairns and Johnston, *Food and Femininity*; Julier and Lindenfeld, "Mapping Men onto the Menu."

8. Sobal, "Men, Meat, and Marriage"; Rozin et al., "Is Meat Male?"; Sumpter, "Masculinity and Meat Consumption"; Adams, *The Sexual Politics of Meat*; Ruby and Heine, "Meat, Morals, and Masculinity"; Bentley, "Men on Atkins"; Gelfer, "Meat and Masculinity in Men's Ministries."

9. DeVault, *Feeding the Family*; Hochschild, *The Second Shift*; Cairns and Johnston, *Food and Femininity*; McPhail, Beagan, and Chapman, "'I Don't Want to be Sexist But . . .'"; Harris and Giuffre, *Taking the Heat*; Druckman, "Why Are There No Great Women Chefs?" For analysis of Black women and foodwork, both domestic and as chefs, see, for example, Williams-Forson, *Building Houses Out of Chicken Legs*; Tipton-Martin, *The Jemima Code*; Nettles-Barcelón et al., "Black Women's Food Work as Critical Space"; Zafar, *Recipes for Respect*.

10. Fry and Cohn, "Women, Men, and the New Economics of Marriage." Please note that my reference to "the institution of marriage between men and women" is meant to qualify these sociological findings. It is not meant to declare that marriage ought to be limited to such arrangements. Love is love.

11. Hoffman, "Visual Persuasion in George W. Bush's Presidency"; Allen and Ratnesar, "The End of Cowboy Diplomacy."

12. Mims, "Thanks to the 'Mancession'"; Rampell, "The Mancession"; Thompson, "It's Not Just a Recession."

13. Negra and Tasker, *Gendering the Recession*; Davies and O'Callaghan, *Gender and Austerity in Popular Culture*; Albrecht, *Masculinity in Contemporary Quality Television*.

14. Leonard, "Escaping the Recession?," 33.

15. Midan's research focused on the meat industry specifically, reporting that in a survey of 900 meat-eating men aged 18 to 64, 47 percent were categorized as manfluencers. Midan Marketing, "New Midan Marketing Research."

16. In this book, I examine the gender discourse of the dude, not dudes themselves. With this distinction in mind, I still use "he" instead of "it" throughout the text for readability. Also, the dude is similar to the "slacker man" analyzed by Albrecht, *Masculinity in Contemporary Quality Television*; Denby, "A Fine Romance"; Leonard, "Escaping the Recession?"; Troyer and Marchiselli, "Slack, Slacker, Slackest."

17. Hill, "You've Come a Long Way, Dude," 322–23.

18. Hill, 324; for a history of coolness, particularly within Black American jazz culture, see MacAdams, *Birth of the Cool*; Peretti, *The Creation of Jazz*.

19. Kiesling, "Dude," 290.

20. Hill, "You've Come a Long Way, Dude"; Kiesling, "Dude"; for a complete analysis of dude films, see Troyer and Marchiselli, "Slack, Slacker, Slackest."

21. Kiesling, "Dude," 283, 298.

22. Cameron, "Guys and Dudes"; Halberstam, *Female Masculinity*; Pascoe, *Dude, You're a Fag*.

23. *Broad City* began as a web series in 2010 and then launched as a TV show on FX in 2014. For examination of Jacobson and Glazer as unruly women with the freedom to "fuck around," see Petersen, *Too Fat, Too Slutty, Too Loud*, 52–54.

24. Comedy Central, "Broad City—Exclusive—Every 'Dude' in Broad City So Far."

25. For more on white masculinity, see Bederman, *Manliness and Civilization*; Pascoe, *Dude, You're a Fag*; Pascoe and Bridges, *Exploring Masculinities*.

26. Here I am inspired by Messner and Montez de Oca's article, "The Male Consumer as Loser," which analyzes "the loser motif" in beer advertisements. Drawing from George Lipsitz's *The Possessive Investment in Whiteness: How White People Profit from Identity Politics*, they write that "the loser motif constructs the universal subject as implicitly white, and as a reaction against challenges to hegemonic masculinity it represents an ongoing possessive investment in whiteness," 1906.

27. The dude's resistance to adult responsibility is much like the "boy-man" that historian Gary Cross identified in his study of modern immaturity. Cross, *Men to Boys*.

28. Johnson, "'Post-Truth' is Oxford Dictionaries' Word of the Year for 2016."

29. For hegemonic masculinity, see Connell, *Masculinities*; for "hybrid masculinities," which would include the dude, see Bridges and Pascoe, "Hybrid Masculinities"; for critiques of hegemonic masculinity, see Connell and Messerschmidt, "Hegemonic Masculinity: Rethinking the Concept"; Summers, *Manliness and Its Discontents*; Pascoe, *Dude, You're a Fag*; Moller, "Exploiting Patterns"; Demetriou, "Connell's Concept of Hegemonic Masculinity." Nevertheless, hegemonic masculinity is a theory well suited to studying food, the body, and the dude. In 2005, Alice Julier and Laura Lindenfeld wrote, "There is a well-articulated ideology of hegemonic masculinity connected to food practices, a kind of 'doing gender' through certain types of foods, cooked in certain ways by particular people, and eaten in certain circumstances. At the same time,

there have been almost no sustained analyses of the changes in this ideology, nor much understanding of how it permeates people's actual activities around food and eating"—a gap to which this book aspires to contribute. Julier and Lindenfied, "Mapping Men onto the Menu."

30. Grindstaff and West, "Hegemonic Masculinity on the Sidelines of Sport," 860.

31. Courtenay, "Constructions of Masculinity and Their Influence on Men's Well-Being"; Courtenay, "Engendering Health."

32. Connell, *Masculinities*, 79.

33. DiAngelo, "White Fragility." For white racial identity, also see Helms, *A Race Is a Nice Thing to Have*.

34. Hall, "Encoding/Decoding."

35. Banet-Weiser, "We Are All Workers," 91.

36. Bederman, *Manliness and Civilization*, 7–8.

37. Bederman, 11.

38. Here I reference in plain terms the concept of intersectionality: the simultaneous, interlocking systems of oppression that create the social conditions of one's lived experience. For intersectionality, see Crenshaw, "Mapping the Margins"; Brah and Phoenix, "Ain't I A Woman?"; for discussion of intersectionality and food studies, see Williams-Forson and Wilkerson, "Intersectionality and Food Studies"; for intersectionality and fat, see Van Amsterdam, "Big Fat Inequalities, Thin Privilege."

39. Connell and Messerschmidt, "Hegemonic Masculinity," 846.

40. Kimmel, *Manhood in America*; Rotundo, *American Manhood*; Bederman, *Manliness and Civilization*.

41. Kimmel, *Manhood in America*.

42. Bederman, *Manliness and Civilization*.

43. Rotundo, *American Manhood*.

44. Rotundo.

45. Schwartz, *Never Satisfied*; Brumberg, *Fasting Girls*; Bordo, *Unbearable Weight*; Stearns, *Fat History*.

46. Bederman, *Manliness and Civilization*; Kasson, *Houdini, Tarzan, and the Perfect Man*; Putney, *Muscular Christianity*; Schuster, *Neurasthenic Nation*.

47. Vester, "Regime Change." See also Tompkins, *Racial Indigestion*.

48. Putney, *Muscular Christianity*, 11.

49. Kasson, *Houdini, Tarzan, and the Perfect Man*, 19.

50. Vester, "Regime Change," 44.

51. Vester, 45.

52. Veit, *Modern Food, Moral Food*; Monaghan and Malson, "It's Worse for Women and Girls.'"

53. Mallyon et al., "I'm Not Dieting, 'I'm Doing It for Science.'"

54. Neuhaus, *Manly Meals and Mom's Home Cooking*; Vester, *A Taste of Power*.

55. Vester, *A Taste of Power*, 132.

56. McGovern, *Sold American*, 3.

57. Scanlon, *Inarticulate Longings*; Scanlon, *The Gender and Consumer Culture Reader*; Sutton, *Globalizing Ideal Beauty*; Marchand, *Advertising the American Dream*; Schudson, *Advertising, The Uneasy Persuasion*; Sturken and Cartwright, *Practices of Looking*.

58. McGovern, *Sold American*; Scanlon, *Inarticulate Longings*; Frederick, *Selling Mrs. Consumer*; Rutherford, *Selling Mrs. Consumer*.

59. Marchand, *Advertising the American Dream*; Scanlon, *Inarticulate Longings*.

60. Pendergast, *Creating the Modern Man*.

61. Breazeale, "In Spite of Women."

62. Brody, "Man in the Kitchenette."

63. Powell, "Cocktail Party, Masculine," 85; Pine, "Women Can't Cook," 51.

64. For midcentury masculinity crisis, see Cuordileone, *Manhood and American Political Culture in the Cold War*; Gilbert, *Men in the Middle*.

65. May, *Homeward Bound*, 11, 12; Meyerowitz, *Not June Cleaver*.

66. For discussion of food, cooking, domesticity, and gender in midcentury America, see Parkin, *Food Is Love*; Neuhaus, *Manly Meals and Mom's Home Cooking*; Neuhaus, "The Way to a Man's Heart"; Shapiro, *Something from the Oven*; Vester, *A Taste of Power*; Hellman, "The Other American Kitchen"; Adler, "Making Pancakes on Sunday"; Gelber, "Do-It-Yourself."

67. Neuhaus, *Manly Meals and Mom's Home Cooking*, 195. For midcentury men, food, and magazines, see chapter 3, "Gourmet Is a Boy," in Elias, *Food on the Page*.

68. Neuhaus, *Manly Meals and Mom's Home Cooking*, 195.

69. See chapter 4 in de la Peña, *Empty Pleasures*; Parkin, *Food Is Love*.

70. Berrett, "Feeding the Organization Man"; Tunc, "The 'Mad Men' of Nutrition."

71. Gill, "Power and the Production of Subjects."

72. Halkitis, "Redefining Masculinity in the Age of AIDS"; Treichler, *How to Have Theory in an Epidemic*.

73. Belasco, *Appetite for Change*; Smith Maguire, *Fit for Consumption*.

74. Feirstein, *Real Men Don't Eat Quiche*.

75. Gill, "Power and the Production of Subjects," 37.

76. Gill, 48.

77. Jeffords, *Hard Bodies*.

78. Shugart, "Managing Masculinities," 283.

79. Johnston, Rodney, and Chong, "Making Change in the Kitchen?," 16–17.

80. For foodies, see Johnston and Baumann, *Foodies*; Rousseau, *Food Media*, 7–12; Finn, *Discriminating Taste*, 179–83.

81. I acknowledge that this version of Spider-Man is not recognized as part of the Marvel Cinematic Universe, but argue that he nevertheless is situated within a twenty-first-century history of superheroes and the dude's bodily ambivalence in popular culture.

82. Stein, "How to Get a Superhero Body."

83. Negra and Tasker, *Gendering the Recession*, 10.

84. Pope, Phillips, and Olivardia, *The Adonis Complex*; Stibbe, "Health and the Social Construction of Masculinity"; Hatton and Trautner, "Equal Opportunity Objectification?"; Bordo, *The Male Body*; Labre, "The Male Body Ideal"; Gill, Henwood, and McLean, "Body Projects and the Regulation of Normative Masculinity." Garner, "Survey Says"; McCabe and Ricciardelli, "Body Image Dissatisfaction among Males"; Tantleff-Dunn, Barnes, and Larose, "It's Not Just a 'Woman Thing'"; Mishkind et al., "The Embodiment of Masculinity"; Markey and Markey, "Relations Between Body Image and Dieting Behaviors."

85. Pope, Phillips, and Olivardia, *The Adonis Complex*; Baghurst, "Muscle Dysmorphia and Male Body Image"; Mitchell et al., "Muscle Dysmorphia Symptomatology"; Donini et al., "Orthorexia Nervosa"; Brytek-Matera et al., "Orthorexia Nervosa and Self-Attitudinal Aspects of Body Image."

86. Metzl and Kirkland, *Against Health*, 1–2; Guthman, *Weighing In*; Biltekoff, *Eating Right in America*.

87. Crawford, "Healthism," 365.

88. Allen, Dickinson, and Prichard, "The Dirt on Clean Eating"; McCartney, "Clean Eating and the Cult of Healthism"; Nevin and Vartanian, "The Stigma of Clean Dieting and Orthorexia Nervosa."

89. Courtenay, "Constructions of Masculinity and Their Influence on Men's Well-Being"; Courtenay, "Engendering Health"; Gough, "'Real Men Don't Diet'"; Gough, "Try to Be Healthy, but Don't Forgo Your Masculinity"; Bennett and Gough, "In Pursuit of Leanness."

90. Foucault, *Discipline and Punish*; Bordo, *Unbearable Weight*; Stinson, *Women and Dieting Culture*; Heyes, "Foucault Goes to Weight Watchers"; Bartky, *Femininity and Domination*.

91. Foucault, *The History of Sexuality*; Rabinow and Rose, "Biopower Today"; for an earlier history of U.S. biopolitics, see Tompkins, *Racial Indigestion*.

92. McGovern, *Sold American*; Cohen, *A Consumers' Republic*.

93. For any reader looking for a clear statement of my methodology, I employ an interdisciplinary methodology that draws from food studies, gender and sexuality studies, media studies, cultural studies, critical nutrition studies, fat studies, and U.S. cultural history. Aiming for breadth and depth, I assess the discourse of the dude in an array of source material, employing close readings at key moments.

94. Bordo, *Unbearable Weight*, 110.

Chapter One

1. In May 2020, the hashtag #dudefood had drawn about 19,000 results, compared to #foodporn's 223 million posts.

2. Mcbride, "Food Porn"; Dejmanee, "'Food Porn' as Postfeminist Play"; Cruz, "Gettin' Down Home with the Neelys"; Contois, "Healthy Food Blogs."

3. Sobal, "Men, Meat, and Marriage"; Rozin et al., "Is Meat Male?"; Sumpter, "Masculinity and Meat Consumption"; Adams, *The Sexual Politics of Meat*; Ruby and Heine, "Meat, Morals, and Masculinity"; Bentley, "Men on Atkins"; Gelfer, "Meat and Masculinity in Men's Ministries."

4. Kiefer, Rathmanner, and Kunze, "Eating and Dieting Differences in Men and Women"; Wardle et al., "Gender Differences in Food Choice."

5. Benwick, "What Is Dude Food, Anyway?"

6. Benwick. For an analysis of food and gender at tailgates specifically, see Veri and Liberti, *Gridiron Gourmet*.

7. Contois, "Dude Food"; Kirkwood, "Dude Food vs Superfood."

8. Erik, "Dude Food."

9. Naccarato and LeBesco, *Culinary Capital*, 86.

10. Canavan, "Gastropubs."

11. Naccarato and LeBesco, *Culinary Capital*, 91.

12. In January 2020 the dude food Instagram account "Fat Fucks Unite" had 56,000 followers, though it topped 68,000 in May 2020. Fat Fucks Unite, 2019 and 2020, http://instagram.com/fatfucksunite.

13. Lawson, "The 25 Most Insane Dude Foods of All Time."

14. Courtenay, "Engendering Health"; Courtenay, "Constructions of Masculinity"; Gough, "'Real Men Don't Diet'"; Sloan, Gough, and Conner, "Healthy Masculinities?"

15. Sax, "How Years of Macho Food Marketing Is Killing Men." Such messages regarding masculinity and eating also appear on food TV shows. See, for example, Eisner-Levine, "Man Versus Food"; Veri and Liberti, "Tailgate Warriors."

16. Bannan, "Dude Food That Is Actually Good for You"; "Diabetic Dude Food"; Best Health, "7 Healthy Dude Foods."

17. Benwick, "What Is Dude Food, Anyway?"

18. Moss, "Pinterest Statistics 2019"; Pew Research Center, "Who Uses Twitter, Pinterest, and Snapchat."

19. Pinterest, "Dude Food."

20. Kita, "In Defense of Dude Food."

21. Kita.

22. Bordo, *The Male Body*; Hatton and Trautner, "Equal Opportunity Objectification?"; Kimmel and Mahalik, "Measuring Masculine Body Ideal Distress"; Murray and Touyz, "Masculinity, Femininity and Male Body Image"; Ridgeway and Tylka, "College Men's Perception of Ideal Body Composition and Shape"; Tager, Good, and Morrison, "Our Bodies, Ourselves Revisited."

23. Monaghan and Malson, "'It's Worse for Women and Girls'"; Rothblum and Solovay, *The Fat Studies Reader*; LeBesco, *Revolting Bodies?*; Lupton, *Fat*; Saguy, *What's Wrong with Fat?*; Braziel and LeBesco, *Bodies out of Bounds*; Farrell, *Fat Shame*; Wann, *FAT!SO?*

24. Bosc, "Man, You Have Moobs!"

25. Pearson, "Why Girls Love the Dad Bod."

26. Pearson, "Why Girls Love the Dad Bod"; Pugh, "Dad Bods Are More Attractive to Women than Rock Hard Abs"; Engel, "Why Women Are Lusting after Dudes with 'Dad Bod'"; Myers, "We're Calling Bullshit on the 'Dad Bod.'"

27. Dominguez, "Let's Stop Pretending Celebrity Dadbods Need Defending."

28. Chaker, "Groceries Become a Guy Thing."

29. Chaker.

30. Wieden + Kennedy, "Work: Kraft, Eat Like That Guy You Know."

31. I use the language of gender "safety" following Irina Mihalache's study of Graham Kerr cooking on television. She argues, "The process of making cooking 'safe' for men included the emphasis on play and experimentation as the main difference between masculine cooking and domestic suburban cooking." Mihalache, "The Chef Who Played Too Much."

32. Minute Rice, "Dude Food."

33. The KFC Survey was conducted in fall 2012 by Wakefield Research among 1,000 participants. EmanatePR, "KFC's Dude Food Etiquette."

34. Schultz, "How Kraft's Lunchables Is Evolving."

35. Moran, "Devour's Racy Launch Campaign Pushes 'Food You Want to Fork.'"

36. Devour, "Lunch Spank" commercial, https://www.youtube.com/watch?v=q_UwjU83I3s; Devour, "Pool Boy" commercial, https://www.adforum.com/creative-work/ad/player/34528852/pool-boy/kraft-devour.

37. Mackinnon, "Sexuality," 204.

38. Notaker, *A History of Cookbooks*; Maynard, "Cookbook Sales Are Jumping."

39. Neuhaus, *Manly Meals and Mom's Home Cooking*, 195.

40. Neuhaus; Vester, *A Taste of Power*.

41. Bowers with Bowers, *Bake It Like a Man*, 1.

42. Rayment, *The Real Man's Cookbook*.

43. D'Agostino, *Eat Like a Man*, 7.

44. Golden, *What the F*@# Should I Make for Dinner?*; Thug Kitchen, *Thug Kitchen*. For analysis of racial privilege and oppression in the *Thug Kitchen* cookbooks, see Twitty, "Thug Kitchen"; Terry, "The Problem with 'Thug' Cuisine."

45. Joachim, *A Man, a Can, a Plan*.

46. Churchill, *DudeFood*.

47. Batali, *Mario Tailgates NASCAR Style*.

48. Benwick, "What Is Dude Food, Anyway?"

49. Steiman and Kita, *Guy Gourmet*, xiv.

50. Wolf, *The Dude Diet*; Wolf, *The Dude Diet Dinnertime*.

51. Bosker, Brooks, and Darmon, *Dude Food*, 7.

52. Steiman and Kita, *Guy Gourmet*, xii.

53. Joachim, *A Man, a Can, a Plan*, i.

54. Raichlen, *Man Made Meals*.

55. Brand, *Cook Like a Man*.

56. Zafar, *Recipes for Respect*; Bower, *Recipes for Reading*; Theophano, *Eat My Words*; Tippen, *Inventing Authenticity*; Neuhaus, *Manly Meals and Mom's Home Cooking*; Leonardi, "Recipes for Reading."

57. Marlboro, *Cook Like a Man Cookbook*.

58. Adams, *The Sexual Politics of Meat*, xviii.

59. Colicchio in D'Agostino, *Eat Like a Man*, 7.

60. Granger in D'Agostino, *Eat Like a Man*, 11.

61. Churchill, *DudeFood*, 5.

62. Madden and Jacques, *Man Meets Stove*. Even though this cookbook is self-published, I included it in my sample because it had eighty-seven customer reviews on Amazon and a 3.9-out-of-5-star average rating as of August 2019, indicating a degree of readership worthy of analysis.

63. D'Agostino, *Eat Like a Man*, 24.

64. Raichlen, *Man Made Meals*, 36.

65. Like most of the photos in *DudeFood*, this topless photo is credited to Karen Watson/Karen Watson Photography. For readers keeping score, *DudeFood* does feature one other photo of a woman in the How to Impress a Girl section: a pair of hands with red painted nails holding a cup of "Coconut Milk Cocoa."

Chapter Two

1. Askari, "How One Man Destroyed the Food Network"; Moskin, "Guy Fieri, Chef-Dude"; Syme, "The Trailer Park Gourmet"; Repanich, "Guy Fieri Is the Hero We Need"; Crowley, "Maybe It's Not Time to Reconsider Guy Fieri After All."

2. The program title changed after season 7 to *Food Network Star*.

3. For definition and discussion of populism, see Canovan, "Trust the People!"; Taggart, *Populism*; Mudde and Kaltwasser, *Populism*; for my analysis of Guy Fieri as a populist culinary figure, see Contois, "Welcome to Flavortown."

4. Lotz, *The Television Will Be Revolutionized*, 3.

5. The colonial fireplace, and later the stove, proved a likely location for these concerns to resonate, as it served as the literal, metaphorical, and later, nostalgic, center of the home, providing a source of heat, light, sustenance, and social connectedness. For more on the cultural role of kitchens, see also Tompkins, *Racial Indigestion*; Plante, *The American Kitchen*; Southerton, "Consuming Kitchens."

6. Goodman, *Radio's Civic Ambition*; Douglas *Listening In*.

7. Boddy, *Fifties Television*, 2; Spigel, *Make Room for TV*.

8. Naccarato and LeBesco, *Culinary Capital*, chapter 3, "Television Cooking Shows."

9. Joyrich, *Re-Viewing Reception*, 9.

10. Collins, "Chapter 3: Julia Child and Revolution in the Kitchen," *Watching What We Eat*; *Gastronomica*, Special Julia Child Issue, vol. 5, no. 3 (Summer 2005); Shapiro, *Julia Child*; Polan, *Julia Child's The French Chef*.

11. Kerr, *The Galloping Gourmet Television Cookbook*, 7.

12. Collins, *Watching What We Eat*; for analysis of race in Food Network programs, see Cruz, "Gettin' Down Home with the Neelys."

13. Collins, *Watching What We Eat*, 167.

14. Poniewozik, "Media Circus."

15. Poniewozik.

16. Collins, *Watching What We Eat*, 214.

17. Moskin, "Guy Fieri."

18. Steinberg, "Food Network Chief Brooke Johnson to Retire."

19. *Next Food Network Star*, season 2, episode 1: "Iron Chef Bootcamp."

20. For example, season 1 winners of *Next Food Network Star*, Dan Smith and Steve McDonagh, won their show *Party Line with the Hearty Boys*, but it aired during an unpopular timeslot on Sunday mornings and ran for only a few seasons. Season 3 winner, Amy Finley, debuted her show *The Gourmet Next Door*, but it only ran for six episodes. While other winners have stayed on the air, Fieri has been the only one to create a food media empire.

21. Pomerantz, "Guy Fieri Would Like You to Stop Talking about the Burgers Please"; Lamare, "The Richest Celebrity Chefs in the World"; Myers, "America's 25 Most Successful Chefs of 2016."

22. Cameron, "Guy Fieri Gets a Star on the Hollywood Walk of Fame"; Calderone, "Guy Fieri Becomes the Third Chef Ever to Receive a Star on the Hollywood Walk of Fame."

23. Murray and Ouellette, *Reality TV*, 2.

24. For brigade de cuisine, see Gillespie, "Gastrosophy and Nouvelle Cuisine."

25. Syme, "The Trailer Park Gourmet."

26. Syme.

27. Mah, "Anthony Bourdain Roars into the Fox Theater, Rips on Guy Fieri."

28. Askari, "How One Man Destroyed the Food Network."

29. Stevens, "Here's a Frosted Tip for You."

30. Stein, "The Crispy Crimes of Guy Fieri."

31. Askari, "How One Man Destroyed the Food Network."

32. Syme, "The Trailer Park Gourmet."

33. *Guilty Pleasures* on Food Network.

34. Syme, "The Trailer Park Gourmet."

35. Crawford, "Healthism and the Medicalization of Everyday Life"; Crawford, "Health as a Meaningful Social Practice."

36. Moskin, "Guy Fieri, Chef-Dude."

37. Forbes, "Watch Bourdain Rip into Guy Fieri's NYC 'Terror-Dome.'"

38. Naccarato and LeBesco, *Culinary Capital*; Johnston and Baumann, *Foodies*.

39. Halberstam, *Female Masculinity*, 4.

40. *Next Food Network Star*, season 2, episode 1: "Iron Chef Bootcamp."

41. Druckman, "Why Are There No Great Women Chefs?"; Harris and Giuffre, *Taking the Heat*.

42. Cairns and Johnston, *Food and Femininity*.

43. *Next Food Network Star*, season 2, episode 5: "Alton Brown TV 101."

44. At the time of filming, Flay already hosted multiple Food Network shows, such as *Boy Meets Grill* (2002–), *BBQ with Bobby Flay* (2004–), and *Iron Chef America* (2004–).

45. Johnston, Rodney, and Chong, "Making Change in the Kitchen?"

46. LaRossa, "Fatherhood and Social Change."

47. Szabo and Koch, eds., *Food, Masculinities, and Home*, 3; see also Marsh, "Suburban Men and Masculine Domesticity"; Gelber, "Do-It-Yourself."

48. Eggebeen and Knoester, "Does Fatherhood Matter for Men?"; Hobson, *Making Men into Fathers*; Leavitt, *Make Room for Daddy*.

49. Paquette, "The Super Bowl Ads Were Right."

50. Paquette; Livingston, "Growing Number of Dads Home with the Kids."

51. Wallace, "'Dad' Gets a Makeover in Super Bowl Ads"; Paquette, "The Super Bowl Ads Were Right."

52. DeVault, *Feeding the Family*; Cairns and Johnston, *Food and Femininity*.

53. Cairns and Johnston, *Food and Femininity*.

54. Cairns, Johnston, and Baumann, "Caring About Food"; DeVault, *Feeding the Family*; Aarseth and Olsen, "Food and Masculinity in Dual-Career Couples"; Aarseth, "From Modernized Masculinity to Degendered Lifestyle Projects"; Sobal, "Men, Meat, and Marriage"; Ketchum, "The Essence of Cooking Shows"; Swenson, "Domestic Divo?"; Hollows, "Oliver's Twist"; Hollows, "The Bachelor Dinner"; Neuhaus, *Manly Meals and Mom's Home Cooking*; Vester, *A Taste of Power*.

55. Fieri and Volkwein, *More Diners, Drive-Ins and Dives*, 3.

56. This is the one and only exclamation point in this book. I hope you agree it's worth it.

57. Fieri and Volkwein, *Guy Fieri Food*, 40–41.

58. Mihalache, "Being Guy Fieri."

59. Miller, "The Birth of the Patio Daddy-O"; Vester, *A Taste of Power*; Veri and Liberti, "Tailgate Warriors"; Deutsch, "'Please Pass the Chicken Tits'"; Sobal, "Men, Meat, and Marriage"; Sumpter, "Masculinity and Meat Consumption."

60. Celebrity chef Jamie Oliver also engages in domestic work, such as feeding his wife and children, in his TV shows. His gender performance, however, reads more closely conventional when compared to Guy Fieri's self-designed rocker persona and unique personal aesthetics. For analysis of Oliver, masculinity, and cooking, see, for example, de Solier, "TV Dinners"; Johnston, Rodney, and Chong, "Making Change in the Kitchen." For other studies of male TV chefs, see Leer, "What's Cooking, Man?"; Holden, "The Overcooked and Underdone."

61. Freedman, *Food*; Levine, *Highbrow Lowbrow*.

62. Laudan, *Cuisine and Empire*, 208, 359.

63. *Diners, Drive-Ins and Dives*, season 14, episode 6: "Unexpected Eats."

64. Fieri and Volkwein, *Guy Fieri Food*, 49.

65. Belasco, *Food*, 16–17.

66. Belasco, 16; Hauck-Lawson, "When Food Is the Voice."

67. *Diners, Drive-Ins and Dives*, season 14, episode 6: "Unexpected Eats."

68. *Next Food Network Star*, season 2, episode 3: "Second Elimination."

69. Bourdieu, *Distinction*; Eisner-Levine, "Man Versus Food."

70. "How Guy Says, 'That's Good.'"

71. Fieri and Volkwein, *Guy Fieri Food*.

72. Pépin, *The Apprentice*, 164–65.

73. Lee, "Dude Food with a Mexican Spin."

74. Moskin, "Guy Fieri."

75. Moskin.

76. Kamp, *The United States of Arugula*.

77. Bestor, "How Sushi Went Global," 56–57.

78. Isle, "Sushi in America."

79. See any of a number of Paul Rozin's articles for discussion of food, disgust, and culture.

80. BuzzFeedVideo, "Americans Try Sushi for the First Time."

81. Oaklander, "Should I Eat Sushi?"

82. As listed at the end of every review, the *New York Times* rating system is as follows: "Ratings range from zero to four stars. Zero is poor, fair or satisfactory. One star, good. Two stars, very good. Three stars, excellent. Four stars, extraordinary."

83. Parker, "Pete Wells Has His Knives Out."

84. Hochman, "At Home with Guy Fieri."

85. Magary, "How Flavortown Mayor Guy Fieri Is Taking Over Wine Country."

86. Diamond, "The Unrecognizable Genius of Guy Fieri."

87. Repanich, "Guy Fieri Is the Hero We Need."

88. Castrodale, "Guy Fieri Spent Yesterday Making Nonstop BBQ for California Fire Victims and First Responders."

89. Rense, "Guy Fieri Is Feeding Wildfire Evacuees Hundreds of Meals in Northern California."

90. Rose, "Guy Fieri Feeds California Fire Evacuees and First Responders."

91. Harrison, "Guy Fieri Feeds First Responders."

92. Harrison.

93. Capatides, "Guy Fieri Serves Barbecue."

94. Fuhrmeister, "Guy Fieri Feeds First Responders."

95. Sherman, "Guy Fieri Feeds Crews."

96. Duffet, *Understanding Fandom*, 2.

97. See, for example, Duffet; Gray, Sandvoss, and Harrington, *Fandom*.

98. Rick, "How It All Began."

99. *Fans of Guy Fieri*.

100. Grella, "'Diners, Drive-Ins and Dives' Adventures."

101. McCormick, "Fieri Fan."

102. McCormick.

103. Nelson, "Fieri Fan Rings in 600 Diners, Drive-Ins and Dives."

104. Gray, "New Audiences, New Textualities"; Gray, "Anti-fandom and the Moral Text"; Click, "Untidy"; Click, *Anti-Fandom*.

105. Norcia, "Inside FieriCon."

106. "About," Fiericon.com, visited November 14, 2019.

107. Gentile, "I, Fieri."

108. Contois, "Welcome to Flavortown."

109. Flager, "How to Dress Up Like Guy Fieri for Halloween."

110. Hallinan, "Guy Fieri Really Digs Your Guy Fieri Halloween Costumes."

111. My friends know that I wore this T-shirt for Christmas 2019.

112. Lana in Macondo, "Frosted Tips," Tumblr post, May 21, 2016, https://lanamacondo.tumblr.com/post/144719920453/frosted-tips.

113. Vain, "Guy Fieri Knows How to Laugh at Himself."

Chapter Three

1. Myers, "Sexist Food Advertisements"; Scherer, "6 Fast-Food Commercials That Are So Sexist."

2. On Cheerios' commercials, see Demby, "That Cute Cheerios Ad"; Townsend, "'The Cheerios Effect' Ad"; Elliott, "An American Family Returns to the Table."

3. For Coke quote, see McWilliams, "Coke Zero Becomes a Hero for Coca-Cola Co"; for Dr. Pepper quote, see "Dr Pepper TEN"; for Powerful Yogurt quote, see Chaker, "Groceries Become a Guy Thing."

4. Hickman, "Introducing 'Bloke Coke.'"

5. "Danone" is the global parent company, but these products are typically branded "Dannon" in the United States, so I have used Dannon throughout this book for consistency.

6. Hopper, "Is Super-Macho Yogurt Sexist?"; Fox News, "'Brogurt'"; Merwin, "Brogurt"; Zuckerman, "Here Comes 'Brogurt.'"

7. For studies finding a relationship between sugar sweetened beverages and weight, see Ludwig et al., "Relation between Consumption of Sugar-Sweetened Drinks and Childhood Obesity"; Malik et al., "Sugar-Sweetened Beverages"; Malik et al., "Intake of Sugar-Sweetened Beverages and Weight Gain."

8. McWilliams, "Coke Zero Becomes a Hero for Coca-Cola Co."

9. McWilliams.

10. Just-Drinks.com Editorial Team, "Just the Facts—Coke Zero."

11. Dr Pepper Snapple Group, "Dr Pepper Snapple Group Annual Report."

12. Bahadur, "Powerful Yogurt."

13. Watson, "The Rise and Rise of Greek Yogurt"; E. J. Schultz, "Dannon Dumps John Stamos for Cam Newton"; Danone, "Mission and Key Figures"; "Powerful Yogurt," *Inc.*

14. de la Peña, *Empty Pleasures*, 194.

15. Bourdieu, *Distinction*.

16. McKay, "Why Coke Indulges (the Few) Fans of Tab"; Plasketes, "Keeping TaB."

17. Moye, "How Coke Zero Became a Hero."

18. Dishman, "Meet the Guy Who Whittled Dr Pepper Down to 10 Calories."

19. Foley, "Best drink out there"; Foley, "Change? Not a chance."

20. FoodBev Media, "The Story Behind the Launch of Powerful Yogurt."

21. Augustynowicz, "Female Food-Induced Dreams in Advertising"; Paiella, "A Brief History of Terrible Yogurt Commercials Targeted at Women."

22. Matgomad, "British Coke Zero Ad"; Carter, "Men Buy Mars, Women Prefer Galaxy."

23. "Global Trends in Protein"; Molyneaux, "Consumer Protein Trends."

24. The Innovation Group, "Summer Fancy Food Show."

25. FoodBev Media, "The Story Behind the Launch of Powerful Yogurt."

26. Best, "Focus."

27. Daniells, "Protein Powders"; "Global Whey Protein Market."

28. National Health and Nutrition Examination Survey, "Protein."

29. See, for example, Tobler, Visschers, and Siegrist, "Eating Green"; Hoekstra and Chapagain, "Water Footprints of Nations."

30. de la Peña, *Empty Pleasures*, 106.

31. Irigaray, *This Sex Which Is Not One*.

32. Scrinis, *Nutritionism*, 13.

33. Mudry, *Measured Meals*, 15. Also see Hayes-Conroy, *Doing Nutrition Differently*.

34. "Products, Yogurt, powerful.co"; Parasecoli, "Feeding Hard Bodies."

35. de la Peña, *Empty Pleasures*.

36. Stinson, *Women and Dieting Culture*.

37. McWilliams, "Coke Zero Becomes a Hero for Coca-Cola Co."; Hart, "Design Review."

38. Moye, "How Coke Zero Became a Hero."

39. This aggressive marketing presence included a simultaneous media buyout on all public TV networks and cable channels to premiere Coke Zero's first commercial on Australia Day in January 2006. Moye, "How Coke Zero Became a Hero."

40. Howard, "Coke Finally Scores Another Winner."

41. Moye, "Summer of Sharing"; Stoeffel, "Nation's Masculinity Intact Thanks to Coke."

42. Copeland, "Is Diet Soda Girly?"

43. "Dr Pepper TEN: It's Not for Women."

44. Chaker, "Groceries Become a Guy Thing."

45. Schultz, "Dannon Dumps John Stamos for Cam Newton."

46. Powerful Yogurt, Facebook Page, https://www.facebook.com/PowerfulYogurt/.

47. Best, "Focus."

48. Wadler, "Judging Men by Their Refrigerators."

49. For more on Coca-Cola's hallmark "Hilltop" commercial, see Frank, *The Conquest of Cool*, chap. 8; Taylor, *The Sounds of Capitalism*, chap. 6.

50. McWilliams, "Coke Zero Becomes a Hero for Coca-Cola Co."; Howard, "Coke Finally Scores Another Winner"; Sampey, "Coke Enlists Crispin for 'Zero' Line Extension."

51. Ebiquity Global Insight, "Coke Zero—Chill."

52. Petersen, "How Millennials Became the Burnout Generation"; World Health Organization, "Burn-out an 'Occupational Phenomenon.'"

53. Coke Zero's 2008 Super Bowl ad referenced another classic Coca-Cola ad featuring Mean Joe Greene as part of the "Have a Coke and Smile" campaign, further demonstrating Coca-Cola's hope that Coke Zero would become an iconic brand and sales success.

54. Messner, *Power at Play*; Messner, *Taking the Field*; Trujillo, "Hegemonic Masculinity on the Mound"; Hartmann, "The Sanctity of Sunday Football."

55. "Coke Zero 400 at Daytona"; *AdWeek* Staff, "Coke Zero Immerses Itself in 'Avatar'"; Nudd, "Coke Zero Gives 'Skyfall' Tickets."

56. Howard, "Coke Finally Scores Another Winner."

57. Nobel, "Should Men's Products Fear a Woman's Touch?"

58. Droga5, "Enjoy Everything."

59. Droga5.

60. Droga5.

61. Socha, "Marc Jacobs Named Diet Coke Creative Director."

62. Socha. Past Diet Coke ads for a female audience incorporated a degree of male objectification. An ad featuring a stripping-to-shirtless Jacobs debuted on YouTube and Diet Coke's Facebook page in 2013. It was inspired by the 1994 "hunk" ads starring Lucky Vanous in which a group of female office workers take an 11:30 Diet Coke break, not to sip themselves, but to ogle a shirtless construction worker drink one.

63. Murnen and Bryne, "Hyperfemininity." "Hyperfemininity" is an "exaggerated adherence to a stereotypic feminine gender role."

64. Zmuda, "Can Dr Pepper's Mid-Cal Soda Score a 10 With Men?"

65. "Dr Pepper TEN: It's Not for Women."

66. Banet-Weiser, *Empowered*.

67. For more on action movies, see Jeffords, *Hard Bodies*.

68. "Dr Pepper TEN: It's Not for Women."

69. Stark, "Is Bro Country Over . . . ?"; Rosen, "Jody Rosen on the Rise of Bro-Country"; Rasmussen and Densley, "Girl in a Country Song."

70. Lukovitz, "'Men-Only' Dr Pepper Ten Ad Pulls Mixed Results."

71. Zmuda, "Can Dr Pepper's Mid-Cal Soda Score a 10 With Men?"

72. Williams, "Dr. Pepper's Commandments of Sexism."

73. Andrew, "Dr. Pepper Ten Review."

74. "Deutsch L.A. Brings Facebook Data to Dr Pepper TEN Brand."

75. "Dr. Pepper: Like Report."

76. Todd, "Dr. Pepper Pisses off Pretty Much Everyone with 'Man'Ments'"; Clarke, "Dr. Pepper Ten: It's 'Not for Women,' Macho Marketing Campaign Says."

77. Condis developed Bro's Law in her study of misogyny within the online gaming community. Condis, *Gaming Masculinity*, 14.

78. For more on misogyny and humor within popular and fan cultures, see Scott, *Fake Geek Girls.*

79. Shek, "Asian American Masculinity."

80. Patel, "Men Can Eat Yogurt Now."

81. "Men Get Their Very Own Yogurt Brand."

82. Schultz, "Dannon Dumps John Stamos for Cam Newton."

83. Buss, "Dannon Turns Yogurt Marketing on Its Head with Men's Health Oikos Ad."

84. Schultz, "Dannon Dumps John Stamos for Cam Newton."

85. "Soda Consumption in America"; Fakhouri et al., "Consumption of Diet Drinks."

86. Howard, "Coke Finally Scores Another Winner."

87. McWilliams, "Coke Zero Becomes a Hero for Coca-Cola Co."

88. Jellyblue, "Poll: Do Guys Eat Yogurt?"

89. This gender is an assumption, based on the fact that reviewers post using female names, such as "Danielle M." and "Lacey V." accompanied by female-presenting profile photos.

Chapter Four

1. ABC News Staff, "100M Fuel $20B Weight Loss Industry."

2. Monaghan and Malson, "'It's Worse for Women and Girls."

3. De Souza and Ciclitira, "Men and Dieting"; Gough, "'Real Men Don't Diet.'"

4. Gough, "'Real Men Don't Diet'"; Courtenay, "Constructions of Masculinity and Their Influence on Men's Well-Being"; Courtenay, "Engendering Health."

5. Schultz, "Weight Watchers Picks a New Target: Men"; Newman, "The Skinny on Male 'Dieting.'"

6. Newman, "The Skinny on Male 'Dieting.'"

7. The 2011 advertising campaign for Weight Watchers Online for Men represented 5–10 percent of the company's total ad budget, which was $117 million in 2010. Olson, "Diet Companies Promote New Ways to Reduce"; Schultz, "New Year Brings New Diet Company Ads, Programs."

8. Biltekoff, "The Terror Within," 43. See also Biltekoff, *Eating Right in America*; Guthman, *Weighing In.*

9. Kleinfield, "The Ever-Fatter Business of Thinness."

10. Jean lost seventy-two pounds, Marty sixty-nine pounds, Albert and Felice together a hundred pounds. For histories of Weight Watchers and Jean Nidetch, see Contois, "Weight Watchers"; Weinraub, "Jean Nidetch"; Hendley, "Weight Watchers at Forty"; Meltzer, *This Is Big*.

11. Van Gelder, "A Real Winner in Weight Losing."

12. Van Gelder.

13. Thomas Jr., "Albert Lippert."

14. Meltzer, *This Is Big*, 195.

15. See, for example, "Chief Evangelist of the Weight Watchers"; Lilliston, "Weight Watchers' Vigil."

16. Ickeringill, "Weight Watchers, Inc."

17. Hall, "Weight Watchers Help Each Other Battle the Bulges"; Clifford, "He Wants to Skip Dessert in the Governor's Mansion."

18. Zyda, "They're Elephants and Proud of It."

19. Mehren, "Apostle of Thin Pays L.A. a Visit."

20. Ames, "One Month Later and Still Resolved to Win the Losing Game."

21. Nidetch, *The Weight Watchers Program Cookbook*, 17–18; Dosti, "Weight Watchers Cookbook."

22. Editor Matty Simmons and publisher Leonard A. Mogel were pictured as the face of the periodical's launch when it was announced in the *New York Times*. Endres and Lueck, "Weight Watchers"; Calta, "New Magazine Aims to Help the Overweight."

23. "Introducing the New Weight Watchers Magazine."

24. Calta, "New Magazine Aims to Help the Overweight."

25. Endres and Lueck, "Weight Watchers," 437–38.

26. Weight Watchers spokeswomen included Jean Nidetch from 1963 and into the 1980s; Lynn Redgrave, starting in 1984; and the Duchess of York, Sarah Ferguson (1997–2008). More recent spokeswomen include Jenny McCarthy (2009–2010), Jennifer Hudson (April 2010–March 2014), Jessica Simpson (2011–2014), and Oprah Winfrey (2015–).

27. Ickeringill, "Weight Watchers, Inc."

28. Johnston, "15,000 Weight Watchers Cheer Svelte Founder and Other Stars."

29. Kleinfield, "The Ever-Fatter Business of Thinness."

30. Klemesrud, "Weight Watcher's Lunch."

31. Lipsyte, "Confronting the Fat in Me."

32. For intersectionality, see Crenshaw, "Mapping the Margins"; Brah and Phoenix, "Ain't I A Woman?" For discussion of intersectionality and food studies, see Williams-Forson and Wilkerson, "Intersectionality and Food Studies."

33. Van Amsterdam, "Big Fat Inequalities." For the history of anti-Black racism in fat phobia, see Strings, *Fearing the Black Body*.

34. Crewe, *Representing Men*.

35. Zinczenko and Spiker, *The Abs Diet*, 5.

36. Hoyt and Kogan, "Satisfaction with Body Image and Peer Relationships for Males and Females in a College Environment"; Pope, Phillips, and Olivardia, *The Adonis Complex*.

37. For "bulimic double bind," see Bordo, *Unbearable Weight*.

38. Weinraub, "Suddenly, It's a Guy Thing"; Zezima, "It Takes a Big Man to Seek Help on Weight Loss."

39. Cordain, *The Paleo Diet*.

40. See, for example, "Nutrition and Physical Degeneration," *JAMA*'s 1940 review of Price; Eaton and Konner, "Paleolithic Nutrition."

41. Schwartz and Stapell, "Modern Cavemen?"

42. Monaghan and Malson, "'It's Worse for Women and Girls'"; Gill, "Body Projects and the Regulation of Normative Masculinity."

43. Weight Watchers, "Announcing the Launch of Weight Watchers Online for Men."

44. Weight Watchers.

45. The "Women's Plans" page on the Nutrisystem website as it appeared on March 10, 2013, http://web.archive.org/web/20130310151716/https://www.nutrisystem.com/jsps_hmr/shop/order_now_secure.jsp?categoryId=353.

46. The "Men's Plans" page on the Nutrisystem website as it appeared on March 10, 2013, http://web.archive.org/web/20130310152110/https://www.nutrisystem.com/jsps_hmr/shop/order_now_secure.jsp?categoryId=358.

47. The "Men's Program" page on the Nutrisystem website as it appeared on February 5, 2008, http://web.archive.org/web/20080205044242/http://www.nutrisystem.com/shop/main.cfm?action=catalog/displayCategoryMembers&category_id=358&template_type_id=2.

48. The homepage of the Weight Watchers Online for Men website as it appeared on January 1, 2013, http://web.archive.org/web/20130101223206/http://www.weightwatchers.com/men.

49. While no longer available, in 2013, a "How Does It Work?" video appeared on the homepages of the "women's" and "men's" Weight Watchers websites at http://weightwatchers.com and http://weightwatchers.com/men. All of the quotes from these videos, attributed to their weight loss stars, Bonnie and Dan, come from these sources.

50. The homepage of the Jenny Craig for Men website as it appeared on February 7, 2011, http://web.archive.org/web/20110207105619/http://jennycraigformen.com/.

51. Deutsch, *Building a Housewife's Paradise*.

52. Cairns and Johnston, *Food and Femininity*; DeVault, *Feeding the Family*.

53. Parasecoli, "Feeding Hard Bodies."

54. Jenny Craig for Men website homepage, February 7, 2011.

55. For "therapeutic culture," see Aubry and Travis, *Rethinking Therapeutic Culture*; Becker, *The Myth of Empowerment*; Wright, "Theorizing Therapeutic Culture." For the influence of therapeutic culture on consumer culture and advertising, see Lears, "From Salvation to Self-Realization."

56. Aubry and Travis, *Rethinking Therapeutic Culture*, 2.

57. A video featuring Charles Barkley appeared on the Weight Watchers Online for Men homepage in January 1, 2013, http://web.archive.org/web/20130101223206/http://www.weightwatchers.com/men.

58. Nutrisystem, "Terry Bradshaw Chose Nutrisystem."

59. Weight Watchers, "Weight Watchers Online: Pete."

60. Weight Watchers, "Weight Watchers Online: Daniel."

61. Weight Watchers, "Kendra."

62. Bartky, *Femininity and Domination*; Bordo, *Unbearable Weight*.

63. Braziel and LeBesco, *Bodies out of Bounds*; Farrell, *Fat Shame*; Kulick and Meneley, *Fat*; LeBesco, *Revolting Bodies?*; Rothblum and Solovay, *The Fat Studies Reader*.

64. Peiss, *Hope in a Jar*; Cahill, "Feminist Pleasure and Feminine Beautification"; Brand, *Beauty Matters*; Vester, "Regime Change."

65. Heyes, "Foucault Goes to Weight Watchers," 145.

66. Bosc, "Man, You Have Moobs!," 69.

67. Crane et al., "A Randomized Trial Testing the Efficacy of a Novel Approach to Weight Loss."

68. Rodin, Silberstein, and Striegel-Moore, "Women and Weight."

69. Weight Watchers, "Rich & Famous."

70. Weight Watchers, "Roll Call."

71. Ostberg, "Thou Shalt Sport a Banana in Thy Pocket."

72. For "male gaze," see Mulvey, "Visual Pleasure and Narrative Cinema."

73. Weight Watchers, "Sir Charles for Weight Watchers."

74. Parasecoli, "Manning the Table."

75. Messner, *Power at Play*; Messner, *Taking the Field*; Trujillo, "Hegemonic Masculinity on the Mound"; Hartmann, "The Sanctity of Sunday Football."

76. Noble, "All About/Weight-Loss Programs"; Newman, "The Skinny on Male 'Dieting.'"

77. Newman, "The Skinny on Male 'Dieting.'"

78. Newman.

79. Parasecoli, "Manning the Table."

80. For history and present of stereotypes affecting perceptions of the Black, male body, see Nagel, *Race, Ethnicity, and Sexuality*; Slatton and Spates, *Hyper Sexual, Hyper Masculine?*

81. Mishra and Kern, "Persuading the Public to Lose Weight," 13. See also Besio and Marusek, "Losing It in Hawai'i."

82. This study included ten magazines. The sample included *Men's Health* and *GQ* to target male audiences, as well as *Latina* (Hispanic and Latina women), *Ebony* (Black/African American men and women), and *Out* (gay and lesbian audiences). Mishra and Kern, "Persuading the Public to Lose Weight."

83. Haupt, "6 Diets for Men."

84. Nutrisystem for Men, "Bradshaw and Marino," commercial, 2012.

85. Nutrisystem, "Up Close & Personal with Terry Bradshaw," commercial, 2012.

86. Business Wire, "Nutrisystem Reports 'Super Monday.'"

87. Business Wire.

88. Zezima, "It Takes a Big Man to Seek Help on Weight Loss."

89. Kirchhoff, "Does Weight Watchers for Men Work?"

90. Kwoh, "Weight Watchers Chief Looks to Men, China for Growth."

91. Sedgwick's *Epistemology of the Closet* provides tools to unpack the purposeful silences of men's weight loss. As she theorized the power relations between homosexuality and heterosexuality, Sedgwick argued that examining "the relations of the

closet" allowed one to address what is unspoken, what is silent, what is closeted, and what is secret — as well as what are constructed and perceived as "ignorances." Sedgwick also addressed the tensions inherent to the closet between subjects and objects, the production of knowledge, and the production of selves. By its very existence, the closet defines what lies inside of it and all that exists outside of it. Men's weight loss programs produced and sustained their power in similar ways to Sedgwick's theorization of heterosexuality's binary dominance over homosexuality and the structure of the closet. Sedgwick, *Epistemology of the Closet*.

92. Newman, "The Skinny on Male 'Dieting.'"

93. Zezima, "It Takes a Big Man to Seek Help on Weight Loss."

94. Zezima.

95. Gaesser, "Is 'Permanent Weight Loss' an Oxymoron?"; Wing and Phelan, "Long-term Weight Loss Maintenance"; Montesi et al., "Long-term Weight Loss Maintenance for Obesity."

96. Lupton, "Quantifying the Body," 396.

97. Dansinger et al., "Comparison of the Atkins, Ornish, Weight Watchers, and Zone Diets."

98. Newman, "The Skinny on Male 'Dieting.'"

99. Mudhustler, "Video from the Bropocalypse Weight Watchers Event."

100. Zezima, "It Takes a Big Man to Seek Help on Weight Loss."

101. According to Giordano, "Mudhustler" references his career as the owner of a concrete company, https://themudhustler.com/.

Conclusion

1. My thanks to Julia Ehrhardt for this observation of George W. Bush as a dude president. I have only presented this idea here. I hope that other scholars might find the dude a useful gender discourse for analyzing political history, among other fields and topics.

2. Pulido et al., "Environmental Deregulation"; Bonilla-Silva, "'Racists,' 'Class Anxieties,' Hegemonic Racism, and Democracy in Trump's America."

3. Kimmel, *Angry White Men*; Banet-Weiser, *Empowered*; Kimmel and Wade, "Ask a Feminist"; Rodino-Colocino, "Me too, #MeToo."

4. Steinmetz, "The Transgender Tipping Point"; Fischer, *Terrorizing Gender*.

5. Merriam-Webster, "Word of the Year: They."

6. Parker, Graf, and Igielnik, "Generation Z Looks a Lot Like Millennials."

7. Kita, *A Man, a Pan, a Plan*, vii.

8. Rifkin, "Majority of Americans Say They Try to Avoid Drinking Soda."

9. Benwick, "What Is Dude Food, Anyway?"

10. Lecklitner, "The Self-Destructive Psychology of 'Dude Food.'"

11. Myers, "We're Calling Bullshit on the 'Dad Bod.'"

12. Pugh, "Dad Bods Are More Attractive to Women Than Rock Hard Ab"; "'Dad Bods' Are More Attractive Than Six Packs, Study Says"; Kacala, "Men with 'Dad Bods' Are Happier and More Attractive to Women, New Survey Finds."

13. LaRosa, "Top 9 Things to Know About the Weight Loss Industry."

14. Symington, "Why Weight Watchers Stock Dropped 50.5% in the First Half of 2019."

15. Schultz, "Anomaly Picks Up Diet Coke as the Soda Eyes Big Changes."

16. Schultz, "Hayley Magnus Dances with Diet Coke in Brand's Social Media-Friendly Super Bowl Spot."

17. ASA and CAP News, "Harmful Gender Stereotypes in Ads to Be Banned."

18. Bryson, "How the Hell Is White Claw Hard Seltzer Outselling Budweiser?"

19. Peltz, "Now That White Claw Summer Is Over, Will Hard Seltzer's Popularity Go Splat?"

20. Bernot, "Why Are People Obsessed with White Claw?"; Hughes, "These Are the Three New White Claw Flavors Coming in 2020"; Rivera, "Ranking Every Flavor of White Claw."

21. Heil, "The Key to White Claw's Surging Popularity."

22. Heil.

23. The Hartman Group, "Insights into the State of Health + Wellness 2019," https://tailorednews.com/u/THG-Publications/JOWeMpSH9ENwXLORX/The-Age-of-Anxiety.htm.

24. See, for example, Goodyear, "California Makes Marijuana a Wellness Industry" or the Hartman Group's 2019 infographic, titled "Out of the Shadows and Into the Mainstream: What's the Future of Edible and Consumable Cannabis Food and Beverage Products?," https://www.hartman-group.com/acumenPdfs/cannabis-and-food-inforaphic.pdf.

25. Duprey, "People Are Still Drinking Massive Quantities of Hard Seltzer During Coronavirus Pandemic."

26. Sidman, "White Claw Is One of the Top Quarantine Drinks of Choice."

27. Rao, "Guy Fieri Is in Quarantine with 400 Goats, a Peacock Problem and a Plan to Help Restaurant Employees."

Bibliography

Aarseth, Helene. "From Modernized Masculinity to Degendered Lifestyle Projects: Changes in Men's Narratives on Domestic Participation, 1990–2005." *Men and Masculinities* 11, no. 4 (2009): 424–40.

Aarseth, Helene, and Bente Marianne Olsen. "Food and Masculinity in Dual-Career Couples." *Journal of Gender Studies* 17, no. 4 (2008): 277–87.

ABC News. "100M Fuel $20B Weight Loss Industry." *ABC News*, May 14, 2012. http://abcnews.go.com/Health/100-million-dieters-20-billion-weight-loss-industry/story?id=16297197.

Adams, Carol. *The Sexual Politics of Meat: A Feminist-Vegetarian Critical Theory.* 25th anniversary ed. New York: Bloomsbury Academic, 2015.

Adler, Thomas A. "Making Pancakes on Sunday: The Male Cook in Family Tradition." *Western Folklore* 40, no. 1 (January 1981): 45–54.

AdWeek. "Coke Zero Immerses Itself in 'Avatar.'" *AdWeek*, November 25, 2009. http://www.adweek.com/news/advertising-branding/coke-zero-immerses-itself-avatar-106839.

Albrecht, Michael Mario. *Masculinity in Contemporary Quality Television.* New York: Routledge, 2015.

Allen, M., Kacie Dickinson, and Ivanka Prichard. "The Dirt on Clean Eating: A Cross Sectional Analysis of Dietary Intake, Restrained Eating and Opinions about Clean Eating among Women." *Nutrients* 10 (2018), doi:10.3390/nu10091266.

Allen, Mike, and Romesh Ratnesar. "The End of Cowboy Diplomacy." *TIME*, July 11, 2006.

Ames, Lynne. "One Month Later and Still Resolved to Win the Losing Game: Calorie Counting at Weight Watchers." *New York Times*, February 7, 1993.

Anderson, Lessley. "Will Eating Luna Bars Make a Guy Grow Breasts?" *Chowhound*, May 22, 2008. https://www.chowhound.com/food-news/54511/will-eating-luna-bars-make-a-guy-grow-breasts/.

Andrew. "Dr. Pepper Ten Review." *Fast Food Geek*, November 1, 2011. http://fastfoodgeek.com/beverage-reviews/dr-pepper-ten-review/.

ASA and CAP News. "Harmful Gender Stereotypes in Ads to Be Banned." *Advertising Standards Authority*, December 14, 2008. https://www.asa.org.uk/news/harmful-gender-stereotypes-in-ads-to-be-banned.html.

Askari, Farsh. "How One Man Destroyed the Food Network: Guy Fieri Has Made Culinary TV into a Viewer's Hell." *Salon*, August 9, 2014. http://www.salon.com/2014/08/08/how_one_man_destroyed_the_food_network_guy_fieri_has_made_culinary_tv_into_a_viewers_hell/.

Aubry, Timothy, and Trysh Travis, eds. *Rethinking Therapeutic Culture.* Chicago: University of Chicago Press, 2015.

Augustynowicz, Nina. "Female Food-Induced Dreams in Advertising: A Case Study of Three Polish TV Commercials." *Acta Philologica* 45 (2014): 85–92.

Avery, Jill. "Defending the Markers of Masculinity: Consumer Resistance to Brand Gender-Bending." *International Journal of Research in Marketing* 29, no. 4 (December 2012): 322–36, https://doi.org/10.1016/j.ijresmar.2012.04.005.

Baghurst, Timothy. "Muscle Dysmorphia and Male Body Image: A Personal Account." *New Male Studies* 1, no. 3 (2012): 125–30.

Bahadur, Nina. "Powerful Yogurt, Yogurt for Men, Now Available." *Huffington Post*, March 15, 2013. http://www.huffingtonpost.com/2013/03/14/powerful-yogurt-for-men_n_2876619.html.

Banet-Weiser, Sarah. *Empowered: Popular Feminism and Popular Misogyny*. Durham, NC: Duke University Press, 2018.

———. "'We Are All Workers': Economic Crisis, Masculinity, and the American Working Class." In *Gendering the Recession: Media and Culture in an Age of Austerity*, edited by Diane Negra and Yvonne Tasker, 81–106. Durham, NC: Duke University Press, 2014.

Bannan, Patricia. "Dude Food That Is Actually Good for You." *Fox News*, June 20, 2015. http://www.foxnews.com/health/2015/06/20/dude-food-that-is-actually-good-for.html.

Barber, Kristen. *Styling Masculinity: Gender, Class, and Inequality in the Men's Grooming Industry*. New Brunswick: Rutgers University Press, 2016.

Bartky, Sandra Lee. *Femininity and Domination: Studies in the Phenomenology of Oppression*. New York: Routledge, 1990.

Batali, Mario. *Mario Tailgates NASCAR Style*. Charlotte, NC: Sporting News, 2006.

Becker, Dana. *The Myth of Empowerment: Women and the Therapeutic Culture in America*. New York: NYU Press, 2005.

Bederman, Gail. *Manliness and Civilization: A Cultural History of Gender and Race in the United States, 1880–1917*. Chicago: University of Chicago Press, 1996.

Belasco, Warren. *Appetite for Change: How the Counterculture Took on the Food Industry*. 2nd ed. Ithaca, NY: Cornell University Press, 2006.

———. *Food: The Key Concepts*. London: Berg, 2011.

Bennett, Eleanor, and Brendan Gough. "In Pursuit of Leanness: The Management of Appearance, Affect and Masculinities within a Men's Weight Loss Forum." *Health: An Interdisciplinary Journal for the Social Study of Health, Illness and Medicine* 17, no. 3 (2013): 284–99.

Bentley, Amy. "Men on Atkins: Dieting, Meat, and Masculinity." In *The Atkins Diet and Philosophy: Chewing the Fat with Kant and Nietzsche*, edited by Lisa Heldke, Kerri Mommer, and Cynthia Pineo, 185–95. Chicago: Open Court, 2005.

Benwick, Bonnie S. "What Is Dude Food, Anyway? We Asked the Experts, and They Fired Away." *Washington Post*, June 19, 2015. https://www.washingtonpost.com/lifestyle/food/what-is-dude-food-anyway-we-asked-the-experts-and-they-fired-away/2015/06/19/91da5fdc-15b5-11e5-89f3-61410da94eb1_story.html.

Bernot, Kate. "Why Are People Obsessed with White Claw?" *The Takeout*, July 26, 2019. https://thetakeout.com/why-are-people-obsessed-with-white-claw-1836670721.

Berrett, Jesse. "Feeding the Organization Man: Diet and Masculinity in Postwar America." *Journal of Social History* 30, no. 4 (1997): 805–25.

Besio, Kathyrn, and Sarah Marusek. "Losing It in Hawai'i: Weight Watchers and the Paradoxical Nature of Weight Gain and Loss." *Gender, Place & Culture* 22, no. 6 (2015): 851–66.

Best, Dean. "Focus: Why the Jury Is Still Out for Danone's Oikos Triple Zero." *just-food*, January 14, 2015. https://www.just-food.com/analysis/why-the-jury-is -out-for-danones-oikos-triple-zero_id128838.aspx.

Best Health. "7 Healthy Dude Foods." *Best Health Magazine Canada*, November 19, 2010. http://www.besthealthmag.ca/best-eats/cooking/7-healthy-dude-foods/.

Bestor, Theodore. "How Sushi Went Global." *Foreign Policy* 121 (2000): 54–63.

Biltekoff, Charlotte. *Eating Right in America: The Cultural Politics of Food and Health.* Durham, NC: Duke University Press, 2013.

———. "The Terror Within: Obesity in Post 9/11 U.S. Life." *American Studies* 48, no. 3 (2007): 29–48.

Boddy, William. *Fifties Television: The Industry and Its Critics.* Urbana: University of Illinois Press, 1992.

Bonilla-Silva, Eduardo. "'Racists,' 'Class Anxieties,' Hegemonic Racism, and Democracy in Trump's America." *Social Currents* 6, no. 1 (2019): 14–31.

Bordo, Susan. *The Male Body: A New Look at Men in Public and in Private.* New York: Farrar, Straus and Giroux, 2000.

———. *Unbearable Weight: Feminism, Western Culture, and the Body.* 10th anniversary ed. Oakland: University of California Press, 2004.

Bosc, Lauren. "Man, You Have Moobs! A Critical Analysis of the Fat, 'Polluted' Body in The Biggest Loser." *Textual Overtures* 2, no. 1 (2014): 65–83.

Bosker, Gideon, Karen Brooks, and Reed Darmon. *Dude Food: Recipes for the Modern Guy.* San Francisco: Chronicle Books, 2000.

Bourdieu, Pierre. *Distinction: A Social Critique of the Judgement of Taste.* Translated by Richard Nice. Cambridge, MA: Harvard University Press, 1984.

Bower, Anne L., ed. *Recipes for Reading: Community Cookbooks, Stories, Histories.* Amherst: University of Massachusetts Press, 1997.

Bowers, David, with Sharon Bowers. *Bake It Like a Man: A Real Man's Cookbook.* New York: William Morrow and Company, 1999.

Brah, Avtar, and Ann Phoenix. "Ain't I A Woman? Revisiting Intersectionality." *Journal of International Women's Studies* 5, no. 3 (2013): 75–86.

Brand, Fritz. *Cook Like a Man: Master Your Kitchen with 78 Simple and Delicious Recipes.* New York: Skyhorse, 2017.

Brand, Peg Zeglin, ed. *Beauty Matters.* Bloomington: Indiana University Press, 2000.

Braziel, Jana Evans, and Kathleen LeBesco. *Bodies out of Bounds: Fatness and Transgression.* Oakland: University of California Press, 2001.

Breazeale, Kenon. "In Spite of Women: *Esquire* Magazine and the Construction of the Male Consumer." In *The Gender and Consumer Culture Reader*, edited by Jennifer R. Scanlon, 226–44. New York: NYU Press, 2000.

Bridges, Tristan, and C. J. Pascoe. "Hybrid Masculinities: New Directions in the Sociology of Men and Masculinities." *Sociology Compass* 8, no. 3 (2014): 246–58.

Brody, Iles. "Man in the Kitchenette." *Esquire*, April 1940, 105.

Broom, Dorothy H., and Jane Dixon. "The Sex of Slimming: Mobilizing Gender in Weight-Loss Programmes and Fat Acceptance." *Social Theory & Health* 6, no. 2 (2008): 148–66.

Brumberg, Joan Jacobs. *Fasting Girls: The History of Anorexia Nervosa*. New York: Vintage, 2000.

Bryson, Lew. "How the Hell Is White Claw Hard Seltzer Outselling Budweiser?" *The Daily Beast*, September 11, 2019. https://www.thedailybeast.com/how-the-hell-is -white-claw-hard-seltzer-outselling-budweiser.

Brytek-Matera, Anna, Lorenzo Maria Donini, Magdalena Krupa, Eleonora Poggiogalle, and Phillipa Ha. "Orthorexia Nervosa and Self-Attitudinal Aspects of Body Image in Female and Male University Students." *Journal of Eating Disorders* 3, no. 2 (2015), https://jeatdisord.biomedcentral.com/articles/10.1186/s40337-015 -0038-2.

Business Wire. "Nutrisystem Reports 'Super Monday' as One of the Top Ten Diet Decision Days of the Year for Men." January 31, 2013. http://www.businesswire .com/news/home/20130131006352/en/Nutrisystem-Reports-"Super-Monday" -Top-Ten-Diet.

Buss, Dale. "Dannon Turns Yogurt Marketing on Its Head with Men's Health Oikos Ad." *Brandchannel*, May 16, 2013. http://brandchannel.com/2013/05/16/dannon -turns-yogurt-marketing-on-its-head-with-mens-health-oikos-ad/.

Butler, Judith. *Gender Trouble: Feminism and the Subversion of Identity.* New York: Routledge, 1990.

BuzzFeedVideo. "Americans Try Sushi for the First Time." YouTube Video, 1:58. September 19, 2014. https://www.youtube.com/watch?v=GoaOfwXvIjk.

Cahill, Ann J. "Feminist Pleasure and Feminine Beautification." *Hypatia* 18, no. 4 (2003): 42–64.

Cairns, Kate, and Josée Johnston. *Food and Femininity*. New York: Bloomsbury Academic, 2015.

Cairns, Kate, Josée Johnston, and Shyon Baumann. "Caring About Food: Doing Gender in the Foodie Kitchen." *Gender & Society* 24, no. 5 (October 1, 2010): 591–615.

Calderone, Ana. "Guy Fieri Becomes the Third Chef Ever to Receive a Star on the Hollywood Walk of Fame." *People*, May 22, 2019. https://people.com/food/guy -fieri-star-hollywood-walk-of-fame/.

Calta, Louis. "New Magazine Aims to Help the Overweight: Weight Watchers, a Journal for Obese, on Newstands." *New York Times*, January 18, 1968.

Cameron, Debbie. "Guys and Dudes." *Language: A Feminist Guide*. February 21, 2016. https://debuk.wordpress.com/2016/02/21/guys-and-dudes/.

Cameron, Meaghan. "Guy Fieri Gets a Star on the Hollywood Walk of Fame." *Food Network*, May 2019. https://www.foodnetwork.com/fn-dish/chefs/2019/5/guy -fieri-gets-a-star-on-the-hollywood-walk-of-fame.

Canavan, Hillary Dixler. "Gastropubs, From London Trend to American Phenomenon." *Eater*, December 5, 2014. https://www.eater.com/2014/12/5 /7329279/gastropubs-history-explained.

Canovan, Margaret. "Trust the People! Populism and the Two Faces of Democracy." *Political Studies* 47, no. 1 (1999): 2–16.

Capatides, Christina. "Guy Fieri Serves Barbecue to Hundreds of California Wildfire Evacuees." *CBS News*, July 30, 2018. https://www.cbsnews.com/news/carr-fire -guy-fieri-serves-barbecue-evacuees-northern-california/.

Capper, J. L. "The Environmental Impact of Beef Production in the United States: 1977 Compared with 2007." *Journal of Animal Science* 89, no. 12 (2011): 4249–61.

Carter, Meg. "Men Buy Mars, Women Prefer Galaxy: Gender Targeting Is Advertising Industry's Secret Weapon." *Independent*, March 17, 2010. http://www .independent.co.uk/life-style/food-and-drink/features/men-buy-mars-women -prefer-galaxy-gender-targeting-is-advertising-industrys-secret-weapon-1922941 .html.

Castrodale, Jelisa. "Guy Fieri Spent Yesterday Making Nonstop BBQ for California Fire Victims and First Responders." *Munchies*, October 13, 2017. https://www.vice .com/en_us/article/7xkgk4/guy-fieri-spent-yesterday-making-nonstop-bbq-for -california-fire-victims-and-first-responders.

Cavazza, Nicolette, Margherita Guidettia, and Fabrizi Buterab. "Ingredients of Gender-based Stereotypes about Food: Indirect Influence of Food Type, Portion Size and Presentation on Gendered Intentions to Eat." *Appetite* 91, no. 1 (2015): 266–72.

Chaker, Anne Marie. "Groceries Become a Guy Thing." *Wall Street Journal*, October 16, 2013. https://www.wsj.com/articles/groceries-become-a-guy-thing -1381964283?tesla=y.

"Chief Evangelist of the Weight Watchers." *Los Angeles Times*, April 10, 1970.

Churchill, Dan. *DudeFood: A Guy's Guide to Cooking Kick-Ass Food*. New York: Simon & Schuster, 2015.

Clarke, Suzane. "Dr. Pepper Ten: It's 'Not for Women,' Macho Marketing Campaign Says." *ABC News*, October 12, 2011. http://abcnews.go.com/blogs/business/2011 /10/dr-pepper-ten-its-not-for-women-macho-marketing-campaign-says/.

Click, Melissa A. "Untidy: Fan Response to the Spoiling of Martha Stewart's Spotless Image." In *Fandom: Identities and Community in a Mediated World*, edited by Jonathan Gray, Cornel Sandvoss, and C. Lee Harrington, 301–15. New York: NYU Press, 2007.

———, ed. *Anti-Fandom: Dislike and Hate in the Digital Age*. New York: NYU Press, 2019.

Clifford, Terry. "He Wants to Skip Dessert in the Governor's Mansion." *Chicago Tribune*, November 23, 1975.

Cohen, Lizabeth. *A Consumers' Republic: The Politics of Mass Consumption in Postwar America*. New York: Alfred A. Knopf, 2003.

"Coke Zero 400 at Daytona." *Daytona International Speedway*. http://www .daytonainternationalspeedway.com/Events/2017/Coke-Zero-400/Coke-Zero-400 .aspx.

Collins, Kathleen. *Watching What We Eat: The Evolution of Television Cooking Shows*. London: Bloomsbury Academic, 2009.

Comedy Central. "Broad City — Exclusive — Every 'Dude' in Broad City So Far." YouTube Video, 1:51. January 1, 2017. https://www.youtube.com/watch?v =PzHmguoLIa4.

Condis, Megan. *Gaming Masculinity: Trolls, Fake Geeks, and the Gendered Battle for Online Culture*. Iowa City: University of Iowa Press, 2018.

Connell, R. W. *Masculinities*, 2nd ed. Oakland: University of California Press, 2005.

Connell, R. W., and James W. Messerschmidt. "Hegemonic Masculinity: Rethinking the Concept." *Gender & Society* 19, no. 6 (December 1, 2005): 829–59.

Contois, Emily. "Blogging Food, Performing Gender." *Cambridge Companion to Food and Literature*. Edited by J. Michelle Coghlan. Cambridge: Cambridge University Press, 2020.

———. "Dude Food: Gender and Health in U.S. Popular Culture." Brown University Research Matters. YouTube Video, 5:39. November 5, 2016. https://youtu.be/m0cR0PV4tRs.

———. "Food Culture at the Margins: Two New Books on Eating Disorders." *Gastronomica: The Journal of Critical Food Studies* 17, no. 3 (2017): 104–5.

———. "Healthy Food Blogs: Creating New Nutrition Knowledge at the Crossroads of Science, Foodie Lifestyle, and Gender Identities." *Yearbook of Women's History* 36 (2016): 129–45.

———. "I Was Trolled—Here's Why I'm Turning It into a Teaching Opportunity." *Nursing Clio*, July 17, 2018. https://nursingclio.org/2018/07/17/i-was-trolled-heres-why-im-turning-it-into-a-teaching-opportunity/.

———. "'Lose Like a Man:' Gender and the Constraints of Self-Making in Weight Watchers Online." *Gastronomica: The Journal of Critical Food Studies* 17, no. 1 (2017): 33–43.

———. "Real Men & Real Food: The Cultural Politics of Male Weight Loss." *Nursing Clio*, August 15, 2017. https://nursingclio.org/2017/08/15/real-men-real-food-the-cultural-politics-of-male-weight-loss/.

———. "The Spicy Spectacular: Food, Gender, and Celebrity on *Hot Ones*." *Feminist Media Studies*, Commentary and Criticism: Food Media Special Issue 18 no. 4 (2018): 769–73.

———. "Weight Watchers." In *Savoring Gotham: A Food Lovers Companion to New York City*, edited by Andrew F. Smith and Garrett Oliver, 638–39. New York: Oxford University Press, 2015.

———. "Welcome to Flavortown: Guy Fieri's Populist American Food Culture." *American Studies*, The Food Issue 57, no. 3 (2019): 143–60.

Copeland, Libby. "Is Diet Soda Girly?" *Slate*, August 12, 2013. http://www.slate.com/articles/double_x/doublex/2013/08/gender_contamination_when_women_buy_a_product_men_flee.html.

Cordain, Loren. *The Paleo Diet: Lose Weight and Get Healthy by Eating the Food You Were Designed to Eat*. New York: Wiley, 2002.

Counihan, Carole M. *The Anthropology of Food and Body: Gender, Meaning and Power*. New York: Routledge, 1999.

Courtenay, Will H. "Constructions of Masculinity and Their Influence on Men's Well-Being: A Theory of Gender and Health." *Social Science & Medicine* 50, no. 10 (2000): 1385–401.

———. "Engendering Health: A Social Constructionist Examination of Men's Health Beliefs and Behaviors." *Psychology of Men & Masculinity* 1, no. 1 (2000): 4–15.

Crane, Melissa M., Lesley D. Lutes, Dianne S. Ward, J. Michael Bowling, and Deborah F. Tate. "A Randomized Trial Testing the Efficacy of a Novel Approach to Weight Loss among Men with Overweight and Obesity." *Obesity* 23, no. 12 (2015): 2398–405.

Crawford, Robert. "Health as a Meaningful Social Practice." *Health* 10, no. 4 (2006): 401–20.

———. "Healthism and the Medicalization of Everyday Life." *International Journal of Health Services: Planning, Administration, Evaluation* 10, no. 3 (1980): 365–88.

Crenshaw, Kimberle Williams. "Mapping the Margins: Intersectionality, Identity Politics, and Violence Against Women of Color." *Stanford Law Review* 43, no. 6 (1991): 1241–99.

Crewe, Ben. *Representing Men: Cultural Production and Producers in the Men's Magazine Market*. New York: Bloomsbury Academic, 2003.

Cross, Gary. *Men to Boys: The Making of Modern Immaturity*. New York: Columbia University Press, 2008.

Crowley, Chris. "Maybe It's Not Time to Reconsider Guy Fieri After All." *Grub Street*, September 13, 2016. http://www.grubstreet.com/2016/09/maybe-its-not-time-to -reconsider-guy-fieri-after-all.html.

Cruz, Ariane. "Gettin' Down Home with the Neelys: Gastro-porn and Televisual Performances of Gender, Race, and Sexuality." *Women & Performance: A Journal of Feminist Theory* 23, no. 3 (2013): 323–49.

Cuordileone, K. A. *Manhood and American Political Culture in the Cold War*. New York: Routledge, 2004.

"'Dad Bods' Are More Attractive Than Six Packs, Study Says." *MSN*, June 18, 2019. https://www.msn.com/en-us/health/health-news/dad-bods-are-more-attractive -than-six-packs-study-says/ar-AAD3K0P.

D'Agostino, Ryan. *Eat Like a Man: The Only Cookbook a Man Will Ever Need*. San Francisco: Chronicle Books, 2011.

Daniells, Stephen. "Protein Powders: The Heavyweight in the $16bn Sports Nutrition Market." *NutraIngredients-USA.com*, September 17, 2015. http://www .nutraingredients-usa.com/Markets/Protein-powders-The-heavyweight-in-the -16bn-sports-nutrition-market.

Danone. "Mission and Key Figures, Danone Dairy Products." 2015. http://www.danone .com/en/for-all/our-4-business-lines/fresh-dairy-products/strategy-key-figures/.

Dansinger, M. L., Joi Augustin Gleason, John L. Griffith, Harry P. Selker, and Ernst J. Shaefer. "Comparison of the Atkins, Ornish, Weight Watchers, and Zone Diets for Weight Loss and Heart Disease Risk Reduction: A Randomized Trial." *JAMA* 293, no. 1 (2005): 43–53.

Davies, Helen, and Claire O'Callaghan, eds. *Gender and Austerity in Popular Culture: Femininity, Masculinity and Recession in Film and Television*. London: I. B. Tauris, 2017.

de la Peña, Carolyn. *Empty Pleasures: The Story of Artificial Sweeteners from Saccharin to Splenda*. Chapel Hill: University of North Carolina Press, 2010.

de Solier, Isabelle. "TV Dinners: Culinary Television, Education and Distinction." *Continuum* 19, no. 4 (2005): 465–81.

De Souza, Paula, and Karen Ciclitira. "Men and Dieting: A Qualitative Analysis." *Journal of Health Psychology* 10, no. 6 (2005): 793–804.

Dejmanee, Tisha. "'Food Porn' as Postfeminist Play: Digital Femininity and the Female Body on Food Blogs." *Television & New Media* 17, no. 5 (2016): 429–48.

Demby, Gene. "That Cute Cheerios Ad with the Interracial Family Is Back." *NPR*, January 30, 2014. http://www.npr.org/sections/codeswitch/2014/01/30/268930004 /that-cute-cheerios-ad-with-the-interracial-family-is-back.

Demetriou, Demetrakis Z. "Connell's Concept of Hegemonic Masculinity: A Critique." *Theory and Society* 30, no. 3 (2001): 337–61.

Dempsey, Sarah E. "The Increasing Technology Divide: Persistent Portrayals of Maverick Masculinity in US Marketing." *Feminist Media Studies* 9, no. 1 (2009): 37–55.

Denby, David. "A Fine Romance: The New Comedy of the Sexes." *The New Yorker*, July 23, 2007.

Deutsch, Jonathan. "'Please Pass the Chicken Tits': Rethinking Men and Cooking at an Urban Firehouse." *Food and Foodways* 13, no. 1–2 (2005): 91–114.

"Deutsch L.A. Brings Facebook Data to Dr Pepper TEN Brand Allows Guys to Test Their Manliness." *AdAge*, January 29, 2013. http://adage.com/print/239353.

Deutsch, Tracey. *Building a Housewife's Paradise: Gender, Politics, and American Grocery Stores in the Twentieth Century*. Chapel Hill: University of North Carolina Press, 2012.

DeVault, Marjorie L. *Feeding the Family: The Social Organization of Caring as Gendered Work*. Chicago: University of Chicago Press, 1991.

Diabetic Gourmet Magazine. "Diabetic Dude Food: Six Healthy Recipes Guys Will Love." *Diabetic Gourmet Magazine*. http://diabeticgourmet.com/articles/784.shtml.

Diamond, Jason. "The Unrecognizable Genius of Guy Fieri." *Esquire*, September 7, 2016. http://www.esquire.com/food-drink/food/a48351/the-genius-of-guy-fieri/.

DiAngelo, Robin. "White Fragility." *The International Journal of Critical Pedagogy* 3, no. 3 (2011): 54–70.

Diners, Drive-Ins and Dives. Season 14, Episode 6: "Unexpected Eats." Aired March 7, 2012, on Food Network.

Dishman, Lydia. "Meet the Guy Who Whittled Dr Pepper Down to 10 Calories." *Fast Company*, September 10, 2012. https://www.fastcompany.com/3000981/meet-guy -who-whittled-dr-pepper-down-10-calories.

Dominguez, Pier. "Let's Stop Pretending Celebrity Dadbods Need Defending." *Buzzfeed News*, July 25, 2019. https://www.buzzfeednews.com/article /pdominguez/lets-stop-pretending-celebrity-dadbods-need-defending.

Donini, Lorenzo Maria, D. Marsili, M. P. Graziani, M. Imbriale, and C. Cannella. "Orthorexia Nervosa: A Preliminary Study with a Proposal for Diagnosis and an Attempt to Measure the Dimension of the Phenomenon." *Eating and Weight Disorders—Studies on Anorexia, Bulimia and Obesity* 9, no. 2 (2004): 151–57.

Dosti, Rose. "Weight Watchers Cookbook: Uncle Sam's 'Full Choice' Food Plan." *Los Angeles Times*, October 29, 1981.

Douglas, Susan J. *Listening In: Radio and the American Imagination*. Minneapolis: University of Minnesota Press, 2004.

"Dr. Pepper: Like Report." *AdAge*, January 10, 2013. https://adage.com/creativity/work /report/30382.

Dr Pepper Snapple Group. "Dr Pepper Snapple Group Annual Report." 2012. http://
investor.drpeppersnapplegroup.com/annual-reports.

"Dr Pepper TEN: It's Not for Women." Dr Pepper Snapple Group website,
October 11, 2011. http://news.drpeppersnapplegroup.com/2011-11-11-Dr-Pepper
-TEN-Its-Not-For-Women.

Droga5. "Enjoy Everything," *Droga5*, 2013. https://droga5.com/work/its-not-your
-fault/.

Druckman, Charlotte. "Why Are There No Great Women Chefs?" *Gastronomica: The
Journal of Critical Food Studies* 10, no. 1 (Winter 2010): 24–31.

Duffett, Mark. *Understanding Fandom: An Introduction to the Study of Media Fan
Culture*. New York: Bloomsbury Academic, 2013.

Duprey, Rich. "People Are Still Drinking Massive Quantities of Hard Seltzer During
Coronavirus Pandemic." *The Motley Fool*, April 7, 2020. https://www.fool.com
/investing/2020/04/07/people-are-still-drinking-massive-quantities-of-ha.aspx.

Eaton, S. B., and M. Konner. "Paleolithic Nutrition. A Consideration of Its Nature
and Current Implications." *The New England Journal of Medicine* 312, no. 5 (1985):
283–89.

Ebiquity Global Insight. "Coke Zero—Chill." YouTube Video, 1:16. May 1, 2013.
https://www.youtube.com/watch?v=eIR8wJ8BIuU.

Eggebeen, David J., and Chris Knoester. "Does Fatherhood Matter for Men?" *Journal
of Marriage and Family* 63, no. 2 (2001): 381–93.

Eisner-Levine, Amy. "Man Versus Food: An Analysis of 'Dude Food' Television and
Public Health." Master's Thesis, University of Western Ontario, 2014. http://ir.lib
.uwo.ca/etd/2124.

Elias, Megan J. *Food on the Page: Cookbooks and American Culture*. Philadelphia:
University of Pennsylvania Press, 2017.

Elliott, Stuart. "An American Family Returns to the Table." *New York Times*,
January 28, 2014. https://www.nytimes.com/2014/01/29/business/media/an
-american-family-returns-to-the-table.html.

EmanatePR. "KFC's Dude Food Etiquette." *Visual.ly*, October 15, 2012. http://visual
.ly/kfcs-dude-food-etiquette.

Endres, Kathleen L., and Therese L. Lueck. "Weight Watchers." In *Women's
Periodicals in the United States: Consumer Magazines*, 436–40. Westport, CT:
Greenwood, 1995.

Engel, Meredith. "Why Women Are Lusting after Dudes with 'Dad Bod.'" *Daily
News*, May 7, 2015.

Erik. "Dude Food: About Me." *Dude Food* (blog), 2010. http://dudefoodnyc.blogspot
.com/p/about-me.html.

Fakhouri, Tala, Brian K. Kit, and Cynthia L. Ogden. "Consumption of Diet Drinks in
the United States, 2009–2010." NCHS Data Brief, October 2012. https://www.cdc
.gov/nchs/products/databriefs/db109.htm.

Fans of Guy Fieri (blog). http://guyfieri.blogspot.com.

Farrell, Amy Erdman. *Fat Shame: Stigma and the Fat Body in American Culture*.
New York: NYU Press, 2011.

Feirstein, Bruce. *Real Men Don't Eat Quiche*. New York: Pocket Books, 1982.

Fieri, Guy, and Ann Volkwein. *Guy Fieri Food: Cookin' It, Livin' It, Lovin' It.* New York: William Morrow Cookbooks, 2011.

———. *More Diners, Drive-Ins and Dives: A Drop-Top Culinary Cruise Through America's Finest and Funkiest Joints.* New York: William Morrow Cookbooks, 2009.

Finn, Margot. *Discriminating Taste: How Class Anxiety Created the American Food Revolution.* New Brunswick, NJ: Rutgers University Press, 2017.

Fischer, Mia. *Terrorizing Gender: Transgender Visibility and the Surveillance Practices of the U.S. Security State.* Lincoln: University of Nebraska Press, 2019.

Flager, Madison. "How to Dress Up Like Guy Fieri for Halloween." *Delish,* July 24, 2019. https://www.delish.com/holiday-recipes/halloween/g21989249/guy-fieri -halloween-costume/.

Foley, Christopher. "Best drink out there if you're looking for 'Coke' taste WITHOUT the sugar, this is it." Amazon.com Customer Review, January 25, 2019. https://www .amazon.com/gp/customer-reviews/R1IP1DC06TL5XT?ref=pf_vv_at_pdctrvw_srp.

———. "Change? Not a chance, same great taste, just different label." Amazon.com Customer Review, January 25, 2019. https://www.amazon.com/gp/customer -reviews/R2SKH5P1KPVXBR?ref=pf_vv_at_pdctrvw_srp.

FoodBev Media. "The Story Behind the Launch of Powerful Yogurt." YouTube Video, 14:36. March 13, 2013. https://www.youtube.com/watch?v=C5MGnEiJ3nM.

Forbes, Paula. "Watch Bourdain Rip into Guy Fieri's NYC 'Terror-Dome.'" *Eater,* September 28, 2012. http://www.eater.com/2012/9/28/6540469/watch-bourdain -rip-into-guy-fieris-nyc-terror-dome.

Foucault, Michel. *Discipline and Punish: The Birth of the Prison.* Translated by Alan Sheridan. Reissue ed. New York: Vintage Books, 1995.

———. *The History of Sexuality, Vol. 1: An Introduction.* Reissue ed. New York: Vintage Books, 1990.

Fox News. "'Brogurt': Greek Yogurt for Men, by Men," *Fox News,* February 26, 2013. http://www.foxnews.com/leisure/2013/02/26/brogurt-greek-yogurt-for-men-by -men/.

Frank, Thomas. *The Conquest of Cool: Business Culture, Counterculture, and the Rise of Hip Consumerism.* Chicago: University of Chicago Press, 1997.

Frederick, Christine. *Selling Mrs. Consumer.* New York: The Business Bourse, 1929.

Freedman, Paul. "How Steak Became Manly and Salads Became Feminine." *The Conversation,* October 24, 2019. https://theconversation.com/how-steak-became -manly-and-salads-became-feminine-124147.

———, ed. *Food: The History of Taste.* Berkeley: University of California Press, 2007.

Fry, Richard, and D'Vera Cohn. "Women, Men, and the New Economics of Marriage." Pew Research Center, January 19, 2010. https://www.pewsocialtrends .org/2010/01/19/women-men-and-the-new-economics-of-marriage/.

Fuhrmeister, Chris. "Guy Fieri Feeds First Responders Battling Northern California Fires." *Eater,* November 13, 2018. https://www.eater.com/2018/11/13/18092728 /guy-fieri-california-wildfires-dave-grohl.

Gaesser, Glenn. "Is 'Permanent Weight Loss' an Oxymoron? The Statistics on Weight Loss and the National Weight Control Registry." In *The Fat Studies Reader,* edited by Esther Rothblum and Sondra Solovay, 37–41. New York: NYU Press, 2009.

Gagliardi, Nancy. "Dieting in the Long Sixties: Constructing the Identity of the Modern American Dieter." *Gastronomica: The Journal of Critical Food Studies* 18, no. 3 (2018): 66–81.

Garner, David. "Survey Says: Body Image Poll Results." *Psychology Today*, February 1, 1997. http://www.psychologytoday.com/articles/199702/survey-says-body-image -poll-results.

Gelber, Steven M. "Do-It-Yourself: Constructing, Repairing and Maintaining Domestic Masculinity." *American Quarterly* 49, no. 1 (1997): 66–112.

Gelfer, Joseph. "Meat and Masculinity in Men's Ministries." *The Journal of Men's Studies* 21, no. 1 (2013): 78–91.

Gentile, Dan. "I, Fieri." *The Austin Chronicle*, October 25, 2018.

Gilbert, James. *Men in the Middle: Searching for Masculinity in the 1950s*. Chicago: University of Chicago Press, 2005.

Gill, Rosalind. "Power and the Production of Subjects: A Genealogy of the New Man and the New Lad." *The Sociological Review* 51, no. S1 (May 1, 2003): 34–56.

Gill, Rosalind, Karen Henwood, and Carl McLean. "Body Projects and the Regulation of Normative Masculinity." *Body & Society* 11, no. 1 (March 1, 2005): 37–62.

Gillespie, Cailein H. "Gastrosophy and Nouvelle Cuisine: Entrepreneurial Fashion and Fiction." *British Food Journal* 96, no. 10 (1994): 19–23.

"Global Trends in Protein." Euromonitor International, March 2016. http://www .euromonitor.com/global-trends-in-protein/report.

"Global Whey Protein Market - Growth, Trends and Forecast (2017–2022)." *Mordor Intelligence*, December 2016. https://www.mordorintelligence.com/industry -reports/global-whey-protein-market-industry.

Golden, Zach. *What the F*@# Should I Make for Dinner?: The Answers to Life's Everyday Question (in 50 F*@#ing Recipes)*. Philadelphia: Running Press, 2011.

Goodman, David. *Radio's Civic Ambition: American Broadcasting and Democracy in the 1930s*. New York: Oxford University Press, 2011.

Goodyear, Dana. "California Makes Marijuana a Wellness Industry." *The New Yorker*, January 31, 2018. https://www.newyorker.com/culture/photo-booth/california -makes-marijuana-a-wellness-industry.

Gough, Brendan. "'Real Men Don't Diet': An Analysis of Contemporary Newspaper Representations of Men, Food and Health." *Social Science & Medicine* 64, no. 2 (January 2007): 326–37.

———. "Try to Be Healthy, but Don't Forgo Your Masculinity: Deconstructing Men's Health Discourse in the Media." *Social Science & Medicine* 63, no. 9 (November 2006): 2476–88.

Graves, Jennifer L., and Samantha Kwan. "Is There Really 'More to Love'?: Gender, Body, and Relationship Scripts in Romance-Based Reality Television." *Fat Studies* 1, no. 1 (2012): 47–60.

Gray, Jonathan. "Anti-fandom and the Moral Text: Television without Pity and Textual Dislike." *American Behavioral Scientist* 48, no. 7 (2005): 840–58.

———. "New Audiences, New Textualities: Anti-fans and Non-fans." *International Journal of Cultural Studies* 6, no. 1 (2003): 64–81.

Gray, Jonathan, Cornel Sandvoss, and C. Lee Harrington. *Fandom: Identities and Communities in a Mediated World*. New York: NYU Press, 2007.

Gray, Kishonna L. "Masculinity Studies." *Feminist Media Histories* 4, no. 2 (2018): 107–12.

Greenebaum, Jessica, and Brandon Dexter. "Vegan Men and Hybrid Masculinity." *Journal of Gender Studies* 27, no. 6 (2018): 637–48.

Grella, Bill. "'Diners, Drive-Ins and Dives' Adventures" (blog), 2011. http://allergb .blogspot.com.

Grindstaff, Laura, and Emily West. "Hegemonic Masculinity on the Sidelines of Sport." *Sociology Compass* 5, no. 10 (2011): 859–81.

Guilty Pleasures on Food Network, accessed November 7, 2016. http://www .foodnetwork.com/shows/guilty-pleasures.html.

Guthman, Julie. *Weighing In: Obesity, Food Justice, and the Limits of Capitalism*. Oakland: University of California Press, 2011.

Hakim, Catherine. *Erotic Capital: The Power of Attraction in the Boardroom and the Bedroom*. New York: Basic Books, 2011.

Halberstam, Judith. *Female Masculinity*. Durham, NC: Duke University Press Books, 1998.

Halkitis, Perry N. "Redefining Masculinity in the Age of AIDS: Seropositive Gay Men and the 'Buff Agenda.'" In *Gay Masculinities*, edited by Peter M. Nardi, 130–51. Newbury Park, CA: Sage, 2000.

Hall, Stuart. "Encoding/Decoding." In *Culture, Media, Language*, edited by Stuart Hall, Dorothy Hobson, Andrew Love, and Paul Willis, 128–38. London: Hutchinson, 1980.

Hall, Thomas. "Weight Watchers Help Each Other Battle the Bulges: Groups Meet Weekly to Check on Progress." *Chicago Tribune*, August 21, 1967.

Hallinan, Bridget. "Guy Fieri Really Digs Your Guy Fieri Halloween Costumes." *Food & Wine*, October 31, 2019.

Hamilton, Carroll. *Affirmative Reaction: New Formations of White Masculinity*. Durham, NC: Duke University Press, 2011.

Harris, Deborah, and Patti Giuffre. *Taking the Heat: Women Chefs and Gender Inequality in the Professional Kitchen*. New Brunswick, NJ: Rutgers University Press, 2015.

Harrison, Olivia. "Guy Fieri Feeds First Responders in Northern California." *Refinery29*, November 14, 2018. https://www.refinery29.com/en-us/2018/11 /216966/guy-fieri-feeds-first-responders-california-camp-fires.

Hart, Fred. "Design Review: Evolution of Caffeine Free Coke Family Branding." *BevReview*, May 8, 2013. http://www.bevreview.com/2013/05/08/design-review -evolution-of-caffeine-free-coke-family-branding/.

The Hartman Group. "Insights into the State of Health + Wellness 2019." https:// tailorednews.com/u/THG-Publications/JOWeMpSH9ENwXLORX/The-Age-of -Anxiety.htm.

Hartmann, Douglas. "The Sanctity of Sunday Football: Why Men Love Sports." *Contexts* 2, no. 4 (2003): 13–21.

Hatton, Erin, and Mary Nell Trautner. "Equal Opportunity Objectification? The Sexualization of Men and Women on the Cover of Rolling Stone." *Sexuality & Culture* 15, no. 3 (September 2011): 256–78.

Hauck-Lawson, Annie. "When Food Is the Voice: A Case Study of a Polish-American Woman." *Food, Culture & Society* 2, no. 1 (1998): 21–28.

Haupt, Angela. "6 Diets for Men." *US News & World Report*, February 10, 2012. http://health.usnews.com/best-diet/articles/2012/02/10/6-diets-for-men.

Hayes-Conroy, Allison. *Doing Nutrition Differently: Critical Approaches to Dietary Intervention.* Oxon: Routledge, 2013.

Heil, Emily. "The Key to White Claw's Surging Popularity: Marketing to a Post-Gender World." *The Washington Post*, September 10, 2019. https://www.washingtonpost.com/news/voraciously/wp/2019/09/10/the-key-to-white-claws-surging-popularity-marketing-to-a-post-gender-world/.

Hellman, Caroline. "The Other American Kitchen: Alternative Domesticity in 1950s Design, Politics, and Fiction." *Americana: The Journal of American Popular Culture, 1900 to Present* 3, no. 2 (2004), http://www.americanpopularculture.com/journal/articles/fall_2004/hellman.htm.

Helms, Janet E. *A Race Is a Nice Thing to Have: A Guide to Being a White Person or Understanding the White Persons in Your Life.* 3rd ed. San Diego, CA: Cognella Academic Publishing, 2019.

Hendley, Joyce. "Weight Watchers at Forty: A Celebration." *Gastronomica* 3, no. 1 (2003): 16–21.

Heyes, Cressida. "Foucault Goes to Weight Watchers," *Hypatia* 21, no. 2 (2006): 126–49.

Hickman, Martin. "Introducing 'Bloke Coke' Is This Now the Real Thing?" *The Independent*, July 3, 2006. http://www.independent.co.uk/news/media/introducing-bloke-coke-is-this-now-the-real-thing-6096336.html.

Hill, Richard A. "You've Come a Long Way, Dude: A History." *American Speech* 69, no. 3 (1994): 321–27.

Hobson, Barbara. *Making Men into Fathers: Men, Masculinities and the Social Politics of Fatherhood.* Cambridge: Cambridge University Press, 2002.

Hochman, David. "At Home with Guy Fieri: The Chef Talks Summer Cooking, Family Fun, and Coping With Critics." *Parade*, May 17, 2014. http://parade.com/292885/davidhochman/at-home-with-guy-fieri-the-chef-talks-summer-cooking-family-fun-and-coping-with-critics/.

Hochschild, Arlie. *The Second Shift: Working Parents and the Revolution at Home.* New York: Viking Adult, 1989.

Hoekstra, A. Y., and A. K. Chapagain. "Water Footprints of Nations: Water Use by People as a Function of Their Consumption Pattern." *Water Resources Management* 21, no. 1 (2007): 35–48.

Hoffman, Karen S. "Visual Persuasion in George W. Bush's Presidency: Cowboy Imagery in Public Discourse." *Congress & the Presidency* 38, no. 3 (2011): 322–43.

Holden, T. J. M. "The Overcooked and Underdone: Masculinities in Japanese Food Programming." In *Food and Culture: A Reader.* 3rd ed., edited by Carole Counihan and Penny Van Esterik, 119–36. New York: Routledge, 2012.

Hollows, Joanne. "The Bachelor Dinner: Masculinity, Class and Cooking in Playboy, 1953–1961." *Continuum: Journal of Media & Cultural Studies* 16, no. 2 (2002): 143–55.

—. "Oliver's Twist: Leisure, Labour and Domestic Masculinity in *The Naked Chef*." *International Journal of Cultural Studies* 6, no. 2 (2003): 229–48.

Hoover, Stewart M., and Curtis D. Coats. *Does God Make the Man: Media, Religion, and the Crisis of Masculinity*. New York: NYU Press, 2015.

Hopper, Nate. "Is Super-Macho Yogurt Sexist?" *Esquire*, February 27, 2013. http://www.esquire.com/is-macho-yogurt-sexist.

"How Guy Says, 'That's Good'" video. Food Network, accessed December 21, 2016. http://www.foodnetwork.com/shows/diners-drive-ins-and-dives/diners-drive-ins-and-dives-video-gallery.html.

Howard, Theresa. "Coke Finally Scores Another Winner." *ABC News*, October 29, 2007. http://abcnews.go.com/Business/story?id=3788224&page=1.

Hoyt, Wendy D., and Lori R. Kogan. "Satisfaction with Body Image and Peer Relationships for Males and Females in a College Environment." *Sex Roles* 45 (2001): 199–215.

Hughes, Ashlie. "These Are the Three New White Claw Flavors Coming in 2020." *VinePair*, November 21, 2019. https://vinepair.com/booze-news/new-white-claw-flavors-watermelon-lemon-tangerine/.

Ickeringill, Nan. "Weight Watchers, Inc.: They Talk Themselves Out of Obesity." *New York Times*, March 20, 1967.

The Innovation Group. "Summer Fancy Food Show: Key Food Trends." *JWT Intelligence*, July 6, 2016. https://www.jwtintelligence.com/2016/07/summer-food-show-key-trends/.

"Introducing the New Weight Watchers Magazine." *New York Times*, March 3, 1968.

Irigaray, Luce. *This Sex Which Is Not One*. Translated by Catherine Porter and Carolyn Burke. Ithaca, NY: Cornell University Press, 1985.

Isle, Ray. "Sushi in America." *Food & Wine*, June 16, 2017. http://www.foodandwine.com/articles/sushi-in-america.

Jane, Emma A. "Back to the Kitchen, Cunt: Speaking the Unspeakable about Online Misogyny." *Continuum: Journal of Media & Cultural Studies* 28, no. 4 (2014): 558–70.

Jeffords, Susan. *Hard Bodies: Hollywood Masculinity in the Reagan Era*. New Brunswick, NJ: Rutgers University Press, 1993.

Jellyblue. "Poll: Do Guys Eat Yogurt?" *The Straight Dope*, April 16, 2009. https://boards.straightdope.com/sdmb/showthread.php?t=514293.

Joachim, David. *A Man, a Can, a Plan: 50 Great Guy Meals Even You Can Make!* Emmaus: Rodale, 2002.

Johnson, Alex. "'Post-Truth' is Oxford Dictionaries' Word of the Year for 2016." *NBC News*, November 16, 2016. https://www.nbcnews.com/news/us-news/post-truth-oxford-dictionaries-word-year-2016-n685081.

Johnston, Josée, and Shyon Baumann. *Foodies: Democracy and Distinction in the Gourmet Foodscape*. New York: Routledge, 2010.

Johnston, Josée, Alexandra Rodney, and Phillipa Chong. "Making Change in the Kitchen? A Study of Celebrity Cookbooks, Culinary Personas, and Inequality." *Poetics* 47 (2014): 1–22.

Johnston, Laurie. "15,000 Weight Watchers Cheer Svelte Founder and Other Stars." *New York Times*, June 12, 1973.

Joyrich, Lynne. *Re-Viewing Reception: Television, Gender, and Postmodern Culture.* Bloomington: Indiana University Press, 1996.

Julier, Alice, and Laura Lindenfeld. "Mapping Men onto the Menu: Masculinities and Food." *Food and Foodways* 13, no. 1–2 (March 9, 2005): 1–16.

Just-Drinks.com Editorial Team. "Just the Facts—Coke Zero." *Just-Drinks*, September 23, 2010. http://www.just-drinks.com/news/just-the-facts-coke-zero_id101930.aspx.

Kacala, Alexandra. "Men with 'Dad Bods' Are Happier and More Attractive to Women, New Survey Finds." *Newsweek*, July 11, 2019. https://www.newsweek.com/men-dad-bods-are-happier-more-attractive-women-new-survey-finds-1448630.

Kamp, David. *The United States of Arugula: How We Became a Gourmet Nation*. New York: Clarkson Potter, 2006.

Kasson, John F. *Houdini, Tarzan, and the Perfect Man: The White Male Body and the Challenge of Modernity in America.* New York: Hill and Wang, 2002.

Kelly, Casey Ryan. "Cooking without Women: The Rhetoric of the New Culinary Male." *Communication and Critical/Cultural Studies* 12, no. 2 (2015): 200–204.

Kerr, Graham. *The Galloping Gourmet Television Cookbook*, Volume 6. London, Fremantle International Inc., 1971.

Ketchum, Cheri. "The Essence of Cooking Shows: How the Food Network Constructs Consumer Fantasies." *Journal of Communication Inquiry* 29, no. 3 (2005): 217–34.

Kiefer, Ingrid, Theres Rathmanner, and Michael Kunze. "Eating and Dieting Differences in Men and Women." *Journal of Men's Health and Gender* 2, no. 2 (2005): 194–201.

Kiesling, Scott F. "Dude." *American Speech* 79, no. 3 (2004): 281–305.

Kimmel, Michael. *Angry White Men: American Masculinity at the End of an Era.* New York: Bold Type Books, 2017.

———. *Guyland: The Perilous World Where Boys Become Men*. New York: Harper, 2008.

———. *Manhood in America: A Cultural History*. New York: Free Press, 1996.

Kimmel, Michael, and Lisa Wade, "Ask a Feminist: Michael Kimmel and Lisa Wade Discuss Toxic Masculinity." *Signs: Journal of Women in Culture and Society* 44, no. 1 (2018): 233–54.

Kimmel, Sara B., and James R. Mahalik. "Measuring Masculine Body Ideal Distress: Development of a Measure." *International Journal of Men's Health* 3, no. 1 (2004): 1–10.

Kirchhoff, David. "Does Weight Watchers for Men Work?" *Men's Health*, May 10, 2012. http://www.menshealth.com/weight-loss/psych-out-fat.

Kirkwood, Katherine. "Dude Food vs Superfood: We're Cultural Omnivores." *The Conversation*, May 26, 2016. http://theconversation.com/dude-food-vs-superfood-were-cultural-omnivores-53978.

Kita, Paul. "In Defense of Dude Food." *Men's Health*, September 19, 2012. http://www.menshealth.com/nutrition/in-defense-of-dude-food.

———. *A Man, a Pan, a Plan*. Emmaus: Rodale Books, 2017.

Kjaer, Meldgaard Katrine, and Jonatan Leer. "Introduction: Food in Gender Studies and Gender in Food Studies." *Women, Gender & Research* 3–4 (2015): 3–7.

Kleinfield, N. R. "The Ever-Fatter Business of Thinness." *New York Times,* September 7, 1986.

Klemesrud, Judy. "Weight Watcher's Lunch: With Spaghetti on Menu?" *New York Times,* January 26, 1972.

Koch, Shelley L. *Gender and Food: A Critical Look at the Food System.* Lanham, MD: Rowman & Littlefield Publishers, 2019.

Kryza, Andy. "11 Foods That No Man Should Eat . . . Ever." *Thrillist,* September 16, 2013. https://www.thrillist.com/eat/nation/foods-that-no-man-should-eat.

Kulick, Don, and Anne Meneley. *Fat: The Anthropology of an Obsession.* New York: Tarcher, 2005.

Kwoh, Leslie. "Weight Watchers Chief Looks to Men, China for Growth." *The Wall Street Journal,* January 9, 2012. http://www.wsj.com/articles/SB1000142405297020 4331304577144613938815858.

Labre, Magdala Peixoto. "The Male Body Ideal: Perspectives of Readers and Non-Readers of Fitness Magazines." *Journal of Men's Health and Gender* 2, no. 2 (2005): 223–29.

Lamare, Amy. "The Richest Celebrity Chefs in the World." *Celebrity Net Worth,* December 4, 2013. http://www.celebritynetworth.com/articles/entertainment -articles/richest-chefs-world/.

LaRosa, John. "Top 9 Things to Know About the Weight Loss Industry." *Market Research Blog,* March 6, 2019. https://blog.marketresearch.com/u.s.-weight-loss -industry-grows-to-72-billion.

LaRossa, Ralph. "Fatherhood and Social Change." *Family Relations* 37, no. 4 (1988): 451–57.

Laudan, Rachel. *Cuisine and Empire: Cooking in World History.* Berkeley: University of California Press, 2013.

Lawson, Sarah. "The 25 Most Insane Dude Foods of All Time." *First We Feast,* February 15, 2013. http://firstwefeast.com/eat/2013/02/the-25-most-insane-dude -foods-of-all-time/.

Lears, T. J. Jackson. "From Salvation to Self-Realization: Advertising and the Therapeutic Roots of the Consumer Culture, 1880–1930." *Advertising & Society Review* 1, no. 1 (2000), doi:10.1353/asr.2000.0009.

Leavitt, Judith Walzer. *Make Room for Daddy: The Journey from Waiting Room to Birthing Room.* Chapel Hill: University of North Carolina Press, 2009.

LeBesco, Kathleen. *Revolting Bodies? The Struggle to Redefine Fat Identity.* Amherst: University of Massachusetts Press, 2003.

Lecklitner, Ian. "The Self-Destructive Psychology of 'Dude Food.'" *MEL Magazine,* 2018. https://melmagazine.com/en-us/story/the-self-destructive-psychology-of -dude-food.

Lee, Debbie. "Dude Food with a Mexican Spin at Guy Fieri's El Burro Borracho." *Las Vegas Weekly,* May 25, 2016. http://lasvegasweekly.com/dining/reviews/2016/may /25/el-burro-borracho-guy-fieri-rio-mexican-food/#/o.

Leer, Jonatan. "What's Cooking, Man? Masculinity in European Cooking Shows after The Naked Chef." *Feminist Review* 114, no. 1 (2016): 72–90.

Leer, Jonatan, and Karen Klitgaard Povlsen, eds. *Food and Media: Practices, Distinctions and Heterotopias*. London: Routledge, 2016.

Leonard, Suzanne. "Escaping the Recession? The New Vitality of the Woman Worker." In *Gendering the Recession: Media and Culture in an Age of Austerity*, edited by Diane Negra and Yvonne Tasker, 31–58. Durham, NC: Duke University Press, 2014.

Leonardi, Susan J. "Recipes for Reading: Summer Pasta, Lobster à La Riseholme, and Key Lime Pie." *PMLA* 104, no. 3 (1989): 340–47.

Levine, Lawrence. *Highbrow Lowbrow: The Emergence of Cultural Hierarchy in America*. Cambridge, MA: Harvard University Press, 1988.

Lewis, Tania, and Michelle Phillipov, eds. "Special Issue: Food/Media: Eating, Cooking, and Provisioning in a Digital World." *Communication Research and Practice* 4, no. 3 (2018): 207–323.

Lilliston, Lynn. "Weight Watchers' Vigil on the Way of All Flesh." *Los Angeles Times*, April 18, 1967.

Lipsyte, Robert. "Confronting the Fat in Me: A Journey Begins." *New York Times*, January 7, 1996.

Livingston, Gretchen. "Growing Number of Dads Home with the Kids." Pew Research Center's Social & Demographic Trends Project, June 5, 2014. http://www .pewsocialtrends.org/2014/06/05/growing-number-of-dads-home-with-the-kids/.

Lotz, Amanda D. *Cable Guys: Television and Masculinities in the 21st Century*. New York: NYU Press, 2014.

———. *The Television Will Be Revolutionized*. 2nd ed. New York: NYU Press, 2014.

Ludwig, David S., Karen E. Peterson, and Steven L. Gortmaker. "Relation between Consumption of Sugar-Sweetened Drinks and Childhood Obesity: A Prospective, Observational Analysis." *The Lancet* 357, no. 9255 (2001): 505–8.

Lukovitz, Karlene. "'Men-Only' Dr Pepper Ten Ad Pulls Mixed Results." *Marketing Daily*, October 14, 2011. http://www.mediapost.com/publications/article/160296 /men-only-dr-pepper-ten-ad-pulls-mixed-results.html.

Lupton, Deborah. *Fat*. 2nd ed. Abingdon: Routledge, 2018.

———. *Food, the Body and the Self*. London: Sage, 1996.

———. "Quantifying the Body: Monitoring and Measuring Health in the Age of mHealth Technologies." *Critical Public Health* 23, no. 4 (2013): 393–403.

MacAdams, Lewis. *Birth of the Cool: Beat, Bebop, and the American Avant Garde*. New York: Free Press, 2001.

Mackinnon, Catherine. "Sexuality." In *Feminist Philosophy Reader*, edited by Alison Bailey and Chris J. Cuomo, 204–22. Boston: McGraw-Hill, 2008.

Madden, Jim, and Thomas Jacques. *Man Meets Stove: A Cookbook for Men Who've Never Cooked Anything Without a Microwave*. Self-published, 2012.

Magary, Drew. "How Flavortown Mayor Guy Fieri Is Taking Over Wine Country." *GQ*, November 13, 2015. http://www.gq.com/story/guy-fieri-wine.

Mah, Evan. "Anthony Bourdain Roars into the Fox Theater, Rips on Guy Fieri and Other Food Celebrities." *Atlanta Magazine*, July 13, 2015. http://www

.atlantamagazine.com/dining-news/anthony-bourdain-roars-into-the-fox
-theater-rips-on-guy-fieri-and-other-food-celebrities/.

Malik, Vasanti S., Barry M. Popkin, George A. Bray, Jean-Pierre Després, and Frank B. Hu. "Sugar-Sweetened Beverages, Obesity, Type 2 Diabetes Mellitus, and Cardiovascular Disease Risk." *Circulation* 121, no. 11 (2010): 1356–64.

Malik, Vasanti S., Matthias B. Schulze, and Frank B. Hu. "Intake of Sugar-Sweetened Beverages and Weight Gain: A Systematic Review." *The American Journal of Clinical Nutrition* 84, no. 2 (2006): 274–88.

Mallyon, Anna, Mary Holmes, John Coveney, and Maria Zadoroznyj. "'I'm Not Dieting, 'I'm Doing It for Science': Masculinities and the Experience of Dieting." *Health Sociology Review* 19, no. 3 (September 2010): 330–42.

Marchand, Roland. *Advertising the American Dream: Making Way for Modernity, 1920-1940*. Oakland: University of California Press, 1986.

Markey, Charlotte N., and Patrick M. Markey. "Relations Between Body Image and Dieting Behaviors: An Examination of Gender Differences." *Sex Roles* 53, no. 7–8 (October 2005): 519–30.

Marlboro. *Cook Like a Man Cookbook*. Phillip Morris USA, 2004.

Marsh, Margaret. "Suburban Men and Masculine Domesticity, 1870–1915." *American Quarterly* 40, no. 2 (1988): 165–86.

matgomad. "British Coke Zero Ad," YouTube Video: 0:40, July 3, 2006. https://www.youtube.com/watch?v=7A8DNWu2c5k.

Matwick, Kelsi, and Keri Matwick. "Cooking at Home: A Multimodal Narrative Analysis of the Food Network." *Discourse, Context & Media* 17 (2017): 20–29.

May, Elaine Tyler. *Homeward Bound: American Families in the Cold War Era*, 20th anniversary ed. New York: Basic Books, 2008.

Maynard, Micheline. "Cookbook Sales Are Jumping, Which Is Great News for Stores That Specialize in Them." *Forbes*, March 10, 2019. https://www.forbes.com/sites/michelinemaynard/2019/03/10/cookbook-sales-are-jumping-which-is-great-news-for-shops-that-specialize-in-them/#423be5f56e54.

Mcbride, Anne. "Food Porn." *Gastronomica: The Journal of Food and Culture* 10, no. 1 (2010): 38–46.

McCabe, Marita P., and Lina A. Ricciardelli. "Body Image Dissatisfaction among Males across the Lifespan." *Journal of Psychosomatic Research* 56, no. 6 (June 1, 2004): 675–85.

McCartney, Margaret. "Clean Eating and the Cult of Healthism." *British Medical Journal* 354 (2016): 4095.

McCormick, Margaret. "Fieri Fan Fuels 500th Foodie Fun." *Syracuse New Times*, May 11, 2016. http://www.syracusenewtimes.com/fieri-fan-fuels-500th-foodie-fun/.

McGovern, Charles F. *Sold American: Consumption and Citizenship, 1890–1945*. Chapel Hill: University of North Carolina Press, 2006.

McKay, Betsy. "Why Coke Indulges (the Few) Fans of Tab." *Wall Street Journal*, April 12, 2001.

McPhail, Deborah, Brenda Beagan, and Gwen E. Chapman. "'I Don't Want to be Sexist But . . .' Denying and Re-Inscribing Gender Through Food." *Food, Culture & Society* 15, no. 3 (2012): 473–89.

McWilliams, Jeremiah. "Coke Zero Becomes a Hero for Coca-Cola Co." *Atlanta Journal-Constitution*, September 16, 2010. https://www.ajc.com/business/coke -zero-becomes-hero-for-coca-cola/K9fdvFfsyjUK32TUgek17M/.

Mehren, Elizabeth. "Apostle of Thin Pays L.A. a Visit: Weight Watchers Get Together to Chew the Fat." *Los Angeles Times*, October 13, 1982.

Meltzer, Marisa. *This Is Big: How the Founder of Weight Watchers Changed the World—and Me*. New York: Little, Brown and Company, 2020.

"Men Get Their Very Own Yogurt Brand." *AdAge*, May 15, 2013. https://adage.com /creativity/work/powerful-yogurt/31599?.

Men's Health Forum. "Luna Bars—Will They Turn Me into a Woman?" *Men's Health* website, April 24, 2007. http://forums.menshealth.com/topic /63643898180487791.

Merriam-Webster. "Word of the Year: They." https://www.merriam-webster.com /words-at-play/word-of-the-year/they.

Merwin, Hugh. "Brogurt, or Greek 'Yogurt for Men,' Is a Real Thing." *Grub Street*, February 25, 2013. http://www.grubstreet.com/2013/02/powerful-yogurt-greek -yogurt-for-men.html.

Messner, Michael A. *Power at Play: Sports and the Problem of Masculinity*. Boston: Beacon Press, 1995.

———. *Taking the Field: Women, Men, and Sports*. Minneapolis: University of Minnesota Press, 2002.

Messner, Michael A., and Jeffrey Montez de Oca. "The Male Consumer as Loser: Beer and Liquor Ads in Mega Sports Media Events." *Signs: Journal of Women in Culture and Society* 30, no. 3 (2005): 1879–909.

Metzl, Jonathan M., and Anna Kirkland, eds. *Against Health: How Health Became the New Morality*. New York: NYU Press, 2010.

Meyerowitz, Joanne. *Not June Cleaver: Women and Gender in Postwar America, 1945–1960*. Philadelphia: Temple University Press, 1994.

Midan Marketing, "New Midan Marketing Research: Manfluence® to Impact Retail Meat Case," August 19, 2013. https://midanmarketing.com/customerinsights /manfluence/.

Mihalache, Irina. "Being Guy Fieri: The 'Chef-Dude' and the Geography of a Bro Kitchen." *Flow Journal*, September 2012. http://www.flowjournal.org/2012/09 /being-guy-fieri/.

———. "The Chef Who Played Too Much: Performing Masculinities in The Galloping Gourmet." *Flow Journal*, September 2012. http://www.flowjournal.org /2012/07/the-chef-who-played-too-much/.

Miller, Tim. "The Birth of the Patio Daddy-O: Outdoor Grilling in Postwar America." *The Journal of American Culture* 33, no. 1 (2010): 5–11.

Mims, Christopher. "Thanks to the 'Mancession,' Metrosexuals Have Become 'Manfluencers.'" *Quartz*, October 24, 2013. https://qz.com/138822/thanks-to-the -mancession-metrosexuals-have-become-manfluencers/.

Minute Rice. "Dude Food." Minute Rice website, accessed July 21, 2016. https://www .minuterice.com/en-us/content/23970/DudeFood.aspx.

Mishkind, Marc E., Judith Rodin, Lisa Silberstein, and Ruth H. Striegel Moore. "The Embodiment of Masculinity: Cultural, Psychological, and Behavioral Dimensions." *American Behavioral Scientist* 29, no. 5 (May 1, 1986): 545–62.

Mishra, Suman, and Rebecca Kern. "Persuading the Public to Lose Weight: An Analysis of a Decade (2001–2011) of Magazine Advertisements." *Journal of Magazine & New Media Research* 16, no. 1 (2015): 1–21.

Mitchell, Lachlan, Stuart B. Murray, Stephen Cobley, Daniel Hackett, Janelle Gifford, Louise Capling, and Helen O'Connor. "Muscle Dysmorphia Symptomatology and Associated Psychological Features in Bodybuilders and Non-Bodybuilder Resistance Trainers: A Systematic Review and Meta-Analysis." *Sports Medicine* 47, no. 2 (2017): 233–59.

Moller, Michael. "Exploiting Patterns: A Critique of Hegemonic Masculinity." *Journal of Gender Studies* 16, no. 3 (2007): 263–76.

Molyneaux, Maryellen. "Consumer Protein Trends." *Natural Products Insider*, October 8, 2015. http://www.naturalproductsinsider.com/articles/2015/10/consumer-protein-trends.aspx.

Monaghan, Lee F. *Men and the War on Obesity: A Sociological Study*. London: Routledge: 2008.

Monaghan, Lee F., and Michael Atkinson. *Challenging Myths of Masculinity: Understanding Physical Cultures*. London: Routledge, 2014.

Monaghan, Lee F., and Helen Malson. "'It's Worse for Women and Girls': Negotiating Embodied Masculinities through Weight-Related Talk." *Critical Public Health* 23, no. 3 (2013): 304–19.

Montesi, Luca, Marwan El Ghoch, uci Calugi, Giulio Marchesini, and Riccardo Dalle Grave. "Long-term Weight Loss Maintenance for Obesity: A Multidisciplinary Approach." *Diabetes, Metabolic Syndrome and Obesity: Targets and Therapy* 9 (2016): 37–46.

Moran, Victoria. "Devour's Racy Launch Campaign Pushes 'Food You Want to Fork.'" *AdAge*, August 1, 2006. https://adage.com/article/cmo-strategy/devour-aims-heat-things-frozen-food-aisle/305249.

Moskin, Julia. "Guy Fieri, Chef-Dude, Is in the House." *New York Times*, August 10, 2010. http://www.nytimes.com/2010/08/11/dining/11Fieri.html.

Moss, Anna. "Pinterest Statistics 2019: Everything Marketers Need to Know." *TechJury*, April 10, 2019. https://techjury.net/stats-about/pinterest/.

Moss, Mark Howard. *The Media and the Models of Masculinity*. Lanham, MD: Lexington Books, 2011.

Moye, Jay. "How Coke Zero Became a Hero: 10 Facts to Mark the Brand's 10th Birthday." Coca-Cola website, June 30, 2015. http://www.coca-colacompany.com/stories/how-coke-zero-became-a-hero-10-facts-to-mark-the-brands-10th-birthday.

———. "Summer of Sharing: 'Share a Coke' Campaign Rolls Out in the U.S." Coca-Cola website, June 10, 2014. https://www.coca-colacompany.com/stories/summer-of-sharing-share-a-coke-campaign-rolls-out-in-the-us.

Mudde, Cas, and Cristobal Rovira Kaltwasser. *Populism: A Very Short Introduction*. 2nd ed. New York: Oxford University Press, 2017.

Mudhustler, "Video from the Bropocalypse Weight Watchers Event," Facebook, August 5, 2017. https://www.facebook.com/mudhustler/posts/here-is-the-live -video-from-the-bropocalypse-weight-watchers-event/1228766317235287/.

Mudry, Jessica J. *Measured Meals: Nutrition in America*. Albany: State University of New York Press, 2010.

Mulvey, Laura. "Visual Pleasure and Narrative Cinema." *Screen* 16, no. 3 (1975): 6–18.

Murnen, Sarah K., and Donn Byrne. "Hyperfemininity: Measurement and Initial Validation of the Construct." *The Journal of Sex Research* 28, no. 3 (1991): 479–89.

Murray, Stuart B., and Stephen W. Touyz. "Masculinity, Femininity and Male Body Image: A Recipe for Future Research." *International Journal of Men's Health* 11, no. 3 (2012): 227–39.

Murray, Susan, and Laurie Ouellette. *Reality TV: Remaking Television Culture*. New York: NYU Press, 2004.

Mycek, Mari Kate. "Meatless Meals and Masculinity: How Veg* Men Explain Their Plant-based Diets." *Food and Foodways* 26, no. 3 (2018): 223–45.

Myers, Dan. "America's 25 Most Successful Chefs of 2016." *The Daily Meal*, March 10, 2016. http://www.thedailymeal.com/eat/america-s-25-most-successful-chefs -2016.

———. "Sexist Food Advertisements That Will Make Your Jaw Drop." *The Daily Meal*, October 9, 2014. https://www.thedailymeal.com/sexist-food -advertisements-will-make-your-jaw-drop.

Myers, Justin. "We're Calling Bullshit on the 'Dad Bod.'" *British GQ*, April 4, 2019.

Naccarato, Peter, and Kathleen LeBesco. *Culinary Capital*. New York: Bloomsbury, 2012.

Nagel, Joane. *Race, Ethnicity, and Sexuality: Intimate Intersections, Forbidden Frontiers*. Oxford: Oxford University Press, 2003.

Nash, Meredith, and Michelle Phillipov, eds. "Eating Like a 'Man': Food and the Performance and Regulation of Masculinities." Special issue, *Women's Studies International Forum* 44 (2014): 205–65.

National Health and Nutrition Examination Survey. "Protein, NCHStats." National Center for Health Statistics, March 30, 2010. https://nchstats.com/category /protein/.

Negra, Diane, and Yvonne Tasker, eds. *Gendering the Recession: Media and Culture in an Age of Austerity*. Durham, NC: Duke University Press, 2014.

Nelson, Hope. "Fieri Fan Rings in 600 Diners, Drive-Ins, and Dives." *Alexandria Gazette Packet*, September 18, 2017.

Nettles-Barcelón, Kimberly D., et al. "Black Women's Food Work as Critical Space." *Gastronomica* 15, no. 4 (2015): 34–49.

Neuhaus, Jessamyn. *Manly Meals and Mom's Home Cooking: Cookbooks and Gender in Modern America*. Baltimore, MD: Johns Hopkins University Press, 2012.

———. "The Way to a Man's Heart: Gender Roles, Domestic Ideology, and Cookbooks in the 1950s." *Journal of Social History* 32, no. 3 (1999): 529–55.

Nevin, Suzanne, and Lenny Vartanian. "The Stigma of Clean Dieting and Orthorexia Nervosa." *Journal of Eating Disorders* 5, no. 37 (2017), doi: 10.1186/ s40337-017-0168-9.

Newman, Andrew Adam. "The Skinny on Male 'Dieting,'" *AdWeek*, April 7, 2008. http://www.adweek.com/news/advertising-branding/skinny-male-dieting-95443.

Next Food Network Star. Season 2, Episode 1: "Iron Chef Bootcamp." Aired March 19, 2006 on Food Network.

Next Food Network Star. Season 2, Episode 3: "Second Elimination." Aired March 26, 2006 on Food Network.

Next Food Network Star. Season 2, Episode 5: "Alton Brown TV 101." Aired April 9, 2006 on Food Network.

Nidetch, Jean. *The Weight Watchers Program Cookbook*. Great Neck: Hearthside Press, Incorporated, 1973.

Nobel, Carmen. "Should Men's Products Fear a Woman's Touch?" *Harvard Business School, Working Knowledge*, November 13, 2013. http://hbswk.hbs.edu/item /should-mens-products-fear-a-womans-touch.

Noble, Barbara Presley. "All About/Weight-Loss Programs; Crash Is Out, Moderation Is In, and Diet Companies Feel the Pinch." *New York Times*, November 24, 1991.

Norcia, Alex. "Inside FieriCon, the World's Only Guy Fieri-Themed Bar Crawl." *Munchies: Food by Vice*, November 20, 2017.

Notaker, Henry. *A History of Cookbooks: From Kitchen to Page over Seven Centuries*. Oakland: University of California Press, 2017.

Nudd, Tim. "Coke Zero Gives 'Skyfall' Tickets to Only the Most Bond-Like People." *AdWeek*, October 22, 2012. http://www.adweek.com/adfreak/coke-zero-gives -skyfall-tickets-only-most-bond-people-144698.

Nutrisystem. "Terry Bradshaw Chose Nutrisystem," commercial, 2012. https://www .youtube.com/watch?v=cIJ5eny6HaY.

Nutrisystem. "Up Close & Personal with Terry Bradshaw," commercial, 2012.

Nutrisystem for Men. "Bradshaw and Marino," commercial, 2012.

"Nutrition and Physical Degeneration: A Comparison of Primitive and Modern Diets and Their Effects by Weston A. Price." *Journal of the American Medical Association* 114, no. 26 (June 29, 1940): 2589.

Oaklander, Mandy. "Should I Eat Sushi?" *TIME*, June 25, 2015. http://time.com /3921573/sushi-fish-sashimi/.

O'Doherty, Jensen K., and Lotte Holm. "Preferences, Quantities and Concerns: Socio-cultural Perspectives on the Gendered Consumption of Foods." *European Journal of Clinical Nutrition* 53, no. 5 (1999): 351–59.

Olson, Elizabeth. "Diet Companies Promote New Ways to Reduce." *New York Times*, January 6, 2011. http://www.nytimes.com/2011/01/07/business/07adco.html.

Ostberg, Jacob. "Thou Shalt Sport a Banana in Thy Pocket: Gendered Body Size Ideals in Advertising and Popular Culture." *Marketing Theory* 10, no. 1 (2010): 45–73.

Paiella, Gabriella. "A Brief History of Terrible Yogurt Commercials Targeted at Women." *The Cut*, June 29, 2016. http://nymag.com/thecut/2016/06/history-of -terrible-yogurt-commercials-for-women.html.

Paquette, Danielle. "The Super Bowl Ads Were Right: Dads in America Really Are Changing Their Act." *Washington Post*, February 2, 2015. https://www .washingtonpost.com/news/wonk/wp/2015/02/02/the-super-bowl-ads-were -right-dads-in-america-really-are-changing-their-act/.

Parasecoli, Fabio. *Bite Me: Food in Popular Culture*. New York: Berg Publishers, 2008.

———. "Feeding Hard Bodies: Food and Masculinities in Men's Fitness Magazines." *Food and Foodways* 13, no. 1–2 (March 9, 2005): 17–37.

———. "Manning the Table: Masculinity and Weight Loss in US Commercials." In *Food and Media: Practices, Distinctions and Heterotopias*, edited by Jonatan Leer and Karen Klitgaard Povlsen, 95–109. New York: Routledge, 2016.

Parker, Ian. "Pete Wells Has His Knives Out." *New Yorker*, September 12, 2016. http://www.newyorker.com/magazine/2016/09/12/pete-wells-the-new-york -times-restaurant-critic.

Parker, Kim, Nikki Graf, and Ruth Igielnik. "Generation Z Looks a Lot Like Millennials on Key Social and Political Issues." Pew Research Center, January 17, 2019. https://www.pewsocialtrends.org/2019/01/17/generation-z-looks-a-lot-like -millennials-on-key-social-and-political-issues/.

Parkin, Katherine. *Food Is Love: Advertising and Gender Roles in Modern America*. Philadelphia: University of Pennsylvania Press, 2007.

Pascoe, C. J. *Dude, You're a Fag: Masculinity and Sexuality in High School*. Oakland: University of California Press, 2007.

Pascoe, C. J., and Tristan Bridges. *Exploring Masculinities: Identity, Inequality, Continuity and Change*. Oxford: Oxford University Press, 2015.

Patel, Ridhi. "Men Can Eat Yogurt Now." *Odyssey*, May 17, 2016. https://www .theodysseyonline.com/men-can-eat-yogurt-now.

Pearson, Mackenzie. "Why Girls Love the Dad Bod." *The Odyssey Online*, March 30, 2015. http://theodysseyonline.com/clemson/dad-bod/97484.

Peiss, Kathy. *Hope in a Jar: The Making of America's Beauty Culture*. Philadelphia: University of Pennsylvania Press, 2011.

Peltz, James F. "Now That White Claw Summer Is Over, Will Hard Seltzer's Popularity Go Splat?" *Los Angeles Times*, October 20, 2019. https://www.latimes .com/business/story/2019-10-20/white-claw-hard-seltzer-fad-or-here-to-stay.

Pendergast, Tom. *Creating the Modern Man: American Magazines and Consumer Culture, 1900–1950*. Columbia: University of Missouri, 2000.

Pépin, Jacques. *The Apprentice: My Life in the Kitchen*. New York: Rux Martin/ Houghton Mifflin Harcourt, 2003.

Peretti, Burton W. *The Creation of Jazz: Music, Race, and Culture in Urban America*. Champaign: University of Illinois Press, 1992.

Petersen, Anne Helen. "How Millennials Became the Burnout Generation." *BuzzFeed News*, January 5, 2019. https://www.buzzfeednews.com/article /annehelenpetersen/millennials-burnout-generation-debt-work.

———. *Too Fat, Too Slutty, Too Loud: The Rise and Reign of the Unruly Woman*. New York: Plum, 2017.

Pew Research Center. "Who Uses Twitter, Pinterest, and Snapchat." February 5, 2018. https://www.pewinternet.org/chart/who-uses-pinterest-snapchat-youtube -and-whatsapp/.

Phillipov, Michelle. *Media and Food Industries: The New Politics of Food*. Cham, Switzerland: Palgrave Macmillan, 2017.

Pine, Dick. "Women Can't Cook." *Esquire*, September 1939, 51.

Pinterest, "Dude Food," accessed July 29, 2019. https://www.pinterest.com/search
/pins/?q=dude%20food&rs=typed&term_meta[]=dude%7Ctyped&term_meta[]
=food%7Ctyped.

Plante, Ellen M. *The American Kitchen: 1700 to the Present: From Hearth to Highrise*.
New York: Facts on File, 1995.

Plasketes, George. "Keeping TaB: A Diet Soft Drink Shelf Life." *The Journal of
American Culture* 27, no. 1 (2004): 54–66.

Polan, Dana. *Julia Child's The French Chef*. Durham, NC: Duke University Press,
2011.

Pomerantz, Dorothy. "Guy Fieri Would Like You to Stop Talking About the Burgers,
Please." *Forbes*, July 18, 2012. http://www.forbes.com/sites/dorothypomerantz
/2012/07/18/guy-fieri-would-like-you-to-stop-talking-about-the-burgers
-please/.

Poniewozik, James. "Media Circus: Full Metal Skillet." *Salon*, September 3, 1997.
http://www.salon.com/1997/09/03/media_210/.

Pope, Harrison G., Katharine A. Phillips, and Roberto Olivardia. *The Adonis Complex:
How to Identify, Treat and Prevent Body Obsession in Men and Boys*. New York: Free
Press, 2002.

Powell, William. "Cocktail Party, Masculine." *Esquire*, September 1936, 85.

"Powerful Yogurt." *Inc.*, 2018. https://www.inc.com/profile/powerful-yogurt.

Powerful Yogurt, Facebook Page. https://www.facebook.com/PowerfulYogurt/.

Pugh, William. "Dad Bods Are More Attractive to Women than Rock Hard Abs:
Survey." *New York Post*, June 17, 2019.

Pulido, Laura, Tianna Bruno, Cristina Faiver-Serna, and Cassandra Galentine.
"Environmental Deregulation, Spectacular Racism, and White Nationalism in the
Trump Era." *Annals of the American Association of Geographers* 109 (2019): 520–32.

Putney, Clifford. *Muscular Christianity: Manhood and Sports in Protestant America,
1880–1920*. Cambridge, MA: Harvard University Press, 2003.

Rabinow, Paul, and Nikolas Rose. "Biopower Today." *BioSocieties* 1, no. 2 (June 2006):
195–217.

Raichlen, Steven. *Man Made Meals: The Essential Cookbook for Guys*. New York:
Workman Publishing Co, 2014.

Rampell, Catherine. "The Mancession." *Economix Blog*, August 10, 2009. https://
economix.blogs.nytimes.com/2009/08/10/the-mancession/.

Rao, Sonia. "Guy Fieri Is in Quarantine with 400 Goats, a Peacock Problem and a
Plan to Help Restaurant Employees." *The Washington Post*, April 7, 2020. https://
www.washingtonpost.com/arts-entertainment/2020/04/07/guy-fieri-interview
-restaurant-relief-fund/.

Rasmussen, Eric E., and Rebecca L. Densley. "Girl in a Country Song: Gender Roles
and Objectification of Women in Popular Country Music across 1990 to 2014." *Sex
Roles* 76, no. 3–4 (2017): 188–201.

Rayment, W. J. *The Real Man's Cookbook: How, When, What, and Why to Cook*.
Tucson, AZ: Hats Off Books, 2000.

Reitz, Julie Kjendal. "Espresso: A Shot of Masculinity." *Food, Culture & Society* 10,
no. 1 (2007): 7–21.

Rense, Sarah. "Guy Fieri Is Feeding Wildfire Evacuees Hundreds of Meals in Northern California." *Esquire*, July 31, 2018. https://www.esquire.com/food-drink/a22601027/guy-fieri-california-wildfire-food-aid/.

Repanich, Jeremy. "Guy Fieri Is the Hero We Need." *Playboy*, December 15, 2015. http://www.playboy.com/articles/in-defense-of-guy-fieri-diners-drive-ins-dives.

Rick. "About: How It All Began," *Flavortown USA* (blog), 2008. https://www.flavortownusa.com.

Ridgeway, Rebekah T., and Tracy L. Tylka. "College Men's Perceptions of Ideal Body Composition and Shape." *Psychology of Men & Masculinity* 6, no. 3 (2005): 209–20.

Rifkin, Rebecca. "Majority of Americans Say They Try to Avoid Drinking Soda." *Gallup*, August 3, 2015. https://news.gallup.com/poll/184436/majority-americans-say-try-avoid-drinking-soda.aspx.

Rivera, Dane. "Ranking Every Flavor of White Claw, America's Hard Seltzer Obsession." *Uproxx*. September 20, 2019. https://uproxx.com/life/white-claw-flavors-ranked/.

Rodin, Judith, L. Silberstein, and Ruth Striegel-Moore. "Women and Weight: A Normative Discontent." *Nebraska Symposium on Motivation. Nebraska Symposium on Motivation* 32 (1984): 267–307.

Rodino-Colocino, Michelle. "Me too, #MeToo: Countering Cruelty with Empathy." *Communication and Critical/Cultural Studies* 15, no. 1 (2018): 96–100.

Rogers, Richard A. "Beasts, Burgers, and Hummers: Meat and the Crisis of Masculinity in Contemporary Television Advertisements." *Environmental Communication* 2, no. 3 (2008): 281–301.

Rose, Lily. "Guy Fieri Feeds California Fire Evacuees and First Responders." *The Daily Meal*, July 31, 2018. https://www.thedailymeal.com/eat/guy-fieri-feeds-california-fire-evacuees/073118.

Rosen, Jody. "Jody Rosen on the Rise of Bro-Country." *Vulture*, August 11, 2013. http://www.vulture.com/2013/08/rise-of-bro-country-florida-georgia-line.html.

Rothblum, Esther, and Sondra Solovay, eds. *The Fat Studies Reader*. New York: NYU Press, 2009.

Rotundo, E. Anthony. *American Manhood: Transformations in Masculinity from the Revolution to the Modern Era*. New York: Basic Books: 1993.

Rousseau, Signe. *Food Media: Celebrity Chefs and the Politics of Everyday Interference*. London: Berg, 2012.

Rozin, Paul, Julia M. Hormes, Myles S. Faith, and Brian Wansink. "Is Meat Male? A Quantitative Multimethod Framework to Establish Metaphoric Relationships." *Journal of Consumer Research* 39, no. 3 (October 1, 2012): 629–43.

Ruby, Matthew B., and Steven J. Heine. "Meat, Morals, and Masculinity." *Appetite* 56, no. 2 (2011): 447–50.

Rutherford, Janice Williams. *Selling Mrs. Consumer: Christine Frederick and the Rise of Household Efficiency*. Athens: University of Georgia Press, 2003.

Saguy, Abigail. *What's Wrong with Fat?* Oxford: Oxford University Press, 2013.

Sampey, Kathleen. "Coke Enlists Crispin for 'Zero' Line Extension." *AdWeek*, March 21, 2005. http://www.adweek.com/news/advertising/coke-enlists-crispin-zero-line-extension-78480.

Sax, David. "How Years of Macho Food Marketing Is Killing Men." *New York Magazine*, Beta Male, June 15, 2016. http://nymag.com/betamale/2016/06/macho -food-marketing-is-killing-men.html.

Scanlon, Jennifer. *Inarticulate Longings: The Ladies' Home Journal, Gender and the Promise of Consumer Culture*. New York: Routledge, 1995.

———, ed. *The Gender and Consumer Culture Reader*. New York: NYU Press, 2000.

Scherer, Josh. "6 Fast-Food Commercials That Are So Sexist You'll Lose Your Burger Craving." *TakePart*, December 11, 2014. http://www.takepart.com/article/2014/12 /11/unappetizingly-sexist-fast-food-commercials.

Schudson, Michael. *Advertising, The Uneasy Persuasion: It's Dubious Impact on American Society*. New York: Basic Books, 1986.

Schultz, E. J. "Anomaly Picks Up Diet Coke as the Soda Eyes Big Changes." *AdAge*, January 23, 2017. https://adage.com/article/agency-news/anomaly-picks-diet -coke-soda-eyes-big/307654.

———. "Dannon Dumps John Stamos for Cam Newton." *AdAge*, January 5, 2015. http://adage.com/article/cmo-strategy/dannon-s-oikos-drops-john-stamos-cam -newton/296438/.

———. "Hayley Magnus Dances with Diet Coke in Brand's Social Media-Friendly Super Bowl Spot." *AdAge*, February 4, 2018. https://adage.com/creativity/work /super-bowl-2018-groove/53804.

———. "How Kraft's Lunchables Is Evolving in the Anti-Obesity Era." *AdAge*, April 19, 2011. http://adage.com/article/news/kraft-s-lunchables-evolving-anti -obesity-era/227075/.

———. "New Year Brings New Diet-Company Ads, Programs." *AdAge*, December 28, 2010. http://adage.com/article/news/marketing-year-brings-diet -company-advertising/147910/.

———. "Weight Watchers Picks a New Target: Men." *AdAge*, April 22, 2011. http://adage.com/article/news/weight-watchers-picks-a-target-men/227155/.

Schuster, David G. *Neurasthenic Nation: America's Search for Health, Happiness, and Comfort, 1869–1920*. New Brunswick, NJ: Rutgers University Press, 2011.

Schwartz, David, and Hamilton Stapell. "Modern Cavemen? Stereotypes and Reality of the Ancestral Health Movement." *Journal of Evolution and Health* 1, no. 1 (2013), https://doi.org/10.15310/2334-3591.1000.

Schwartz, Hillel. *Never Satisfied: A Cultural History of Diets, Fantasies and Fat*. New York: Free Press, 1986.

Scott, Joan W. "Gender: A Useful Category of Historical Analysis." *The American Historical Review* 91, no. 5 (1986): 1053–75.

Scott, Suzanne. *Fake Geek Girls: Fandom, Gender, and the Convergence Culture Industry*. New York: NYU Press, 2019.

Scrinis, Gyorgy. *Nutritionism: The Science and Politics of Dietary Advice*. New York: Columbia University Press, 2013.

Sedgwick, Eve Kosofsky. *Epistemology of the Closet*. Oakland: University of California Press, 1990.

Shapiro, Laura. *Julia Child*. New York: Viking, 2007.

————. *Something from the Oven: Reinventing Dinner in 1950s America*. New York: Penguin Books, 2005.

Shek, Yen Ling. "Asian American Masculinity: A Review of the Literature." *The Journal of Men's Studies* 14, no. 3 (Fall 2006): 379–91.

Sherman, Elisabeth. "Guy Fieri Feeds Crews Fighting California Wildfires." *Food and Wine*, July 30, 2018. https://www.foodandwine.com/news/guy-fieri-feeds-crews -fighting-california-wildfires.

Shugart, Helene. "Managing Masculinities: The Metrosexual Moment." *Communication and Critical/Cultural Studies* 5, no. 3 (2008): 280–300.

Sidman, Jessica. "White Claw Is One of the Top Quarantine Drinks of Choice." *Washingtonian*, April 7, 2020. https://www.washingtonian.com/2020/04/07/white -claw-is-one-of-the-top-quarantine-drinks-of-choice/.

Singer, Ross. "Neoliberal Backgrounding, the Meatless Monday Campaign, and the Rhetorical Intersections of Food, Nature, and Cultural Identity." *Communication, Culture & Critique* 10, no. 2 (2017): 344–64.

Slatton, Brittany C., and Kamesha Spates. *Hyper Sexual, Hyper Masculine? Gender, Race and Sexuality in the Identities of Contemporary Black Men*. London: Routledge, 2014.

Sloan, Claire, Brendan Gough, and Mark Conner. "Healthy Masculinities? How Ostensibly Healthy Men Talk about Lifestyle, Health and Gender." *Psychology & Health* 25, no. 7 (September 2010): 783–803.

Smith Maguire, Jennifer. *Fit for Consumption: Sociology and the Business of Fitness*. London: Routledge, 2007.

Sobal, Jeffery. "Men, Meat, and Marriage: Models of Masculinity." *Food and Foodways* 13, no. 1–2 (2005): 135–58.

Socha, Miles. "Marc Jacobs Named Diet Coke Creative Director." *WWD*, February 6, 2013. http://wwd.com/business-news/marketing-promotion/marc-jacobs-named -diet-coke-creative-director-6699440/.

"Soda Consumption in America: Who's Drinking Regular and Diet?" *Huffington Post*, August 16, 2013. http://www.huffingtonpost.com/2013/08/16/soda-america -consumption-habits_n_3768480.html.

Southerton, Dale. "Consuming Kitchens Taste, Context and Identity Formation." *Journal of Consumer Culture* 1, no. 2 (2001): 179–203.

Spigel, Lynn. *Make Room for TV: Television and the Family Ideal in Postwar America*. Chicago: University of Chicago Press, 1992.

Stark, Phyllis. "Is Bro Country Over . . . And What Is Its Lasting Legacy?" *Billboard*, August 19, 2015. http://www.billboard.com/articles/columns/country/6670362/is -bro-country-over-and-what-is-its-lasting-legacy.

Stearns, Peter N. *Fat History: Bodies and Beauty in the Modern West*. 2nd ed. New York: NYU Press, 2002.

Steiman, Adina, and Paul Kita. *Guy Gourmet: Great Chefs' Best Meals for a Lean & Healthy Body*. Emmaus: Rodale Books, 2013.

Stein, Joel. "How to Get a Superhero Body." *GQ*, July 21, 2015. http://www.gq.com /story/fitness-how-to-get-chris-pratt-fit.

Stein, Joshua David. "The Crispy Crimes of Guy Fieri: Junk Food T.V. Star Takes Times Square." *Observer*, October 2, 2012. http://observer.com/2012/10/the -crispy-crimes-of-guy-fieri/.

Steinberg, Brian. "Food Network Chief Brooke Johnson to Retire." *Variety*, August 19, 2015. http://variety.com/2015/tv/news/food-network-brooke-johnson -1201573441/.

Steinmetz, Katy. "The Transgender Tipping Point." *TIME*, May 29, 2014.

Stevens, Ashlie. "Here's a Frosted Tip for You, Food Network: Stop Trying to Find the Next Guy Fieri." *Slate*, July 4, 2015. http://www.slate.com/blogs/browbeat /2015/07/04/guy_fieri_imitators_are_not_what_food_network_needs_opinion .html.

Stibbe, Arran. "Health and the Social Construction of Masculinity in Men's Health Magazine." *Men and Masculinities* 7, no. 1 (July 1, 2004): 31–51.

Stinson, Kandi. *Women and Dieting Culture: Inside a Commercial Weight Loss Group.* New Brunswick, NJ: Rutgers University Press, 2001.

Stoeffel, Kat. "Nation's Masculinity Intact Thanks to Coke for 'Bros.'" *The Cut*, August 26, 2014. https://www.thecut.com/2014/08/nations-masculinity-intact -with-bros-coke.html.

Strings, Sabrina. *Fearing the Black Body: The Racial Origins of Fat Phobia.* New York: NYU Press, 2019.

Sturken, Marita, and Lisa Cartwright. *Practices of Looking: An Introduction to Visual Culture.* 2nd ed. New York: Oxford University Press, 2009.

Summers, Martin. *Manliness and Its Discontents: Black Middle Class & the Transformation of Masculinity, 1900–1930.* Chapel Hill: University of North Carolina Press, 2004.

Sumpter, Kristen C. "Masculinity and Meat Consumption: An Analysis Through the Theoretical Lens of Hegemonic Masculinity and Alternative Masculinity Theories." *Sociology Compass* 9, no. 2 (2015): 104–14.

Sutton, Denise H. *Globalizing Ideal Beauty: Women, Advertising, and the Power of Marketing.* New York: Palgrave Macmillan, 2009.

Swenson, Rebecca. "Domestic Divo? Televised Treatments of Masculinity, Femininity and Food." *Critical Studies in Media Communication* 26, no. 1 (2009): 36–53.

Syme, Rachel. "The Trailer Park Gourmet." *The Daily Beast*, November 10, 2009. http://www.thedailybeast.com/articles/2009/11/10/the-glenn-beck-of-food.html.

Symington, Steve. "Why Weight Watchers Stock Dropped 50.5% in the First Half of 2019." *Yahoo Finance*, July 10, 2019. https://finance.yahoo.com/news/why-weight -watchers-stock-dropped-140603974.html.

Szabo, Michelle. "Foodwork or Foodplay? Men's Domestic Cooking, Privilege and Leisure." *Sociology* 47, no. 3 (2012): 623–38.

———. "'I'm a real catch:' The Blurring of Alternative and Hegemonic Masculinities in Men's Talk about Home Cooking." *Women's Studies International Forum* 44, no. 1 (2014): 228–35.

———. "Men Nurturing Through Food: Challenging Gender Dichotomies Around Domestic Cooking." *Journal of Gender Studies* 23, no. 1 (2014): 18–31.

Szabo, Michelle, and Shelley Koch, eds. *Food, Masculinities, and Home*. New York: Bloomsbury Academic, 2017.

Tager, David, Glenn E. Good, and Julie Bauer Morrison. "Our Bodies, Ourselves Revisited: Male Body Image and Psychological Well-Being." *International Journal of Men's Health* 5, no. 3 (2006): 228–37.

Taggart, Paul A. *Populism*. Maidenhead: Open University Press, 2000.

Tantleff-Dunn, Stacey, Rachel D. Barnes, and Jessica Gokee Larose. "It's Not Just a 'Woman Thing': The Current State of Normative Discontent." *Eating Disorders* 19, no. 5 (December 2011): 392–402.

Taylor, Timothy D. *The Sounds of Capitalism: Advertising, Music, and the Conquest of Culture*. Chicago: University of Chicago Press, 2012.

Terry, Bryant. "The Problem with 'Thug' Cuisine." *CNN*, October 10, 2014. https://www.cnn.com/2014/10/10/living/thug-kitchen-controversy-eatocracy/index.html.

Theophano, Janet. *Eat My Words: Reading Women's Lives Through the Cookbooks They Wrote*. 2nd ed. New York: Palgrave Macmillan, 2002.

Thomas Jr., Robert McG. "Albert Lippert, 72, a Founder of Weight Watchers, Is Dead." *New York Times*, March 3, 1998.

Thompson, Derek. "It's Not Just a Recession. It's a Mancession!" *The Atlantic*, July 9, 2009. https://www.theatlantic.com/business/archive/2009/07/its-not-just-a-recession-its-a-mancession/20991/.

Thug Kitchen. *Thug Kitchen: The Official Cookbook: Eat Like You Give a F*ck*. Emmaus, PA: Rodale Books, 2014.

Tippen, Carrie Helms. *Inventing Authenticity: How Cookbook Writers Redefine Southern Identity*. Fayetteville: University of Arkansas Press, 2018.

Tipton-Martin, Toni. *The Jemima Code: Two Centuries of African American Cookbooks*. Austin: University of Texas Press, 2015.

Tobler, Christina, Vivianne H. M. Visschers, and Michael Siegrist. "Eating Green: Consumers' Willingness to Adopt Ecological Food Consumption Behaviors." *Appetite* 57, no. 3 (December 2011): 674–82.

Todd, Anthony. "Dr. Pepper Pisses off Pretty Much Everyone with 'Man'Ments.'" *Chicagoist*, October 11, 2011. http://chicagoist.com/2011/10/11/doctor_pepper_pisses_off_pretty_muc.php.

Tompkins, Kyla Wazana. *Racial Indigestion: Eating Bodies in the 19th Century*. New York: NYU Press, 2012.

Townsend, Megan. "'The Cheerios Effect' Ad Features Gay Dads and Their Daughter." GLAAD, October 6, 2014. http://www.glaad.org/blog/cheerios-effect-ad-features-gay-dads-and-their-daughter.

Treichler, Paula A. *How to Have Theory in an Epidemic: Cultural Chronicles of AIDS*. Durham, NC: Duke University Press, 1999.

Troyer, John, and Chani Marchiselli. "Slack, Slacker, Slackest: Homosocial Bonding Practices in Contemporary Dude Cinema." In *Where the Boys Are: Cinemas of Masculinity and Youth*, edited by Murray Pomerance and Frances Gateward, 264–76. Detroit, MI: Wayne State University Press, 2005.

Trujillo, Nick. "Hegemonic Masculinity on the Mound: Media Representations of Nolan Ryan and American Sports Culture." *Critical Studies in Mass Communication* 8, no. 3 (1991): 290–308.

Tunc, Tanfer Emin. "The 'Mad Men' of Nutrition: The Drinking Man's Diet and Mid-Twentieth-Century American Masculinity." *Global Food History* 4 (2018): 189–206.

Twitty, Michael. "Thug Kitchen: It's Not Just about Aping and Appropriation, It's about Privilege." *Afroculinaria*, October 22, 2014. https://afroculinaria.com /2014/10/22/thug-kitchen-its-not-just-about-aping-and-appropriation-its-about -privilege/.

Vain, Madison. "Guy Fieri Knows How to Laugh at Himself. That's Why He Has Instagram's Best Meme Account." *Esquire*, October 10, 2019.

Van Amsterdam, Noortje. "Big Fat Inequalities, Thin Privilege: An Intersectional Perspective on 'Body Size.'" *European Journal of Women's Studies* 20, no. 2 (2013): 155–69.

Van Gelder, Lawrence. "A Real Winner in Weight Losing." *New York Times*, March 25, 1975.

Veit, Helen Zoe. *Modern Food, Moral Food: Self-Control, Science, and the Rise of Modern American Eating in the Early Twentieth Century*. Chapel Hill: University of North Carolina Press, 2013.

Veri, Maria J., and Rita Liberti. *Gridiron Gourmet: Gender and Food at the Football Tailgate*. Fayetteville: University of Arkansas Press, 2019.

———. "Tailgate Warriors: Exploring Constructions of Masculinity, Food, and Football." *Journal of Sport & Social Issues* 37, no. 3 (2013): 227–44.

Vester, Katharina. "Regime Change: Gender, Class, and the Invention of Dieting in Post-Bellum America." *Journal of Social History* 44, no. 1 (2010): 39–70.

———. *A Taste of Power: Food and American Identities*. Oakland: University of California Press, 2015.

Wadler, Joyce. "Judging Men by Their Refrigerators." *New York Times*, July 18, 2014. http ://www.nytimes.com/2014/07/20/fashion/judging-men-by-their-refrigerators.html.

Wallace, Kelly. "'Dad' Gets a Makeover in Super Bowl Ads." *CNN*, January 31, 2015. https://www.cnn.com/2015/01/30/living/feat-super-bowl-dads-ads/index.html.

Wann, Marilyn. *FAT!SO?: Because You Don't Have to Apologize for Your Size*. New York: Ten Speed Press, 1998.

Ward, Jane. "Dude-Sex: White Masculinities and 'Authentic' Heterosexuality Among Dudes Who Have Sex with Dudes." *Sexualities* 11, no. 4 (2008): 414–34.

Wardle, Jane, Anne M. Haase, Andrew Steptoe, Maream Nillapun, Kiriboon Jonwutiwes, and France Bellisle. "Gender Differences in Food Choice: The Contribution of Health Beliefs and Dieting." *Annals of Behavioral Medicine* 27, no. 2 (2004): 107–16.

Watson, Elaine. "The Rise and Rise of Greek Yogurt. But Is the Growth Sustainable?" *Food Navigator USA*, April 8, 2013. https://www.foodnavigator-usa.com/Article /2013/04/09/The-rise-of-Greek-yogurt.-But-is-the-growth-sustainable.

Weber, Christopher L., and H. Scott Matthews. "Food-Miles and the Relative Climate Impacts of Food Choices in the United States." *Environmental Science & Technology* 42, no. 10 (2008): 3508–13.

Weight Watchers. "Announcing the Launch of Weight Watchers Online for Men Battling the Bulge Not Just a Female Issue—Men Do It Differently." Weight Watchers website, March 29, 2007. https://www.weightwatchers.com/about/prs/wwi_template.aspx?GCMSID=1149551.

Weight Watchers. "Kendra," commercial, 2013. https://www.ispot.tv/ad/7wqu/weight-watchers-kendra-song-by-vv-brown.

Weight Watchers. "Rich & Famous," commercial, 2012. https://www.ispot.tv/ad/7LC8/weight-watchers-online-featuring-charles-barkley.

Weight Watchers. "Roll Call," commercial, 2013. https://www.youtube.com/watch?v=zQnZuxBCT2E.

Weight Watchers. "Sir Charles for Weight Watchers," commercial, 2013. https://www.youtube.com/watch?v=rB08F9S5EHU.

Weight Watchers. "Weight Watchers Online: Daniel," commercial, 2013.

Weight Watchers. "Weight Watchers Online: Pete," commercial, 2013.

Weinraub, Judith. "Jean Nidetch." In *Savoring Gotham: A Food Lovers Companion to New York City*, edited by Andrew F. Smith and Garrett Oliver, 428–29. New York: Oxford University Press, 2015.

———. "Suddenly, It's a Guy Thing. In the Beginning, Before Low-Carb Eating, It Wasn't Manly to Watch Your Weight." *Washington Post*, April 30, 2012. http://www.washingtonpost.com/wp-co/hotcontent/index.html?section=health/nutrition.

West, Candace, and Don H. Zimmerman. "Doing Gender." *Gender & Society* 1, no. 2 (1987): 125–51.

Wieden + Kennedy. "Work: Kraft, Eat Like That Guy You Know." August 22, 2012. http://www.wk.com/campaign/eat_like_that_guy_you_know.

Williams, Mary Elizabeth. "Dr. Pepper's Commandments of Sexism." *Salon*, October 12, 2011. http://www.salon.com/2011/10/12/dr_peppers_commandments_of_sexism/.

Williams-Forson, Psyche. *Building Houses Out of Chicken Legs: Black Women, Food, and Power*. Chapel Hill: University of North Carolina Press, 2006.

Williams-Forson, Psyche, and Abby Wilkerson. "Intersectionality and Food Studies." *Food, Culture & Society* 14, no. 1 (2011): 7–28.

Wing, Rena R., and Suzanne Phelan. "Long-term Weight Loss Maintenance." *The American Journal of Clinical Nutrition* 82, no. 1 (2005): 222S–5S.

Wolf, Serena. "The Dude Diet." *Domesticate ME!* (blog), September 19, 2012. http://domesticate-me.com/the-dude-diet-one/.

———. *The Dude Diet*. New York: Harper Collins, 2016.

———. *The Dude Diet Dinnertime*. New York: Harper Collins, 2019.

World Health Organization. "Burn-out an 'Occupational Phenomenon': International Classification of Diseases." World Health Organization website, May 28, 2019. https://www.who.int/mental_health/evidence/burn-out/en/.

Wright, Katie. "Theorizing Therapeutic Culture: Past Influences, Future Directions." *Journal of Sociology* 44, no. 4 (2008): 321–36.

Zafar, Rafia. *Recipes for Respect: African American Meals and Meaning*. Athens: University of Georgia Press, 2019.

Zezima, Katie. "It Takes a Big Man to Seek Help on Weight Loss." *New York Times*, November 8, 2007.

Zinczenko, David, and Ted Spiker. *The Abs Diet: The Six-Week Plan to Flatten Your Stomach and Keep You Lean for Life.* Emmaus: Rodale Books, 2005.

Zmuda, Natalie. "Can Dr Pepper's Mid-Cal Soda Score a 10 With Men?" *AdAge*, February 21, 2011. https://adage.com/article/news/dr-pepper-10-avoid-marketing-missteps-pepsi-coke/148983.

Zuckerman, Esther. "Here Comes 'Brogurt.'" *The Wire*, February 24, 2013. http://www.theatlanticwire.com/entertainment/2013/02/here-comes-brogurt/62495/.

Zyda, Joan. "They're Elephants and Proud of It." *Chicago Tribune*, June 14, 1976.

Index

diet programs, 89–91; advertising campaigns, 106–110; gender difference and, 98–106, *100, 101, 103,* 110–13, *113–16*; online programming, 110–13; social media and, 114–16. *See also* dieting; diets; Jenny Craig; Nutrisystem; Weight Watchers

diets, 97–98. *See also* dieting; diet programs

diet soda, 64, 66–69, 70, 74–76, 79–84, 87–88, 119–20, 123–25, 133n4. *See also* Coca-Cola products; Coke Zero; Diet Dr. Pepper; Dr. Pepper Ten

Diners, Drive-Ins and Dives, 41, 43, 49–50, 53. *See also* Guy Fieri

domesticity, 2, 11–12, 33–34, 49, 101–2, 138n31, 140n5. *See also* cooking; fatherhood

Dr. Pepper products, 64, 65–66, 68, 69, 119–20, 76, 76, 81–84, 123–24. *See also* diet sodas

Dr. Pepper Ten, 65–66, 68, 119–20, 123; advertising campaigns, 64, 69, 81–84; packaging *76, 76. See also* Diet Dr. Pepper; diet soda; Dr. Pepper products

dude food, 19–26, 116, 120; dieting and, 97, 99, 115; Guy Fieri and, 43, 55–56

dude, 4–7, 13–16, 67, 78, 91, 106, 117–18. *See also* advertising campaigns; Guy Fieri; male body; masculinity

Esquire, 11, 12, 28–29. *See also* magazines, men's

excess, 21–22, 43. *See also* dude food; Guy Fieri, cuisine; healthism

Facebook, 84, 113, 145n62. *See also* social media

fatness, 10, 109. *See also* thinness

fat stigma, 23, 94–95, 102–3, 104–6, 116. *See also* thinness

fatherhood, 47, 48–52, 58, 142n60

Feig, Paul, 124–25

femininity, 5, 6, 8, 9, 12, 17, 44, 49, 52, 72–73; advertising campaigns and, 12, 70, 81, 82, 84, 86. *See also* masculinity

Fieri, Guy, 37, 40–44, *41*, 57–60, 129–30, 142n82; cookbooks, 49–51, *50*; cuisine of, 52–57, *54; Diners, Drive-Ins and Dives,* 41, 43, 49–50, 53; fandom of, 60–62, 115, 143n111; fatherhood and, 47, 48–52, 58; *Next Food Network Star* 37, 39–40, 44–48, *46,* 53

film(s), 4, 5, 13, 14–15, 136n81

flavor, xii, 2, 19–20, 32, 53–54, 99, 100–101, 126–27; diet soda; 66–69, 70, 74, 75, 123, 125; yogurt, 66–67, 73–74

Flay, Bobby, 40, 48, 141n44

food. *See* diet foods; dude food

foodies, 14, 44, 56–57

Food Network, 38–40, 43; *Next Food Network Star,* 37, 39–40, 44–48, *46,* 53, 140n20. *See also* Guy Fieri

food packaging, 74–78

food porn, 19, 26, 54, 82

French Chef, The (TV series), 38

frozen meals, 25–26

Galloping Gourmet, The (TV series), 38

gastropubs, 20

gastrosexual, 13, 14

gender, 8; coding, 10–11, 33, 49, 64, 66, 70, 73, 89; contamination, 1–4, 17, 28, 88, 116, 118, 125; crisis, 7–16; neutrality (in marketing), 118–21, 121–23; scripts, 2, 133n5. *See also* femininity; masculinity

Giordano, Jonathan, 113, 115–16, 150n101

Great Recession, 3, 7–8, 25, 31, 49, 52, 91, 98, 118. *See also* 2000s

grilling, 32–33, 34, 51. *See also* cooking; meat; protein

Guy's American Kitchen and Bar, 57, 142n82

Oliver, Jamie, 142n60
Oscar Mayer Portable Protein Packs, 25.
  See also protein

packaging, 69, 74–78, *75, 76, 77. See also*
  advertising campaigns
Paleo Diet, 97–98
Pépin, Jacques, 55
Pinterest, 22. *See also* social media
populism, 37, 56, 57, 115, 129. *See also*
  Guy Fieri.
Powerful Yogurt, 64, 66, 69, 70, 71, 72,
  73–74, 121; advertising campaigns,
  84–86, *86*; packaging, 77, *77–78.*
  See also yogurt
Pratt, Chris, 14
Prescott, Dak (spokesperson), 121
presidential election (2016), 117, 130.
  See also 2000s, post-2016; Donald J.
  Trump
protein, 25, 66, 70–72, 97. *See also*
  grilling; meat

Queer Eye for the Straight Guy
  (TV series), 13

race, 3, 5–6, 9–10, 17, 53, 95, 134n26;
  advertising campaigns and 65–66, 85,
  109; body ideals and, 15, 23–24;
  consumerism and, 8, 11. *See also*
  Blackness; whiteness
Ray, Rachel, 40
Real Men Don't Eat Quiche (Feirstein), 13
Recession, The Great (2007–2009), 3,
  7–8, 25, 31, 49, 52, 91, 98, 118. *See also*
  2000s
regional food, 21. *See also* dude food

Sedgwick, Eve, 110, 149n91. *See also*
  weight loss closet
seduction, *35, 35–36,* 85. *See also*
  heteronormativity; misogyny
separate spheres, xiii, 7, 9, 18, 33;
  dieting and, 101–2, 104, 106; fatherhood and, 49, 52. *See also* gender

Seward, Carissa, 45, 46, 47. *See also Next*
  Food Network Star
sexuality, 4, 5, 8, 9, 12, 23, 31; advertising campaigns and, 64, 73; dieting
  and, 93, 95; relational 44, 45–47.
  See also heteronormativity
sexualization, 25–26, 34, 35–36. *See also*
  heteronormativity; misogyny
slacker, 4, 24–25, 78, 80–81, 124,
  134n16. *See also* dude
social media, 59–60, 77, 84, 115–16, 121;
  diet programs and, 114–16; Facebook,
  84, 113, 145n62; Instagram, 19, 62,
  114–16, 127–28, 137n1, 138n12;
  Pinterest, 22. *See also* technology,
  dieting and
South Beach Diet, 97
Southerland, Reggie, 45–47, *46. See also*
  Next Food Network Star
spokespeople, 147n26; Bob Hope, 94; Cam
  Newton, 86, 121; Charles Barkley, 90,
  90, 104, 106–9, *107,* 110; Dak Prescott,
  121; Dan Marino, 108, *109;* Jason
  Alexander, 108–9; John Stamos, 86;
  Terry Bradshaw, 104, 108, 110. *See also*
  advertising campaigns; Nidetch, Jean
Stamos, John (spokesperson) 86
sugar, 65, 68, 75, 119. *See* artificial
  sweeteners
Super Bowl commercials, 26, 49, 86,
  124, 145n53. *See also* advertising
  campaigns
superhero, (body ideal), 14–15
sushi, 56
Symons, Michael, 34

taste (cultural), 11–12, 17, 43, 45, 48, 54, 56
technology, dieting and, 110–13. *See also*
  dieting; social media
television, food, 37–40. *See also* Food
  Network
thinness, 10, 23, 65; advertising
  campaigns and, 70, 71, 73, 75; dieting
  and, 95, 102, *103,* 104–6, 113–14.
  See also fatness; fat stigma

transgender visibility, 117–18
Trump, Donald J., 21, 43, 59, 117

weight loss closet, 110–13. *See also* diet
  foods; dieting; diet programs
Weight Watchers, 89–90, 97, 98–104,
  100–101, 103, 112, 122; advertising
  campaigns, 90, *90*, 106–10, *107*,
  113, 146n7; history of, 91–95,
  147n10, 147n22. *See also* diet
  programs
Wells, Pete, 57, 142n82
White Claw, 126–29, *127*

whiteness, 2, 5–6, 7, 9–10, 11, 17,
  23–24, 41 117, 134n26; advertising
  campaigns and 65–66, 85; dieting
  and, 91, 96, 109. *See also* race

yogurt, 64, 65–67, 69–74, 88, 121, 143n5;
  advertising campaigns, 84–88;
  packaging, 76–78. *See also* Oikos
  Triple Zero; Powerful Yogurt

zero (marketing concept), 69, 72–74,
  100, 107, 122. *See also* healthism;
  nutritionism

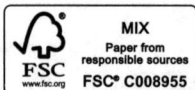